# Hypoactive Sexual Desire

*Integrating Sex and Couple Therapy*

ALSO BY GERALD WEEKS AND NANCY GAMBESCIA

*Erectile Dysfunction:*
*Integrating Couple Therapy, Sex Therapy, and Medical Treatment*

A NORTON PROFESSIONAL BOOK

# Hypoactive Sexual Desire

*Integrating Sex and Couple Therapy*

GERALD R. WEEKS, PH.D.
NANCY GAMBESCIA, PH.D.

W. W. Norton & Company
New York • London

For information about permission to reproduce
selections from this book, write to
Permissions, W. W. Norton & Company, Inc.,
500 Fifth Avenue, New York, NY 10110

**Library of Congress Cataloging-in-Publication Data**

Weeks, Gerald R., 1948–
    Hypoactive sexual desire : integrating sex and couple therapy / Gerald R.
Weeks, Nancy Gambescia.
        p. cm.
    Includes bibliographical references and index.
    ISBN 0-393-70344-4
    1. Sexual desire disorders.   2. Marital psychotherapy.   I. Gambescia,
Nancy.   II. Title.

RC560.S46 W44 2002
616.85′830651—dc21                                                        2001054621


W. W. Norton & Company, Inc., 500 Fifth Avenue, New York, N.Y. 10110
www.wwnorton.com

W. W. Norton & Company Ltd., Castle House, 75/76 Wells Street,
London W1T 3QT

1 2 3 4 5 6 7 8 9 0

# Contents

# Acknowledgments

THE AUTHORS WOULD LIKE TO EXPRESS gratitude to the many individuals and couples we have treated in our practices over the past decades. They have generously shared the many joys, worries, and concerns about their intimate and sexual relationships. We feel fortunate to have known and worked with them. We appreciate the others who have helped to review and edit the manuscript such as Sherrie Burch and Susanne Methven who were invaluable as research assistants, proofreaders, and keeping the document organized and formatted. Also, we wish to recognize the support of many of our colleagues who have contributed ideas about various aspects of the book such as Judith Kastenberg, Sharon Youcha, and Amy Ellwood. The senior author would also like to thank Dean Martha Watson for her ongoing support at the University of Nevada Las Vegas and acknowledge the assistance of others such as Sandie M. Smith and Jennifer March. We value our ongoing association with Norton through the publication of two books. Our editors at Norton, Susan Munro and Deborah Malmud continued to provide excellent feedback on this manuscript as they did with the *Erectile Dysfunction* text. Finally, the support and understanding of those close to us were essential to the success of this project. We thank Kathy Weeks, Michael Chenet, and Matt and Lauren Gambescia.

# Preface

THE LACK OF SEXUAL DESIRE, known clinically as hypoactive sexual desire (HSD) or hypoactive sexual desire disorder (HSDD) is generally recognized as the most common sexual problem in America. According to an analysis of the United States National Health and Social Life Survey by Laumann, Paik, and Rosen (1999), it effects almost 20% of men and 33% of women in the general population. An earlier study of the frequency of sexual dysfunctions in "normal" couples found similar results (Frank, Anderson, and Rubinstein, 1978). The incidence of HSD is higher in clinical practice than in the general population. In fact, over 50% of couples presenting for treatment will complain of insufficient sexual desire in one or both partners or a discrepancy in sexual appetite between partners (Segraves & Segraves, 1991). Thus, clinicians are very likely to encounter HSD in their individual and especially couple therapy practices. Unfortunately, most therapists have had little training in the physiological aspects of sexual functioning and the practice of sex therapy. Typically, a cursory assessment is made and the individual or couple is then referred to a physician or a sex therapist. In the worst-case scenario, an inexperienced, untrained, and unsupervised clinician attempts to treat the HSD, fails, and the couple believes the situation is hopeless.

A great deal of research has been done since Kaplan originally identified the lack of sexual desire as a distinct clinical entity in 1979. However, only a few texts have been devoted exclusively to HSD and these tend to emphasize etiology rather than treatment. Furthermore, the research and clinical literature have not been presented systematically in one publication. Our text presents an integrated approach that examines the physiological and the psychological factors that can cause or interfere with sexual desire. Also, we offer a treatment model based on the integration of medical and psychological interventions developed specifically for HSD. The purpose of this volume is to provide clinicians with the theoretical and practical tools required for understanding and treating this complex problem.

This manual incorporates many principles for the assessment and treatment of erectile dysfunction proposed in a recent text by Weeks and Gambescia (2000). The foundation of our model is the intersystemic approach developed by Weeks (1994) that views every problem in terms of its individual, interactional, and intergenerational components. (The individual component includes both the biological and psychological factors.) The role of the couple's relationship is viewed as a major contributing factor in both the etiology and treatment of HSD. Relational risk factors are discussed and couple therapeutic techniques described. Also, situations originating within the family-of-origin such as negative sexual messages are included under the intergenerational understanding of the problem.

The authors have many years of experience specializing in couple and sex therapy involving the treatment of all types of relational and sexual difficulties. We recognize that HSD:

- is one of the most complex of all the problems we treat,
- requires an integrative approach,
- is a difficulty resulting from a confluence of factors, and
- is embedded in the couple's dynamics.

We are also interested in the medical factors that contribute to HSD as well as the biological approaches to this dilemma. Other than Viagra, which promotes sexual arousal, the medical community has not yet discovered a pill to *restore* desire for most men and women. Low testosterone levels may contribute to this problem and replacement therapy may prove successful in a limited number of cases. However, the popular literature has grossly oversimplified the accepted understanding of HSD, promoting it as a solely organic problem that will respond to medical treatment alone. If anything, medical remedies are often one of the primary causes of HSD. As we will demonstrate, many commonly used drugs, especially antidepressants, adversely affect sexual desire, yet doctors are reluctant to inform patients about this side effect.

Our experience and most of the literature regarding the treatment of lack of sexual desire have been about heterosexual individuals or couples. This volume assumes a heterosexual relationship; however, we have successfully applied the same principles to working with homosexual couples in our practices. A brief overview of the chapters is included below.

*Chapter 1* provides general background regarding the lack of sexual desire. Definitions are clarified, gender differences described, and the incidence of the problem is reviewed. The general framework of the problem is established in this chapter.

*Chapter 2* gives the reader a better theoretical understanding of sexual desire, satisfaction, and HSD. Theories regarding the presence, absence, and normative amounts of sexual desire are reviewed. We discuss the fact that partners are rarely in sync when sexual desire is experienced. Finally, we review the indicators of sexual desire such as sexual fantasies, interest, and solo sexual activity rather than using the frequency of sexual relations alone as an assessment measure.

*Chapter 3* covers factors that contribute to the lack of sexual desire from the individual perspective. Nonpsychiatric and psychiatric factors are examined in this discourse.

*Chapter 4* includes the relational factors that place the couple at risk for developing HSD. Our belief is that couple-related risk factors, particularly the lack of control in one partner or chronically suppressed anger, play major roles in the lack of sexual desire. Empirical research and our own clinical observations are integrated in this chapter.

*Chapter 5* deals with the intergenerational risk factors in the development of HSD. These factors have been underemphasized in the literature and include the sexual ramifications of events within the family-of-origin such as parentification, sexual secrecy, ignorance, and trauma.

*Chapter 6* reviews the physiology of sexual desire and the biological factors that can diminish desire such as hormonal deficiencies, chronic illnesses, and the sexual side effects of some commonly prescribed medications. Some of the drugs and devices that theoretically restore desire are also discussed.

*Chapter 7* describes a comprehensive approach for assessing HSD, which includes the couple's overall and sexual relationships. A cognitively oriented rapid assessment technique is reviewed in order to help the clinician move quickly from assessment to beginning treatment.

*Chapter 8* provides the reader with the basic principles and strategies for treating HSD. It is a broad, lengthy chapter that includes some ideas that are not found anywhere in the literature. The framework is both comprehensive and integrative, focusing on the behavioral, cognitive, and affective aspects of this problem. It includes the use of the therapeutic reframe, homework exercises, and strategies to promote sexual intimacy. Chapter 8 furnishes the overall framework for all the treatment chapters to follow.

*Chapter 9* concentrates on the identification and treatment of multiple risk factors found in the couple. Problems with commitment, intimacy, and passion often contribute to a lack of sexual desire. The various presentations of underlying fears of intimacy are revealed and their treatment discussed.

*Chapter 10* reviews some of the traditional sex therapy techniques as well as some of the strategies that were developed by the authors such as creating a sexual environment, the use of fantasy work, and the expression of desire through solo sex.

*Chapter 11* concludes the book with some of the more advanced techniques for the couple. The particular elements of sensate focus exercises are described thoroughly. In fact, our version is unique because of the attention to the details involved in the proper implementation of this classic exercise. The creation of affectional intimacy as opposed to sexual intimacy is discussed and the problematic relationship between these two is revealed as a factor that contributes to lack of desire.

Treating lack of sexual desire is one of the most challenging, yet rewarding of all the problems with which we work. Couples enter therapy with a great deal of pessimism and often have given up the hope of having a satisfying sexual relationship. Frequently, they have failed to achieve results with other therapists who are wedded to a singular theoretical approach. We invite readers to join us in learning to treat a problem in ways that will stretch their theoretical limits and usually result in a couple reviving their sexual relationship in the context of a significantly enhanced couple relationship.

# Hypoactive Sexual Desire

*Integrating Sex and Couple Therapy*

# 1

# Overview

SEX THERAPISTS GENERALLY REGARD hypoactive sexual desire (HSD) or hypoactive sexual desire disorder (HSDD) as one of the most common problems in our practices. Unfortunately, the treatment of this disorder is remarkably challenging, complex, and lengthy compared to other sexual dysfunctions. In the Preface, we mentioned that the aim of this text is to present an *integrative* and *comprehensive* analysis of this problem. Our primary goals of this chapter are to:

- discuss the ways in which HSD is currently being defined,
- explain how this problem was first recognized and defined, including the evolution of the concept over time, and
- support the claim that HSD is common in the population and in clinical practices.

(We will use the term HSD throughout this text except for discussion of the diagnostic criteria for HSDD.)

## DEFINITION

The 2000 edition of the *Diagnostic and Statistical Manual of Mental Disorders (DSM-IV-TR)* (APA, 2000) provides a definition of HSDD and lists three criteria that must be met in order to diagnose this condition:

1. There is a "deficiency or absence of sexual fantasies and desire for sex-ual activity" (p. 539).
2. The disorder must produce marked personal distress or interpersonal distress.
3. The condition must not be a result of another Axis I disorder (except another sexual dysfunction) or a by-product of a general medical condi-tion or the result of substance use (medications or alcohol or drug abuse).

This definition raises a number of clinical and theoretical issues. The authors of the *DSM-IV* clearly state that the terminology leaves much to the judgment of the clinician. For example, in assessing "absence or defi-ciency" of sexual fantasies and desire, factors such as *age* and the context of the person's life are to be taken into account. Of course, questions about what constitutes "normal" frequency of sexual activity and fantasy are not answered. These are empirical issues that will be discussed later. Addition-ally, very little empirical research has been performed on gender-based trends regarding the *type* of sexual fantasies experienced. Moreover, there is the ever-present dilemma concerning what is a "normal" fantasy and why we would wish to change or modify something that is working for the individual. Thus, the subject of sexual fantasy has been virtually ignored in the sex therapy literature (Loren & Weeks, 1986).

The second part of the definition, personal or interpersonal distress, can also be perplexing in certain cases. Suppose both partners lacked desire and neither one wished to feel any sexual desire. While they would obviously be in sync with each other and there would be no personal or interpersonal distress, are they not still experiencing HSD? In some cases we have seen, individuals have sought out other individuals with no desire in order to avoid dealing with their sexuality or to ensure a comfortable level of inti-macy. Are we to call this type of conscious or unconscious collusion healthy from a sexual perspective?

The fact is two discrepancies may exist where there is HSD. In one in-stance, there exists a dilemma for the *individual* who wishes to feel desire, but cannot experience or sustain the feeling. This lack of desire can repre-sent a change from the normal sexual appetite of the individual. Further-more, this change can exist globally, in all situations, or be specific to the intimate partner. Nonetheless, the individual has the *desire for desire* and is very distressed about *not* being able to experience a more robust sexual appetite or recapture sexual desire for the partner.

The second situation is when there is *relationship* distress or discord as a result of a difference between partners with respect to sexual desire. In a common scenario, one partner lacks desire and the other experiences desire. Naturally, the partner who has a sexual appetite wants to engage in sexual interaction while the other partner avoids sexual intimacy as a result of the lack of interest. These couples suffer from the marked discrepancy in their levels of desire. Sometimes the partner who experiences desire has an extraordinarily high level of desire and may "accuse" the other person of lacking desire. The clinician must determine the level of desire for both partners in order to determine whether there has been a change in the status quo of the relationship. Another clinical manifestation of discordant levels of desire is when the tables have been turned such that the real problem is hypersexuality rather than hyposexuality. The partner with more sexual desire, in this instance, presents the partner as having an "abnormally" low level of desire.

In some cases, the person with the lowest level of desire in the relationship also lacks any interest in experiencing desire. They feel no longing. This *individual* will not experience an internal discrepancy, thus there is no internal distress. There may be *interpersonal* difficulty however, due to the extent the partner chooses to make lack of sexual interaction an issue.

The third criterion is that the lack of desire not be a result of:

- another Axis I problem such as depression,
- a general medical condition, or
- substance use (medications or alcohol or drug abuse).

It is presumed that if one or more of these conditions were resolved, the individual would experience "normal" desire. This assumption may or may not be true. For instance, we have seen many individuals taking medications known to interfere with sexual desire, but once the medications were changed or eliminated, the person still did not experience any desire. (See Chapter 6 for a more detailed discussion of the effects of medications on sexual functioning). Thus, the HSDD must have another cause. We can assume any of the conditions mentioned above may inhibit sexual desire, but the clinician should be cautious to not to summarily rule out the possibility of HSDD as the underlying cause.

In addition, *DSM-IV* (APA, 1994) identifies several types of HSDD. Two opposing types are lifelong versus acquired and generalized versus situational.

Lifelong would refer to a lack of desire from puberty forward. Typically, the individual with *lifelong* HSDD does not experience a change in appetite. In fact, the lack or absence of desire is a "normal" state of affairs for the person. When an individual has experienced a change in his or her sexual appetite, the term *acquired* is used. This individual has felt sexual desire in his or her lifetime, normally for a period of several years, but has lost or has had a noticeable decline in sexual desire over time. The change can be gradual or precipitous, perhaps resulting from life cycle issues, aging, or the loss of a partner.

The *DSM-IV* (APA, 1994) states that an individual with *generalized* lack of desire does not feel desire under any circumstances regardless of the partner or situation. Typically, this individual does not engage in sexual fantasy or any type of self-pleasuring. The *situational* type, on the other hand, is marked by selective or situational desire. This person may feel desire in certain situations or with certain people, but not always or with every partner. For example, the person might feel desire when alone, but not with one's mate, or one might feel desire toward an affair partner, but not with one's established partner.

Although *DSM-IV* refers to a relationship between HSD and other sexual problems such as lack of orgasm, this association is not defined in terms of direction of causality or the frequency with which any two or more given sexual problems may be related (APA, 1994). *DSM-IV* also fails to address the relationship between HSD and the paraphilias. As yet, this area is unexamined with the exception of a short clinical article by Moser (1992). Moser helps to define some of the issues and suggests that when sexual desire goes "awry" such as in the case of a fetish, it is very difficult to change.

It should also be noted that HSDD was differentiated from sexual aversion disorder in *DSM-IV* (APA, 1994). Some clinicians have been confused by the similarity of these two concepts. Sexual aversion disorder is more severe than HSDD. The main criterion, which differentiates the two disorders, is, with sexual aversion, there is an active loathing or disgust with regard to genital sexual contact. Thus, in sexual aversion the avoidance of sexual intimacy is more pronounced than with HSDD. For the reader who wants to gain a quick understanding of sexual aversion, Crenshaw (1985) published one of the early articles describing both primary and secondary sexual aversion in males and females.

## CONCEPTUAL ISSUES

An interesting study challenges the idea that sexual desire is a unidimensional concept. Spector, Carey, and Steinberg (1996) conducted a factor analytic study of sexual desire. They found there are basically two types of sexual desire, solitary and dyadic. Solitary sexual desire refers to having sex with oneself often using masturbation and sometimes sexually arousing material. The purpose of this activity is often tension release. Dyadic sexual desire refers to partnered sex and is designed to facilitate an emotional and physical connection with another person. In our clinical experience, it is certainly possible for a person to lack desire in either or both of these areas. In fact, a common presentation is a couple in which a partner is interested in solo sex, but not partnered sex. Other cases show a pattern of lack of interest in solo sex, but an emergent interest when the partner initiates some form of affectional, sensual, or sexual contact. Obviously, when assessing lack of sexual desire it is important to inquire about both solitary and dyadic types.

One of the authors' cases illustrates the preference in one partner for solo sex. John and Jane, married for 10 years, presented after a 2-year period of weekly conjoint therapy with another therapist. The couple had worked with their former therapist on many issues such as communication, resentment, and unmet expectations. Nonetheless, they were at an impasse because John no longer experienced sexual desire for Jane. He was, however, sexually active several times a week, masturbating to stimulating pornography in magazines, videotapes, and on the Internet. Essentially he now lacked dyadic desire. This was very distressing to Jane who believed that he was not interested in her sexually because she was inherently inadequate or unappealing. Later in the therapy, as the couple achieved more differentiation, Jane was able to see John's lack of desire as more his problem than hers.

The therapy then focused on the many of factors that contributed to John's lack of desire for Jane and the resulting decline in sexual frequency. From an intergenerational perspective, each came from a family of origin in which emotional intimacy was not demonstrated. Their relationship represented a "safe haven." Originally each partner rescued the other in order to escape from damaging and oppressive families of origin. Thus, their marital bond was more parental than passionate. In addition, there were individual restrictions brought to the relationship by each partner, such as Jane's fear of loss of control and her discomfort in experiencing pleasure. An overbearing mother and critical father had traumatized John. He consistently kept a distance from Jane in order to protect himself from criticism and abandonment. She maintained the distance in order to feel safe and in control. Finally, the couple had built a long list of relational issues that contributed to their problems. Jane had been disinterested in sexual intimacy during the first few years of their marriage. Resentful and unable to "change" Jane, John had an early extramarital affair and threatened to leave the marriage. Each of these issues contributed greatly to the couple's emotional distance although Jane eventually became very interested and

experimental with sex and John resolved the affair. They were bound together in a relationship that was safe yet disappointing in terms of emotional and sexual intimacy.

## GENDER DIFFERENCES AND SEXUAL DESIRE

There are many problems in trying to conceptualize sexual desire and lack
of sexual desire as a unitary concept. *DSM-IV* (APA, 1994) implicitly assumes that men and women experience sexual desire and lack of desire in
the same way. Research has also shown some significant gender differences
associated with sexual desire. Leiblum and Rosen (1988) found that male
sexual desire appears to be more constant and genitally focused, whereas
women appear to be more variable in their levels of sexual desire and are
influenced by social and interpersonal factors to a greater extent. In fact,
sexual desire for women is often related to nonsexual variables such as
trust and comfort in their intimate relationships (Basson, 2000; Regan &
Berscheid, 1996). Instead of experiencing an overwhelming hunger or an
insatiable drive towards physical release, the female sexual appetite is more
responsive to factors between herself and her partner. If the relationship is
safe, loving, and caring, she can begin to experience sexual fantasies and
feel the bodily sensations that coincide with sexual desire. In essence, sexual appetite is more related to the expectation of emotional intimacy than
the pressing urge for sexual release.

Basson (2000) proposed a model examining the underlying forces that
motivate sexual desire in women. She postulated that in long-term relationships, sexual appetite is more *responsive* than spontaneous. That is, women
are not necessarily motivated to experience unconstrained sexual arousal
or even orgasm for the sake of physical pleasure alone. Instead, they are
more enticed by the expectation that they can be vulnerable in an affectionate relationship. In essence, they are *responsive to* the anticipated pleasures
related to emotional intimacy. In addition, Basson expands upon the concept of a *normal* sexual appetite by proposing that women are capable of
experiencing an unlimited range of sexual thoughts, dreams, and fantasies,
provided the nonsexual climate is safe.

Regan and Berscheid (1996) conducted an interesting study that suggests
significant gender differences with respect to sexual desire. Ninety percent
of the subjects in this study used motivational, cognitive, emotional, or
other subjective experiences in their definition of desire. Only a small percent defined desire in terms of physiological arousal or sexual activity. The
researchers found that women were much more likely to "romanticize"
sexual desire while men tended to "sexualize" sexual desire. Essentially,
women viewed sexual desire in terms of love, emotional intimacy, or com-

mitment. Men, however, experienced sexual desire as a state of sexual interest leading to sexual activity. The object of women's desire could be an established partner or someone they did not know, while men were more likely than women to state the object of their desire is a physically or sexually attractive partner. The authors summarized their findings by stating women tend to view sexual desire from more of a *relational* perspective while men experience it from a *recreational* or body-centered orientation. That is, men are more able to enjoy the pleasurable sensations from sex regardless of the context while women need the relational issues to be under control before they can lose themselves in sexual gratification.

Donahey and Carroll (1993) found several differences between men and women in reporting lack of sexual desire. Men noted the duration of their HSD to be 3.4 years while women reported 4.7 years. Men with HSD tended to be older. The mean age for men was 50 and for women 33. Women also tested as having a much higher level of psychological distress and more psychological symptoms. They were higher on depression, anxiety, hostility, and paranoid thinking, and slightly higher on obsessive-compulsive indices, interpersonal sensitivity, and phobic anxiety. Women accounted for more stress than men did over home-related issues and finances and were significantly more dissatisfied with the quality of the marital relationship. Men also noted that their lack of desire coincided with another sexual dysfunction, that is, an erectile dysfunction. Interestingly, both men and women focused more on their sexual dysfunction than on their other psychiatric symptoms. Regardless of gender, the research by Donahey and Carroll pointed out three clinical implications related to HSD:

1. It is primary and contributes to other problems.
2. The HSD is secondary and results from other problems.
3. There is a global inhibition of sexual response, and one problem is the focal point for the individual's distress.

A puzzling aspect of HSD has been the absence of the feminist voice in understanding this problem. Only one article published by Richgels (1992) addresses this issue. Rather than challenge how men and women might differentially define desire, Richgels chose to focus on the lack of social/cultural attention paid to this disorder. Her main thesis was that in traditional patriarchal societies, rigid and narrowly defined sex roles have severely limited the range of sexual expectations for women. Sexual desire has historically been viewed as a male privilege, and the purpose of sexual activity has been for procreation or for the satisfaction of men alone. Sexual pleasure as a goal state has been virtually ignored for women. Thus, female sexual expression has been a neglected factor in the understanding of HSD.

## A Brief Historical Perspective

The sexual response was originally understood as a series of physiological stages beginning with arousal and ending after orgasm. In 1966, William Masters and Virginia Johnson, in the book *Human Sexual Response*, published the results of their study of *physical* reactions to sexual stimulation in men and women. They described four distinct stages of the sexual response cycle:

1. excitement
2. plateau
3. orgasm
4. resolution

Masters and Johnson (1966) did not recognize sexual desire as a stage that triggered the physical responses to sexual stimulation. Later, Harold Lief identified sexual desire as an integral component of the sexual response (Lief, 1977, 1985). Helen Singer Kaplan (1979) then identified sexual desire as the first stage of the sexual response cycle. She reconceptualized the sexual response cycle using a "triphasic" model, by adding the important *psychological* stage of sexual desire to the Masters and Johnson physical formulation. Thus, the three phases became:

1. desire
2. arousal (replacing excitement and plateau)
3. orgasm (replacing orgasm and resolution)

This book immediately became the standard text in the field for understanding the *lack of* sexual desire.

Kaplan (1979) used the phrase "hypoactive sexual desire" and "inhibited sexual desire" to describe the lack of or reduction in sexual appetite. Both Lief and Kaplan independently reached the conclusion that HSD was one of the most pervasive and intractable of any sexual difficulties. The term hypoactive sexual desire did not gain widespread acceptance and legitimacy until the publication of *DSM-IV* in 1994. Prior to that time, the phenomenon was most commonly referred to as Inhibited Sexual Desire (ISD) or HSD. Kaplan (1979) stated the term ISD should be used when the etiology of the low libido was unclear. Obviously, she believed that in the majority of the cases discussed in her book, the etiology was known. Kaplan believed that "involuntary and unconscious but active suppression of sexual desire" (p. 83) is the immediate cause or antecedent of ISD. Kaplan also described primary, secondary, generalized, and situational ISD. Her ideas about ISD and HSDD were later incorporated in *DSM-III* and *DSM-IV*.

ISD became an official diagnosis in the *DSM-III* (APA, 1980). It was defined as a "persistent and pervasive inhibition of sexual desire" (p. 278). A further revision was made in *DSM III-R* (APA, 1987) when the terms "Hypoactive Sexual Desire Disorder" and "Sexual Aversion Disorder" were included. The definition of HSD was the same as appears in *DSM-IV* (APA, 1994).

Researchers and clinicians differ on the importance of being able to operationalize the term *hypoactive sexual desire*. LoPiccolo and Friedman (1988) have argued for more precision in the definition and assessment of HSD. They appear to represent the research-oriented group. Clinicians are more tolerant of this lack of precision. They argue their clinical judgment is sufficient and that most couples subjectively define the problem for themselves. In our experience, it is rare that an individual will self-diagnosis with HSD when it is not present. One recent case is illustrative and somewhat humorous. The wife, who was also a therapist, with just a little training in sex therapy, stated she had HSD. She further said she only wanted sex about once a week and that her level of desire distressed her husband. Once this couple was educated about the "normal" range of desire and frequency, they agreed HSD was not their problem.

## INCIDENCE

Numerous reports have been made about the incidence of HSD. Recall from the historical overview, that the term used to describe a lack of desire would reflect the era in which the study was conducted. Some studies to be discussed have examined clinical populations while others have examined nonclinical populations. Of course, good data are difficult to obtain because of the nature of the problem being assessed. Each study will have its strengths and weaknesses. Perhaps the best approach is to review a number of the studies in order to determine whether the statistics begin to converge.

## Nonclinical Samples

Frank, Anderson, and Rubinstein (1978) conducted one of the earliest and best studies reporting the frequency of sexual dysfunction. The sexual part of the study was one component of a much larger study on family life. This team of researchers was interested in the incidence of sexual dysfunction among "normal couples." They were able to recruit 100 couples from and around the University of Pittsburgh campus. Their sample was far from being representative of the overall American population. For instance, the couples were mostly white, middle to upper-middle class, and very well educated. A strength of the study, however, was that the marriages represented varied in length of time from a few years to over 20 years. The main criterion for participating in the study was the couple's perception that their marriage was working.

Bahr and Weeks (1989) replicated the study by Frank and colleagues (1978) using a sample of 100 gay couples. The results were fairly similar to those obtained using the heterosexual couples. The gay men reported a great deal of overall relationship and sexual satisfaction. However, when asked about specific sexual problems they reported rates similar to that of the heterosexual group:

- About 20% reported an erectile problem.
- 19% ejaculated too quickly.
- 17% had difficulty ejaculating.
- 20% reported being sexually disinterested and 9% felt "turned off."

Also of interest was the fact that almost 1 out of 5 felt there was too little foreplay or afterplay. Compared to the heterosexual sample studied by Frank and others (1978) the following differences were noted in homosexual men:

- 4% reported sexual contact daily compared to 1% for the heterosexual group.
- 9% reported sex 4–5 times a week compared to 12% for heterosexual men.
- 35% reported sex 2–3 times per week compared to 31% for heterosexual men.
- 25% reported sex once per week compared to 24% for heterosexual men.
- 11% reported sex 2–3 times per month compared to 23% for heterosexual men.
- 17% reported sex less than once a month compared to 10% for heterosexual men.

Given the demographics of the sample by Frank and colleagues (1978) one might suspect little sexual dysfunction. However, this situation was not the case. Although the couples reported overall *relationship* satisfaction, sexual dysfunction for the *women* was as follows:

- 48% reported difficulty getting aroused.
- 33% had difficulty maintaining sexual arousal.
- 11% reached orgasm too quickly.
- 46% had difficulty reaching an orgasm.
- 15% reported being unable to have an orgasm at all.

The *men* in the Frank, Anderson, and Rubinstein (1978) study also reported an unexpected incidence of sexual dysfunction despite *relationship* contentment:

- 7% had difficulty getting an erection.
- 9% reported difficulty maintaining an erection.
- 36% ejaculating too quickly.
- 4% had difficulty reaching orgasm.

The researchers defined the problems identified above as *major* sexual dysfunctions. The reader will notice, however, that lack of sexual appetite or desire was not included in the list. Remember, in 1978, ISD had not yet been identified as a major dysfunction when the study began. Thus, Frank and colleagues (1978) identified the information that is of interest to us as "sexual difficulties."

There were two items under "sexual difficulties" that give us some idea about the frequency of HSD. Roughly 35% of women and 16% of men reported being *disinterested* and 28% of women and 10% of men reported feeling *turned off*. Of the sexual dysfunctions, disinterest was one of just a few problems related to depressed sexual satisfaction.

What is also interesting in the study by Frank and others (1978) is that the overwhelming majority of men and women reported being happy or satisfied with their marriages. Apparently, in this sample, couples were able to isolate their sexual problems from their marriage in general and in large measure from their perceived level of sexual satisfaction. This study also shows that the probability of multiple sexual dysfunctions exists for every relationship, including those that are perceived to be working well.

In 1986, Nathan investigated the epidemiology of the *DSM-III* psychosexual dysfunctions. She reanalyzed data from 22 general population studies. For HSD, she found the studies ranged from 1%–15% for men and 1%–35% for women. One year later, an article published in *Newsweek* on lack of desire placed the incidence between 20% to 50% of the general population at some time and to some degree. The researchers, Gelman, Doherty, Murr, Drew, and Gordon (1987) estimated that during the past half century the estimate would be up to 15% for men and 35% for women.

One of the most recent studies to stir interest was conducted by Michael, Gagnon, Laumann, and Kolata (1994). The study was published in a popular book entitled, *Sex in America* and also in an academic text called *The Social Organization of Sexuality* (Laumann, Gagnon, Michael, & Michaels, 1994). This study, conducted by a group of sociologists, was a large-scale investigation using good sampling techniques and multiple ways of collecting data. Generally speaking, their data are similar to that found in 1978 by Frank and colleagues. One major difference did exist, however. The researchers only asked about sexual problems experienced during the *past year*. In spite of wording the question in that way, they found that about 15% of men and 33% of women reported a lack of desire. However, we should keep in mind that problems with sexual desire could be persistent and recurrent, generally lasting for a considerable duration of time. It is entirely possible that an individual experiencing a lack of desire for 10 years was included in the 1-year group. Thus, factors related to intensity and duration might have been underestimated. Moreover, this study supports the idea that it is highly probable that couples reporting one sexual problem might have more than one, given the frequency with which problems are reported.

A very recent large-scale study on sexual satisfaction was conducted in England using 4,000 adult respondents and their partners (Dunn, Croft, & Hackett, 2000). About 25% of the respondents reported being dissatisfied with their sex lives. Men were less content than women were, especially with the frequency of intercourse. In general, 24% of the respondents reported not having intercourse at all during the previous 3 months. Only 53% noted a frequency of up to once per week, and 23% reported having sex more than once a week. Interestingly, the men and women agreed in their recording of the frequency of intercourse. We could assume the group who did not have sexual relations in the past 3 months (24%) were probably experiencing a problem with lack of sexual desire. This percentage would be considered low in any age group.

About 80% of the respondents thought their partners were sexually gratified, which was higher than the actual reports of sexual satisfaction. Subjects were more likely to think their partners were not fulfilled if they were experiencing a sexual problem themselves. In order to assess sexual dysfunction more accurately, it is essential to actually examine the actual frequency or percentage of sexual problems by asking about them directly. General questions about sexual satisfaction tend to elicit responses that "look good" but do not accurately reflect the incidence of dysfunction. When asked about specific sexual problems, the following picture emerged:

*Men*
- erection problems (48%)
- premature ejaculation (43%)
- sex not pleasant (45%)

*Women*
- inhibited female orgasm (39%)
- dyspareunia or painful intercourse (24%)
- vaginal dryness (21%)
- arousal problems (51%)
- sex not pleasurable (47%)

Clearly, the overall level of sexual satisfaction is inconsistent with the frequency of reported sexual difficulties. Therefore, this finding is consistent with other studies mentioned above in that simply having a sexual problem does not fully predict sexual dissatisfaction. The data also suggest that the participants were not asked specifically about sexual desire. Therefore, a substantial number of men and women must be experiencing desire problems within the context of other sexual difficulties or other life-cycle issues.

## Clinical Samples

Due to the incidence of HSD in the general population, we would expect this problem to be common in clinical practices. Data from both early and more recent studies supports this idea. Harold Lief, one of the originators of the concept of HSD, conducted two surveys of patients treated at the Marriage Council of Philadelphia where he served as director in the late 1970s. He found 20% of men and 37% of women reported a lack of desire (Lief, 1977). In a later study, he found the HSD rate to be 14% for men and 31% for women (Lief, 1985). Subsequent studies conducted at the Stony Brook Center for Sex Therapy showed higher rates. LoPiccolo (1980) examined 37 cases in treatment and found HSD in 63% of men and 37% of women. Schover and LoPiccolo (1982) did a larger scale study in 1982 with 152 couples. In this study 38% of men and 49% of women were found to be experiencing HSD. In addition, 18% of the women were diagnosed with a sexual aversion disorder.

Rosen, Leiblum, and Hall (1987) believe HSD is about twice as common in women than men based on their clinical experience. They also noted that many men with this diagnosis are also likely to report an erectile dysfunction. One survey of sex therapists (Kilmann, Boland, Norton, Davidson, & Caid, 1986) also found that 28% of patients complained about a lack of desire and 31% complained about the discrepancy in levels of sexual desire between partners. Therefore, the incidence of HSD in clinical samples appears to be even higher than reported in the more current studies.

Segraves and Segraves (1991) conducted a more recent large-scale study of the incidence of HSD in the clinical population. A pharmaceutical company studying the effectiveness of a drug that might affect desire, arousal, and orgasm difficulties conducted this study at various sites. HSD was the primary diagnosis in 65% of the 906 subjects. A significant gender difference was noted with respect to HSD: 81% of the women in this study were diagnosed with HSD as opposed to 30% of the men. These percentages may be inflated due to the fact that the study would have attracted patients seeking help for sexual desire or arousal disorders. In fact, 40% of the subjects reported another sexual dysfunction in addition to HSD. Nonetheless, the data reported by Segraves and Segraves (1991) support the suspected higher incidence of HSD in the clinical population.

According to the authors of one popular textbook on human sexuality, the prevalence of HSD appears to have increased from the early seventies into the nineties (Wincze & Carey, 1991). There are several reasons why this might be the case. First, researchers and clinicians, now aware of the problem, are asking more questions about sexual functioning in general. Second, clients may be more willing to admit that this problem exists due to the fact that it has received so much attention in the popular press, especially in women's magazines. Third, more clients may be seeking help for this problem because of awareness in the public's mind due to recent advances in the treatment of other sexual dysfunctions (Weeks & Gambescia, 2000). Fourth, sexual expectations for women are constantly expanding to include sexual enjoyment as a goal state. Also, the power structure in relationships is changing to a more egalitarian system, which impacts the sexual relationship. Fifth, with the increasing incidence of dual-career marriages, unfortunately, fatigue becomes a real variable that can adversely influence sexual desire. And, finally, the change in the incidence may not be a real change, but an artifact of some of the factors mentioned above. Now that clinicians are able to identify HSD and a public awareness of the problem is obvious, reporting rather than actual incidence may have increased. Although studies on this phenomenon have temporarily ceased, research tends to go in cycles, and we can expect a new round of investigations in the next few years to give us a more contemporary picture.

## CONCLUSION

In this chapter, we have attempted to show that the concept of HSD is one that is evolving. Some researchers will continue to try to further refine and operationally define this concept using more sophisticated diagnostic systems. Clinicians tend to work with what the client(s) subjectively perceive to be their problems. They are unlikely to have much interest in researching this aspect of HSD. Nonetheless, all sex therapists will be interested to see how common this problem becomes and how it is tied to various demographic factors such as age, gender, and relationship status, for example. In addition, the clinician is alerted to the coincidence of HSD and other sexual dysfunctions. Finally, the general public has an ongoing interest in HSD now that it has been identified and they can label and recognize it as a real problem. Additionally, many women are now waiting and laboring under the misconception that Viagra will be approved for them in the hopes that it may increase their desire. We are realizing, as a result of a growing body of research, that there is no "quick fix" for HSD in men or women and that Viagra is a remedy for arousal (not desire) phase disorders in men as well as women.

As clinicians, we will be interested in the content of the next chapter where we discuss issues related to the varied case presentations involving the experience of sexual desire. Differences within and between individuals with respect to sexual appetite will be considered. Also, we contemplate the nature of sexual desire, what is "normal," and how individuals go about subjectively assessing their desire.

# 2

# Perspectives on Sexual Desire

THE CONCEPT OF SEXUAL DESIRE is relatively new in the medical and psychological literature. Unlike the excitement and orgasm phases of the sexual response cycle, where there are marked anatomic changes and physiological events that are easily observed and measured, the desire phase is physically elusive. It is a psychological state much like an appetite that ebbs and flows with the physical and emotional circumstances of the individual. Also, sexual desire is extremely subjective and idiosyncratic, responding to the tastes and preferences of the individual at a given time. Furthermore, there exist mild to profound variations in sexual desire within and between individuals. It is no surprise that, in the clinical setting, the lack of or decrease in sexual desire is a common complaint for the individual or the couple.

When she first described sexual desire in 1979, Kaplan hypothesized a phase based on clinical rather than scientific evidence, but her ability to describe this state was limited in specifying any psychological feeling. Nonetheless, Kaplan astutely noted that the lack of a sexual appetite constituted a significant entity in itself and that desire was a necessary condition for the sexual response to continue through the arousal and orgasm phases. This was a significant contribution to the earlier investigations of the human sexual response cycle by Masters and Johnson (1966, 1970). Through her clinical observations, Kaplan described sexual desire in terms of "specific sensations that move the individual to seek out, or become receptive to, sexual experiences" (p. 10). She went on to say that when individuals are in a state of desire they may feel "horny," sexy, receptive to sex, or perhaps restless. It is clear that she conceptualized an emotional state that represented a hunger, longing, or wish that could be satiated by sex. Sexual desire, therefore, includes emotions, cognitions, and fantasies that activate the sexual appetite. None of these processes can be measured or observed directly as we can now do with arousal and orgasm.

Thus, the concept of sexual desire continues to be elusive. Of course, Freud (1962) was one of the first physicians to describe this phenomenon in general terms. He believed the libido represented a fundamental drive or life force in humans. Like other theorists, Freud recognized that sexual desire was a *normal* state and lack of desire resulted from some type of inhibition or intrapsychic conflict. Rather than dwell on historical ideas about libido, it will be more useful to discuss the ideas of contemporary theorists and clinicians interested in HSD.

In 1988, Leiblum and Rosen published an edited volume regarding sexual desire disorders. Several contributors to this volume offered their *ideas* on the nature of sexual desire. Yet throughout the book there was not a consistently used *definition* for sexual desire throughout the book. The editors of the volume acknowledged the inherent difficulties in developing a universally accepted definition. Nonetheless, in the introduction they set the stage for the book by offering their own meaning of sexual desire. Interestingly, many, in fact, most of the contributors, did not offer an exposition of sexual desire, but chose to discuss their concept of a *lack of* desire. The reader, therefore, is forced to infer from other aspects of the chapters what the authors mean by desire.

Leiblum and Rosen (1988) stated sexual desire was "a subjective feeling state that may be triggered by both internal and external cues, and that may or may not result in overt sexual behavior" (p. 5). Their definition assumes an intact and functional vascular, endocrine, and central nervous systems. Additionally, they stress the fact that desire is basically a feeling that may be triggered by such internal psychological cues such as fantasy, vasocongestion, or perhaps a sensual or sexual situation such as a romantic dinner. It is interesting to note that in a subsequent chapter in the text, Lieblum and Rosen discuss sexual desire from a "scripting" approach. Script theory has become a major force in conceptualizing sexual behavior by placing more emphasis on cognitions than affect (Weiss, 1998). In other words, the individual internalizes various messages about sexuality learned early in life in the form of cognitions or thoughts. Later these thoughts become an integral component of sexual scripts and determine how sexual behaviors and feelings are enacted. According to Lieblum and Rosen,

sexual scripts provide the "cognitive organization of sexual interactions—
defining the situation as sexual, naming the actors, and directing the behavior" (p. 169).

Lazarus (1988) addresses the issue of sexual desire in his "multimodal
model" of psychotherapy. He formulated the BASIC ID model in which
the therapist assesses and treats the problem from various aspects including
behavior, affect sensation, imagery, cognition, interpersonal relationships,
and biological factors such as medications. Once again, the issue of sexual
desire was addressed by defining the *lack of* desire in terms of a low interest
in sex. It would certainly make sense that sexual desire could be determined
in some fashion through each of the BASIC ID categories. Although Lazarus clearly suggests that treatment should involve attending to each of these
areas, he fails to develop a conceptualization of sexual desire.

Schwartz and Masters (1988) also describe the new Masters and Johnson model of treating HSD. They state that sexual desire is a *natural* function, much like the sexual act. Further, individuals will experience sexual
desire if they do not experience or construct psychological roadblocks. Examples of roadblocks could include such factors as inadequate parenting
or gender identity problems. Their position is forcefully stated: Sex is a
natural function like other customary functions such as respiration, bowel
movements, and bladder activity. Obviously, they see sexual desire and
sexual performance as basic biological functions.

Levin (1984, 1988) has written the most elaborate theory on sexual
desire. His work is from the perspective of a theoretician and clinician,
rather than a researcher. Levin (1988) believes that sexual desire is "the
psychobiological energy that precedes and accompanies arousal and tends
to produce sexual behavior" (p. 23). This definition contains three basic
elements:

1. Sexual desire is that which precedes and accompanies arousal.

2. Sexual desire is the psychobiological propensity to engage in sex.

3. The energy brought to a sexual interaction *is* sexual desire.

Levin also added that sexual desire fluctuates and is often personally
baffling. He discusses several dimensions of sexual desire (1984, 1988).
One of these dimensions is sexual "drive." Drive is the neurological and
endocrine generator of the sexual impulses. It is an internal physical state
that may create genital tingling or erotic fantasy. It is believed to fluctuate
based on various bodily cycles. Sexual drive is a difficult concept to operationalize and to assess.

The second aspect of desire is the concept of sexual "wish." Wish refers
to wanting to be with another person sexually for a variety of reasons. It

might be related to the desire to feel good physically and/or to please the sexual partner.

A third dimension of desire is that of sexual "motive." Levin roughly equates motivation with sexual willingness and discusses four major determinants in his theory. These are:

1. sexual identity
2. quality of the nonsexual relationship
3. self and partner regulation
4. transference from past attachments

These four factors take into account such phenomena as the person's comfort with their sexual identity, the quality of the overall relationship, using sex to ease pain, creating greater comfort and intimacy, expressing affection, and transferring positive images of significant past attachments. Levin does not claim to have a comprehensive or scientific theory. He appears to view it from a heuristic perspective, offering us a guide to begin understanding the experience of sexual desire.

One of the most interesting studies on sexual desire dealt with identifying the factors that individuals use to assess their *own* level of sexual desire (Beck, Bozman, & Qualtrough, 1991). This empirically based investigation employed several measures of love, sex, and social desirability. In general, the men in the study experienced sexual desire slightly more often than the women did. However, within both samples of men and women, large individual variations were reported with respect to sexual appetite. This finding substantiates our clinical observation that sexual desire may change for the individual, depending on circumstances such as fatigue and stress. The participants in this study (144 college students) could easily differentiate between desire and sexual activity and reported that the two did not necessarily co-occur. For instance, sometimes the sole purpose of sexual activity was to please the sexual partner. We will elaborate on this point a little later in this chapter.

Men and women did differ somewhat in how they assessed their feelings of desire. Men tended to rely on fantasies, daydreams, and genital arousal as an indicator of their level of sexual desire. Women typically preferred genital arousal, intercourse, and sexual daydreams to indicate their level of sexual interest. The fact that women relied on genital sensations at all was interesting in light of some prior research, which showed women often have difficulty judging their level of genital arousal (Rosen & Beck, 1988; Laan & Everaerd, 1995).

The most unexpected finding from this investigation was the poor correlation between love and sex. Perhaps, this sample of college students is

representative of young adults experimenting with sex in uncommitted relationships. Overall, however, the conclusions indicate that nonprofession-
als use an amalgamation of experience to define their sexual desire,
including physical as well as psychological indices. Thus, the conceptualization of sexual appetite is broader than we realized, and definitions of desire
do not adhere to gender-based expectations. The subjective experience
(feeling) of desire alone is only a part of the client's assessment process;
therefore, therapeutic assessment of sexual desire should incorporate the
parameters identified by Beck, Bozman, and Qualtrough (1991).

A final implication of this study is that the stages of sexual desire and
arousal may not be as distinct as postulated by Kaplan (1979). There may
be considerable overlap of the psychological state of fantasy and the physical sensations that accompany sexual images, thoughts, and feelings. It may
also be the case that the processes of desire and arousal actually represent
a third deeper operation for which we have no term or language. Nonetheless, the complexity of the sexual appetite is once again affirmed.

## DESIRE AND SEXUAL SATISFACTION

Researchers have discovered some gender differences between sexual desire, marital satisfaction, and sexual satisfaction. Hurlbert and Apt (1994)
explored the relationship between *low* sexual desire, relationship dissatisfaction, and sexual dissatisfaction. For men, both marital *and* sexual dissatisfaction was associated with low levels of sexual desire. For women, *only*
marital dissatisfaction was associated with low levels of desire. In other
words, women tend to evaluate their levels of desire with the overall quality
of the marital relationship rather than with their sexual satisfaction. Men
are much more concerned with their level of sexual satisfaction in determining whether they feel desire. This finding once again confirms the idea
that for women sex is more relationally oriented than it is for men. In
addition, a woman's desire for sexual activity may be an indicator of her
emotional satisfaction with the relationship while for men it may only be
an indicator of his sexual satisfaction. This finding has been supported in
several similar studies including those by Rosenzweig and Dailey (1989);
Hurlbert and Whittaker (1991); Regan and Bercheid (1996); and Basson
(2000). In addition, women's sexual satisfaction may also be a function of
how sex is *initiated* by her partner (Byers & Heinlein, 1989). This observation is not an uncommon theme in our clinical practices. That is, many
women complain about the fact that sex is initiated without any "warming
up" period and sometimes in a manner that is perceived as hurried or even
rough. Thus, women often can become simply "turned off" by a series of

initiation behaviors, even if they experience an appetite for sex. These women do not *lack* desire. Instead, they come to anticipate that unsatisfying caressing and touch will follow sexual desire. If the faulty sexual initiation happens often enough, such women will inevitably develop anticipatory anxiety regarding sexual contact with her partner.

For women the relationships between sexual satisfaction, marital satisfaction, sexual desire, sexual arousal, and orgasm are complex. Researchers have not yet been able to tease apart all the various factors and give each one some normative weight. It is clear they are all somehow intermingled. Predicting sexual satisfaction for women appears to involve the quality of her relationship, her attitudes toward sex (personality variables, cultural messages, religious beliefs), and to some degree sexual satisfaction. Even in situations where women cannot consistently reach an orgasm via intercourse, they report that if the overall relationship is working, they feel satisfied sexually (Frank et al., 1978; Hurlbert, Apt, & Rabehl, 1993). Also, these studies tell us that orgasm during intercourse is still not that common an experience and that the ability to reach an orgasm consistently is not used as a major index of sexual satisfaction for women.

## Sexual Asynchrony and Desire

Earlier in the first chapter, we discussed the various definitions of desire and HSD. At this point, the reader should have some understanding about what it means to *lack* desire. We pointed out that a lack of desire could be experienced as an internal or external discrepancy in the normal sexual appetite. That is, in the case of internal discrepancy, the *individual* experiences a level of desire that is discordant with his or her own wishes. This condition could represent a change from the person's normal state or it could be an ongoing disappointment (wanting to feel desire and not being able to). In the case of an external discrepancy, there is a *relationship* asynchrony. One partner consistently has a greater sexual appetite than the partner that generally lacks desire does. There is, however, one other situation to consider when assessing for HSD. The partners may simply not be "in sync" with each other much of the time.

We mentioned above that couples might have sex when desire and activity do not co-occur. Researchers interested in understanding why individuals have sex when they are not necessarily in the mood have focused on the topics of "unwanted" or "compliant" sexual relations (Shortland & Hunter, 1995; Sprecher, Hatfield, Cortese, Potapova, & Levitskaya, 1994). The results revealed that it was surprisingly common for the subjects to consent to undesired sexual relations. In an investigation of this topic using

80 male and 80 female heterosexual college students, O'Sullivan and All-geier (1998) found similar results. The subjects were asked to report about a 2-week period during their relationship. One third or 38% of the subjects had engaged in some form of "unwanted" sexual activity during this time.

- 20% of the women and 8.7% of the men engaged in unwanted inter-course.
- About 16% of the women and 13% of the men engaged in unwanted hugging or making out.
- Roughly 16% of the women and 8% of the men reported unwanted fondling of breasts.

These statistics show us that a number of sexual interactions occur without the benefit of desire. When the students were asked why these interactions were permitted they gave a number of reasons. The two main reasons were 1) to satisfy the partner, and 2) to avoid tension in the relationship. Most of the reasons given by the subjects involved altruistic motives rather than coercion by a partner, although respondents of another study reported feelings of inadequacy as well as peer pressure (Poppen & Segal, 1988).

In particular, the study by Sprecher and colleagues (1994) reported results that were similar to those found by O'Sullivan and Allgeier (1998). In fact, the former study found that 35% of college men and 55% of college women had engaged in nonconsensual sexual behavior. The reader is cautioned, however, that generalizing from studies using college students in short-term relationships has many problems. Nonetheless, these studies do raise some important questions about how we go about defining desire or lack thereof. Moreover, implications for assessment and treatment of HSD are generated by such investigations.

We believe asynchrony is a fact of sexual life. Sometimes couples connect sexually when they are both in the mood and sometimes they do not. Many couples do intuitively understand this lack of synchrony and accept it as a fact of life. Unfortunately, more couples are unfamiliar with this concept and do not communicate sexually anyway. The absence of communication in couples who are also sexually uninformed is a dangerous combination. It can lead to some very inaccurate conclusions. Some view the lack of synchrony as having a much darker meaning. They do not believe their partner is *ever* interested in them. A more serious scenario occurs when couples panic and inaccurately assume that they are not "in love."

In our clinical experience, we know that at least part of the time partners engage in various sexual activities in order to please the other partner. Typical reasons for complying with the sexual desires of the partner with the greater sexual appetite include the avoidance of relationship conflict, sexual disappointment, or disapproval from the other partner. These are altruistic strategies employed by many couples in an effort to maintain relationship equilibrium. In fact, they can be fruitful provided that one partner is not violating the boundaries of the other with unwanted nonconsensual sexual activity.

Sexual asynchrony is a common experience in couples that has been ignored in clinical literature and only rarely discussed in research literature. Sex therapists frequently hear the complaint that one is ready for sexual intimacy when the other is not. For example, one partner likes to have sex in the morning and the other at night. We must be careful not to confuse asynchrony with HSD and fortunately some of the same techniques we used to treat HSD may be useful with this problem. How does the clinician differentiate between a lack of a desire in the individual and a couple that is out of sync? What implications do we see for treatment of HSD?

Understanding of asynchrony has broadened our definition of what is the "normal" sexual appetite. Thus, treatment options are also based on this awareness. For example, one of the goals for the couple would be to try to *create* some sexual synchrony in their intimate relationship. Treatment, therefore, would include educating the couple about each individual's particular sexual rhythm and how these are sometimes different. It is much easier to accept occasional asynchrony given this information. The clinician can help the couple to get in sync by:

• reviewing the concept of sexual asynchrony,

• promoting sexual communication,

• suggesting scheduling of sexual opportunities (this concept will be described in detail in a later chapter),

• teaching the partners how to "read" each others sexual moods more effectively, and

• learning how to create seduction rituals in order to facilitate synchrony of desire.

A seduction ritual is simply a set of behaviors that helps to promote sexual desire. As an example, one couple lived apart during the week due to the husband's job out of state. When he would arrive home on Thursday night, he would almost immediately want some form of sexual interaction. He felt desire for, in fact, fantasized about sex with his wife on the 3-hour trip home, and expected her to be in the same mood. Typically, his wife would work until he arrived home and then stop. She was *not* in the mood for sex at that time. The husband interpreted her rejection of his sexual advances as an indication that she did not like him, did not want to please him, and that she was just not as sexual a person as he was. His wife explained that she could not stop work and just turn herself on for him. She also let him know that she missed him, wanted to spend time with him having dinner and relaxing, and then she would be in the mood. She had, in fact, described the seduction ritual for him. The husband thought about what she said and changed his approach. With some fine-tuning, this ritual began to work effectively leading to sexual desire and sexual satisfaction for each partner. Once they had achieved this goal, it was easier for both of them to have sexual interactions when they were not initially in the mood.

## What Is Normal?

The question of what is normal is one that is asked frequently in the research literature and is also a question that clients bring to therapy. In many cases, the partners will debate about the "normalcy" of level of sexual desire, frequency of sexual activity, and types of sexual behaviors. It is useful for the clinician to have some idea about what is statistically normal in the general population. These usually very broad parameters are representative of what would be considered normal within the statistical model. However, as sex and marital therapists, we are not trying to fit everyone to one model. In practice, we tend to blend the statistical model with the personal comfort/discomfort model. In other words, each individual has some range of behavior within which they feel comfortable and outside of that, they begin to feel uncomfortable. The same is true for couples. In fact, it is more important for the therapist to learn from the couple about what is sexually typical for them. Of particular interest would be departures from their "normal" state in terms of desire, frequency, and kinds of behaviors. The couple's sexual parameters or their desire for sexual activity may change dramatically over time. For instance, it is not uncommon for young, newly formed couples to have sex multiple times per week, sometimes multiple times per day. Within a period of a couple of years, however, this frequency may have significantly dropped, yet each partner may be satisfied with the frequency of sexual interaction.

In this final section, we will not provide a detailed and comprehensive overview of the research, but mention some of the major studies that would be of use to the clinician. Clinicians interested in additional information can consult any number of general undergraduate texts for these statistics. Oddly enough, most texts on sex therapy only discuss pathology and fail to review any statistics on what is normative behavior. While the focus of this book is on desire and lack thereof, the reader will remember that individuals use several indexes by which to gauge desire. Therefore, we will review some of these behaviors in this section.

## Sexual Desire and Frequency

Surprisingly, only one study has investigated the relationship between sexual desire and the frequency of sexual intercourse. With all the attention being paid to sexual desire in the last decade it is remarkable that more research has not been conducted on measuring the actual "behaviors" which express desire. LoPiccolo and Friedman (1988) carried out this study using 93 nonclinical married couples. The mean age for the men was 34, for the women 32; the mean length of marriage was 9 years with 2.6 children; and a family income of $33,000 was the average. The study compared the frequency of desire with the "actual" frequency of intercourse.

*Men*
- About 12% reported desiring sex *more than once a day*. The actual frequency of intercourse was 2% of the times it was desired.
- About 29% said they desired sex *once a day* but had intercourse about 2% of the times it was desired.
- About 42% desired sex *three or four times a week*. In this group, intercourse occurred about 36% of the desired frequency.
- About 12% wanted sex *twice a week*, but had it that often only about 30% of the time.
- About 4% wanted sex *once a week*, but had sex that often only about 16% of the time.

*Women*
- About 3% desired sex *more than once a day* and only 1% reported having intercourse that often.
- About 20% wanted sex *once a day* but had it that often only 3% of the time.
- About 51% wanted sex *three or four times a week* and only 40% reported having intercourse that frequently.
- About 17% said they wanted sex *twice a week* and only 24% reported having intercourse that often.
- 9% desired sex *once a week* and had intercourse that often 21% of the time.

This study showed that men *wanted* sex more frequently than women did. It also showed that the *actual frequencies* reported were about the same for women and men. Therefore, *both* genders exerted an influence on how often sex occurred, especially at the extremes of the sampling distribution where men were more responsible for increases and women for decreases.

## Fantasy and Sexual Desire

Kaplan (1995) views sexual fantasy as the "mental representation" of the sexual appetite. It is a necessary condition for sexual desire and so critical to the sexual appetite that Kaplan uses the terms fantasy and desire synonymously. Fantasy involves the application of mental processes such as cognitions, images, and feelings in order to trigger the sexual response, fuel sexual arousal, or promote orgasm (Sue, 1979; Loren & Weeks, 1986). The individual is free to experiment with desired behaviors or to alter the physical attributes of the self or the partner. Fantasy can embellish the sexual repertoire and promote passion to the extent that the individual is comfortable. In addition, it can provide a safe antidote for sexual boredom or habituation. Studies conducted by Sue, Loren and Weeks, and Masters and Johnson (1979) concluded that the older, more sexually experienced subjects often shifted their fantasies from an established partner to a replacement partner. It appears, therefore, that an important part of the arousal mechanism is sexual variety. Variety can be achieved by virtually exchanging partners, doing different things with one's partner, or most simply and safely, having a sexual fantasy that introduces some variety. The three studies cited above also revealed a commonly held clinical assumption that a great deal of variety in sexual fantasies exists within and among most individuals. Although there is tremendous variety, the basic purpose or function of sexual fantasy remains the same—to promote arousal. The extent to which the individual creating the fantasy shares or enacts it with a partner is a matter of choice and discretion (Carnes, 1997).

The following findings are of interest regarding the role of fantasy in sexual desire:

1. 95% of men and women have sexual fantasies (Leitenberg & Henning, 1995).

2. It appears that as sexual experience increases so does the frequency of sexual fantasies (Gold & Chick, 1988).

3. The content of fantasies varies greatly and differs for men and women mostly in terms of the frequency with which a particular fantasy occurs. About 70% to 75% of men and women fantasize about their

loved one, but 33% of men and 18% of women fantasize about sex with more than one person (Hunt, 1974).

4. The range of sexual fantasies is tremendous, and all are basically considered normal unless they are personally distressing to the individual or the individual feels compelled to act on fantasy material that is inappropriate.

5. The primary function of fantasy is to increase feelings of sexual desire, increase the partner's attractiveness, or imagine activities one would like to try (Sue, 1979; Loren and Weeks, 1986).

6. In a sample of college students who were relatively sexually inexperienced, the types of fantasies men and women reported were remarkably similar (Sue, 1979). For example, they fantasized about:
   - a past sexual experience,
   - an ideal sexual experience,
   - being sexually irresistible,
   - having sex in different places, and
   - having oral-genital sex.

7. About 1 out of 5 men and women reported feeling uncomfortable with their sexual fantasies (Loren & Weeks, 1986).

8. Each gender overestimated the frequency with which the other had fantasies (Loren & Weeks 1986).

9. Women also thought men must enjoy their fantasies more (Loren & Weeks, 1986).

10. Masters and Johnson (1979) conducted a study using sexually experienced, mature individuals. They found that heterosexual men and women shared the same top three sexual fantasies. These were:
    - replacement of one's established partner,
    - a forced sexual encounter, and
    - observing someone else having sex.

Group sex and homosexual fantasies were fairly common in the Masters and Johnson (1979) sample. It should be noted these fantasies were assessed between 1957 and 1968. Fantasies may change over the course of time depending upon the culture and, in our clinical experience, what is portrayed in the media, especially pornography.

ABSENCE OF SEXUAL FANTASIES

As we stated previously, the main feature of HSDD is the deficiency or absence of sexual fantasies (APA, 1994). If we think of sexual fantasies as thoughts involving mental images, then our assertion that fantasies are an important part of the etiology is consistent with our theory that positive sexual thoughts are also of key importance. An absence of sexual fantasy is functionally the same as an absence of sexually positive thoughts. In spite of the fact that the lack of fantasies is an integral component of the definition of HSDD, very little literature has been published on this phenomenon as part of a lack of desire. Of all the chapters on lack of desire in Leiblum and Rosen's (1988) book, only one theorist mentioned fantasy as an element of treatment and none discussed it as part of the etiology of HSD. Our clinical experience with HSD suggests the definition is correct in including an absence of fantasies. Most of the clients we have treated report the absence of or infrequency of sexual fantasies. It is one of the most striking features of this disorder. Many also report never having had an active fantasy life in spite of the fact that the disorder may be secondary rather than primary. Other clients with situational HSD may have fantasies about other people, but almost never about their established partner.

There is one notable exception in the area of research on fantasy and sexual dysfunction. Nutter and Condron (1985) investigated the sexual fantasies of men with erectile dysfunction and/or HSD. The men in the HSD group showed a lower rate of sexual fantasy during daydreaming, foreplay, intercourse, and masturbation when compared to a control group. The fantasies of the men included the following themes. The most frequent themes appear first and follow in descending order:

- kissing the genitals of a woman,
- being kissed on the genitals,
- sex with a replacement partner,
- reliving a past sexual experience, and
- imagining having sex with the established partner.

As a side note, the men in the HSD group have higher rates of masturbation when compared to those in the control group.

Nutter and Condron (1983) conducted an earlier study with female subjects experiencing HSD and found exactly the same pattern as men in their lack of sexual fantasies. In both studies, the participants with HSD did report some fantasies, but significantly less than in the control group. Obviously, much more research remains to be done in this area. Studies need to be much larger, to differentiate among the different types of HSD, and to present more detailed information about the types of fantasies.

## Frequency of Solitary Sex

Masturbation or self-pleasuring is clearly an activity that is more common in men than in women (Kinsey, Pomeroy, & Martin, 1948; Kinsey, Pomeroy, Martin, & Gebhard, 1953). Kinsey found that by the age of 20, 92% of men had masturbated compared to only one third of the women. By the age of 40, the number of women who masturbated was 62%. Hunt (1974) made almost identical findings some 20 years later. Atwood and Gagnon (1987) also found that about twice as many college men masturbate, as do college women. Additionally, Kinsey and colleagues and Hunt and colleagues found that men are not only more likely to masturbate, but are also likely to masturbate two to three times more frequently. It is also interesting to note that being partnered and having a high degree of partnered sex tends to increase, not decrease, the frequency of masturbation (Laumannn, Gagnon, Michael, & Michaels, 1994). Also, 60% of men and 40% of women under the age of 60 had reported masturbating during the last year (Laumannn et al., 1994).

## Frequency of Dyadic Sex

Dyadic sex, specifically, marital sex, has been the subject of many studies over the past five decades. Three of the major studies showed a remarkable consistency in the measured frequency of marital sex (Kinsey et al., 1948; Kinsey et. al., 1953; Smith, 1991; Westoff, Bumpass, & Ryder, 1969). These researchers showed that younger married couples had sex about 2.5 times per week. Our clients often cite this number as being the average they should aspire to because they have seen it so many times in popular literature. As age increases, the frequency of sex decreases gradually. For middle-aged couples the frequency drops to about 2 times per week, and by the later years to about once per week.

In terms of which partner initiates sexual behavior, Blumstein and Schwartz (1983) found that in married couples 33% report that men and women initiate in equal proportions. In 51% of the couples, husbands were more likely to initiate, and in 16% of couples the wife was the initiator. As stated above, initiative behaviors are often a reflection of sexual desire and in fewer instances, the aspiration to pleasure the more-interested partner.

Laumann, Paik, and Rosen (1999) conducted the most comprehensive and recent survey of sexual function and dysfunction. In general, they found that partnered individuals were the most sexually active. In short, being married increases the chances of having sex. They also found that the oldest and the youngest in their sample experienced less sexual activity due to a lack of partner availability. Moreover, the level of sexual satisfaction was highly correlated with the person's overall level of life satisfaction. Unlike many of the other studies mentioned, Laumann, Paik, and Rosen assessed that:

- about a third of couples have sex a few times a week,
- a few couples have sex a few times a month, and
- a few have sex a few times a year.

Unfortunately, the authors only reported general statistics. It is difficult to know what they mean by the use of the term "a few."

Our assumption is that given the incidence of HSD reported earlier, it should be no surprise that many couples are only having sex a few times a year.

## CONCLUSION

This chapter shows us that there is much more work to do in developing a research-based approach to defining sexual desire. A theory of sexual desire needs to be developed in conjunction with research and clinical literature. This approach should include the ways in which sexual desire is related to: the couple's relationship, sexual satisfaction, personal preferences, and the asynchrony that occurs between partners. In spite of these theoretical short-comings, the clinician who understands the issues described in this chapter will be in a good position to help the couple sort out the severity of their problem, normalize that which is commonplace, and identify real and po-tential problems.

# 3

# Etiology: Psychological
# Risk Factors

WE HAVE LEARNED MORE ABOUT the psychogenic etiology of HSD, as the incidence of this phenomenon has become a frequently noted clinical presentation. Initially, Kaplan (1979) drew our attention to HSD in a text devoted to the understanding and treatment of desire phase disorders. At the time, she formulated a psychoanalytically based etiology rooted in her belief that feelings of sexual desire are *actively suppressed* in individuals with HSD. She postulated that the *immediate* cause of HSD is an involuntary or unconscious coping mechanism in which the individual defends against and avoids erotic fantasies and feelings. Avoidance of sexual desire can take many forms such as focusing on the negative characteristics of the partner or evoking negative "countererotic" memories or images. A range of deeper conflicts was believed by Kaplan to trigger the immediate causes. Regardless of the source of the conflict, anxiety was considered a key feature of the individual's need to avert feelings of sexual desire.

In 1987, Weeks presented another formulation of HSD in a chapter in *Integrating Sex and Marital Therapy* (Weeks & Hof, eds.). He used an *integrative* model to organize the etiology of this problem from three perspectives:

1. individual (factors such as personality style)

2. interactional (the relationship)

3. intergenerational (internalized messages from the families-of-origin)

At the time this chapter was written, few articles had been published on the etiology of HSD.

Leiblum and Rosen's (1988) book contained many chapters that described various etiologies and treatments for the lack of sexual desire. With the exception of Lazarus (1988), each of the models in the Leiblum and Rosen volume stressed a particular theoretical approach such as biological, cognitive, analytic, systems, and scripting. In 1995, Kaplan produced another book dealing with the various complexities of sexual desire disorders. With almost two decades of additional clinical experience, she developed the "multiple-layer" model for determining etiology. This paradigm is based on the psychoanalytic concept, which distinguishes immediate from deeper psychogenic causes of HSD (Kaplan, 1995). In 1989, Weeks wrote once more about the etiology of HSD in another edited volume, *Treating Couples*, in which he again used the model that integrates the three elements mentioned above: the individual, the couple, and the family-of-origin. In 1994, much more was known about the etiology of HSD. Weeks was able to offer a number of original ideas based on his clinical observations (Weeks & Hof, 1994). We will discuss this in greater detail later.

Beginning with Kaplan's (1979) book, and moving forward, everyone who has written about lack of desire appears to agree that assessing the factors that contribute to this issue is difficult and time consuming, and that the problem is a multifactorial one. In other words, HSD rarely occurs due to one element, but, rather, to a confluence of elements. Problems having multiple causes are difficult to assess. The clinician may believe he or she has found the key factor only to find it is embedded within a much larger picture. Sometimes the factor that stands out most is being used as the justification for the problem by the individual, but is not the root of the problem. Thus, the assessment phase of treating HSD may be extended and arduous for clients who need a good deal of probing before the problem is fully understood.

Before describing the specific factors that may contribute to HSD, we would like to provide a brief overview of some of the major theoretical models employed in this field and then describe our own approach. One approach is the *biological/hormonal* one. One's sexual desire is in part viewed as a function of normally functioning central nervous (brain and spinal cord), vascular, and hormonal systems. When a problem exists such as a lack of testosterone, desire begins to diminish. Obviously, research in this area is medically oriented and psychological factors are virtually ignored. Traditional *psychoanalytic* models look for a "deeper" cause for the lack of desire. They focus on intrapsychic conflicts that have an historical basis in the early years. Apfelbaum (1988) formulated a more contemporary analytic or intrapsychic approach focusing on extreme performance anxiety based largely on societal expectations. Of course, the major problem with analytic approaches is that they tend to ignore the current dynamics of the problem and do not consider the role the current relationship plays in the problem. Scharff's (1988) work is based on an *object relations* approach. This approach postulates various developmental and familial processes in the infant that shape the sense of self, including attraction, fear, and sexual desirability. Verhulst and Heiman (1988) were two of the first theorists to propose a model that was based on systems theory. They described interpersonal dynamics such as deficiencies in affective communication and power imbalances as factors in lack of desire. Levin (1984, 1988) believed that biological, intrapsychic, and interpersonal factors were involved. His theory is closest to ours in organizing etiologic factors.

## AN INTEGRATED ETIOLOGICAL MODEL:
## INDIVIDUAL RISK FACTORS

Weeks (1989, 1994) developed an integrative approach to treatment called the *intersystems* model in which the therapist assesses and treats the client from multiple perspectives. At the heart of this theory is the idea that the clinician evaluates the factors producing the problem from an individual (biological, psychological), interactional (dyadic), and intergenerational (family-of-origin) perspective. Once the factors producing a problem have been identified, the therapist then links treatment techniques or strategies to *each* factor. Utilizing this theory is challenging because it demands that the therapist is well versed in several therapeutic modalities (individual, couple, and family therapy) and in the theories, techniques, and research based on these approaches. Rarely are therapists so well trained in spite of the fact that most therapists define themselves as "eclectic."

The truth, as we perceive it, is that most therapists operate within one modality at a time, using only a few models of treatment. We have seen many seasoned individual therapists in clinical programs seeking training in couples' work who are wedded to a singular theory. It may prove that an individually oriented therapist will have more difficulty dissecting the couple's relationship or understanding early impact of family dynamics on the dyadic problem. We have found that it is not easy for therapists to expand their repertoire to include several formulas for assessment and treatment and to be flexible in their choice of approach. We assert that the therapy must be designed for the individual or couple and that the client(s) should not be "forced" into some therapeutic mold or framework limited by the therapists vision. By organizing the etiologic factors using the intersystems approach, we hope the therapist will be able to "see" the various factors at work in contributing to the problem. Only well-seasoned, highly experienced, and highly trained therapists are capable of using the intersystems model effectively. Yet, some understanding is better than no understanding, and we hope this text will be helpful in laying the foundation for treatment and that appropriate referrals can be made when the scope of practice exceeds that of the therapist.

The intersystems approach may also help the therapist grow in new directions as well as promote flexibility in choosing treatment options. As therapists, each of us operates with an implicit model of how clients function, what produces pathology, what is healthy, and how clients change. When we change our implicit model in compliance with a broader explicit model, we are able to change ourselves and learn new ideas that can benefit our clients. Treating HSD for over 20 years has proven to be challenging and has led to our significant growth as therapists.

In previous chapters, we discussed the various perspectives and presentations of HSD. The material in this chapter represents our observations of many cases over the years as well as clinical reports and empirical studies in the literature. Empirical studies have clearly not kept pace with the clinical observations. Thus, we will mention many possible contributors that have not yet been empirically investigated. In all probability, it may take years for the research to examine all the various ideas about etiology. Clinical presentations vary as societal expectations of men and women change. Currently, our clinical practices are flooded with an epidemic of HSD in women of childbearing ages and women in the perimenopausal years. We also treat an alarming number of men who present with nonorganic HSD or HSD of mixed etiology. In the meantime, we must continue to exercise our clinical judgment and caution in discerning which factors contribute to this problem, the significance of each of these factors, and how best to treat each factor. The list of risk factors identified below is not exhaustive, as clients respond to different risks in different ways. This chapter will focus on the individual psychological factors. The relationship and the family-of-origin risk factors will be discussed subsequently. Medical risk factors will also be discussed in Chapters 3 and 6.

## Nonopsychiatric Factors

A host of risk factors for HSD could be considered nonpsychiatric. These are conditions that do not meet the diagnostic criteria of *DSM-IV* (1994), but are commonly seen in clinical practice. Some of these problems may be normative such as life-cycle changes involving marriage, divorce, having children, or trying to have children. Sometimes the risk factor is as simple as a fear of pregnancy. The client(s) may not realize they have a strong fear of being a parent, thus they avoid sex. In one of our cases, a woman stated explicitly that she did not want to have children. Whenever she had sex, she feared that she might become pregnant. She started to avoid sex in order to avoid pregnancy. Her husband kept insisting on wanting to make her pregnant. The more he pressured her, the less interested she became in sex. She was telling him sexually that she was refusing to have children.

Many problems we treat are simply caused by the individual client's personal distresses whereas another client might not be so severely affected or see the problem as being so great. A mother might be overly distressed over a sick child or over a comment made by her boss. A man might be inordinately disturbed by a downturn in his business or the fact that he is not receiving as much recognition at work as he thinks is warranted. Risk factors that cause personal distress have a cumulative effect in some cases. One or two events may not be enough to produce much anxiety, but when several stressors are accumulated over a brief period of time the magnitude of effect is exponential.

ANXIETY

In one way or another, anxiety is a pervasive factor in the development and maintenance of most sexual difficulties (Masters & Johnson, 1970; Kaplan, 1983, 1985). Apfelbaum (1988) developed a novel concept for the specific type of anxiety felt by an individual with HSD. He called this emotional reaction "response anxiety" which is similar to *performance anxiety*, an old and well-understood term in the field of sex therapy. Masters and Johnson (1970) used the term *performance anxiety* consistently in describing the reaction of an individual who is fearful that he or she will not be able to carry out a specific sexual behavior. For instance, men sometimes fear they will not be able to sustain or maintain an erection. They then worry about their sexual performance, thereby becoming "spectators" rather than participants in the sexual act. They try to *force* a particular behavior such as an erection or perhaps orgasm rather than letting it occur naturally as a result of sexual enjoyment. This term *performance anxiety* is used to refer to some particular *behavior* such as erection or ejaculation.

More broadly, *response anxiety* refers to a particular *emotional response* rather than a specific behavior. Specifically, when an individual with low or a lack of sexual desire tries to feel desire or force herself to feel desire, she begins to feel anxious that she is not feeling desire. In these cases, the client:

1. wants to feel desire,
2. misses feeling desire,
3. believes she should feel desire for her partner or for her own sake, and,
4. worries about not feeling that which she wants to feel or thinks she should feel.

The client then becomes trapped in a vicious cycle. In virtually every case of HSD we have seen in which the client wishes to feel desire, we have noted *response anxiety*. Sexual desire and *response anxiety* cannot coexist in the individual at the same time. The more *response anxiety* the client feels the more difficult it is for him or her to feel desire. This description suggests that a common or universal effect of HSD is *response anxiety* especially for clients who experience the internal discrepancy between what they think they should feel and what they actually feel. Apfelbaum (1988) believes it is not only an effect, but also a cause of lack of sexual desire. This belief is consistent with our clinical experience in which we have noted throughout the years that clients with HSD become entrapped in this viscous, self-defeating cycle.

The mechanism that underlies anxiety in sexual dysfunction is slowly being investigated empirically. Barlow (1986) published an article that reviewed research in this area and from that research developed a working model for viewing sexual dysfunctionality, including lack of sexual desire. He stated that four factors differentiated individuals who functioned sexually from those who do not. Sexually dysfunctional individuals:

1. showed more negative affect in a sexual context,
2. underreported their level of sexual arousal,
3. were distracted by outside stimuli, and
4. were distracted by performance-related sexual anxiety, which inhibits arousal.

The model proposed by Barlow (1986) suggests that anxiety and cognitive interference work together in a vicious cycle producing sexual dysfunction. The fourth point made above is consistent with Apfelbaum's (1988) theory of *response anxiety*. The individual with a lack of desire (not feeling turned on) is distracted by concerns about sexual performance.

Needless to say, many individuals with a lack of desire will still engage in a sexual encounter without deriving much pleasure or having an orgasm during it. In our experience, it is also much more likely that the female will not have an orgasm. These women then begin to feel anxious about not having an orgasm for their partner, and some men fuel this anxiety by pressing their partners to have an orgasm each time they have sex. Women are now faced with experiencing both response anxiety (not feeling turned on) and performance anxiety (not having an orgasm.)

A 29-year-old woman, Michele, described an example of this kind of nonpsychiatric sexual anxiety. She has been married for 10 years and has three children under the age of 6 years. In an individual session, she recounted that sexual relations with her husband felt like a chore, similar to folding the laundry. Michele felt that she could not rest until all of her chores were completed. When she knew that her husband wanted sex, she would avoid going to bed or she would comply without much genuine enthusiasm. She feared that he would notice her lack of desire despite her feigned interest in sex. She was anxious about not enjoying sexual relations, wanted to want sex, and was worried that she would disappoint her husband, Dan. In a subsequent session, Dan discussed how sad he felt that his exhausted wife did not seem to enjoy sex with him. The couple had not discussed this problem together prior to counseling.

LoPiccolo and Friedman (1988) also noted that religious orthodoxy plays a strong role in HSD. Of course, in many partners it does not have an effect. In cases where it does play a role, the partner has been exposed to a variety of sexually negative messages in a religious context. Of course, two of those messages are that sex is bad before marriage, and sexual thoughts and desire are sinful. It is difficult to suddenly switch these beliefs following marriage.

Our culture is sexually saturated at one level. Messages about being sexual are pervasive in popular media. In our experience, without the benefit of accurate information or discussion among people, many people think that everyone else is "sexier." In other words, people feel the need to present themselves as being sexually interested. Moreover, one of our strongest beliefs about marriage is that it involves a sexual relationship based on mutual attraction and desire. Some individuals do not and cannot feel as sexy as they think the culture or their spouse demand. When these individuals begin to dwell on this idea, it simply creates more pressure and anxiety to be that which one is not.

NEGATIVE COGNITIVE DISTORTIONS

Kaplan (1979) postulated that an active mental mechanism was at the root of HSD. However, she never described what that mechanism might be. Our theory is that sexual desire is based at least in part on having positive sexual cognitions. The positive cognitions fall into three categories:

1. thoughts about self
2. thoughts about partner
3. thoughts about the relationship

Some of these thoughts may be in our conscious awareness. We may think about having sex or about some aspect of sex during sex or positively anticipate a sexual interaction. Many times these thoughts are "transparent," meaning we do not realize we are thinking about them. They are a part of the automatic process that precede and occur during and even after a sexual experience. For example, we do not stop to think about what we are going to say to someone or to our spouse. We simply say what we were "thinking." If we are going out to a favorite place such as a park, beach, or an eatery, we might think about being there before we arrive. This state of *positive anticipation* can create a positive mood and even sensory experiences such as feeling the warmth of the sun, having a sense of relaxation, or tasting the food we plan to order. The reverse process can also occur. Rather than thinking positive thoughts and positively anticipating the experience, we may think overt and covert negative thoughts.

An integral part of our theory is that clients with HSD experience a preponderance of negative cognitions compared to positive cognitions about sex. These cognitions may be about the self, partner, or relationship and usually include all three categories. In every case we have assessed, we have uncovered a number of negative cognitions. These negative cognitions form the basis for the "turn off" mechanism. As long as the client is automatically thinking those negative thoughts, or experiencing *negative anticipation* they will not be able to feel much desire. It is similar to swimming upstream. The feelings follow the cognitive stream. The thoughts tend to fall into two broad categories:

1. thoughts that have no basis in reality
2. thoughts that are reality based

The effect of each type is the same, but the treatment differs significantly. In the chapter on assessment, we will discuss how to uncover these thoughts and give numerous case examples in order to provide you with a sense of the kinds of *negative anticipation* we often see. Later, in the treatment chapters, we will discuss how to work with these negative thoughts therapeutically.

SEXUAL IGNORANCE AND MYTHOLOGY

Masters and Johnson (1970) stated that one of the risk factors for clients with sexual problems was a lack of appropriate sex education. This was a simple idea that had a great deal of appeal in explaining sexual problems. They did not elaborate on this idea, perhaps due to the fact that little was actually known about the effects of sexual ignorance and sexual mythology. In our thinking, sexual ignorance would refer to someone who has acquired *inaccurate* beliefs about sexuality or who does not have a fund of knowledge with which to base an opinion about sexual convictions and behaviors. The fact is that everyone has many opinions about sexuality, which are acquired through our culture. If the schools do not have sex education children learn about it from their peers in the schoolyard and elsewhere. As children develop, they are exposed to more and more of the culture, particularly the popular culture. Sex is implicitly or explicitly embedded in music, movies, printed material, and the Internet. Those who want to view it, especially with the advent of the Internet, easily acquire pornography. In a recent survey of college students by Ballard and Morris (1998) regarding *where* they believed they obtained their knowledge about sex, the three primary sources were:

1. same-sex peers
2. the media
3. parents (mostly mothers)

Unfortunately, many of the messages embedded in this material are not based in fact. Mythology fuels many predominant beliefs about sex, particularly the notion that sex is something everyone should want. Men's magazines provide unrealistic images about how they are to look, how large the penis should be, and how they should be sexual supermen and conquerors. A quick scan of women's magazines quickly reveals that women are focusing on how to get the maximum pleasure out of sex, how to provide the ultimate pleasure to the man, or how to keep a man. In the last few years, both men's and women's magazines have gradually provided some factually based information with sex columns written by or in consultation with sexuality experts. Nonetheless, letters to magazines like *Penthouse* and similar forums just give men more reason to believe they are somehow falling short of what they should be sexually. Being bombarded with these messages does not create ignorance, but instead, promotes misinformation in clients who carry sexual mythology as truth.

The extent and effect of this misinformation was not empirically examined until Mosher (1979) carried out a landmark survey. He found that college students were highly misguided about sex and that the effects of this misinformation elevated sexual guilt and sexual anxiety. His study filled the gap between lack of education and sexual dysfunction. The mediators of sexual dysfunction may then be ignorance, guilt, and anxiety. Anxiety has a good deal of theoretical and empirical support. Accurate information tends to reduce anxiety. Guilt certainly makes sense from a logical perspective, but needs empirical validation. We often encounter clients with HSD that have an inordinate amount of sexual guilt. Their view of sex is that it is just bad, wicked, sinful, or dirty. In spite of the fact that some of these clients were reared in families that tried to protect them from "bad" messages about sex, the implicit message from the family turned out to be paradoxically that sex must be bad if we (the family) can't discuss it.

BODY IMAGE

American culture has become obsessed, preoccupied, and bombarded with messages about body image. Everyone knows what is expected in terms of the ultimate or idealized body representation based on what is portrayed in magazines and other media. Even the model with the most symmetrical and "perfect" body is now computer-enhanced in order to eliminate any flaw and to exacerbate those features that are deemed to be attractive. Women's bodies are objectified, evaluated, and sexualized in our culture through various routes such as magazines that focus on selling fashion, diet programs, and exercise programs. This objectification becomes internalized, and in many cases, leads to lowered sexual self-esteem and sexual dysfunction (Dove & Wiederman, 2000). It is difficult to tell how much body image disappointment is a risk factor for HSD as opposed to other sexual dysfunctions, but it often appears as a theme in many of our cases. In its simplest form, these women focus on their limitations or perceived imperfections, becoming self-conscious during physical intimacy with their partners. This clinical observation was confirmed by a study of young, white, heterosexual women by Wiederman (2000). These women monitor themselves during the sexual act, and fail miserably to lose themselves in the moment just as Masters and Johnson (1970) has pointed out. They are overly aware of how their bodies appear to others, particularly their sexual partners (Fredrickson & Roberts, 1997). This version of body image self-consciousness creates performance anxiety that directly interferes with the pleasurable aspects of sex. Another researcher found that clients with HSD report poorer body images overall (Schiavi, Karstaedt, Schreiner-Engel, & Mandeli, 1992). They found about the same degree of body image dissatisfaction for both men and women.

In our experience, many clients with HSD *do* have significantly distorted images of their bodies; some even suffer from body dysphoria. The clinical presentation is an individual, usually a woman, who often has an average or even thin somatotype and actually sees something different when she looks in the mirror or fantasizes. She will try to convince the listener that she is fat or physically undesirable. Clients with body image problems do not like their bodies and cannot imagine anyone else finding them attractive or sexually appealing, and thus have an extremely low sexual self-esteem. They will sometimes report getting dressed and undressed in private and they often avoid being seen in the nude by their partners. It is important to assess the extent to which the client's body image is translated into *not feeling* sexual desire or not perceiving oneself to be sexually attractive.

In some cases, the problem invades the relationship and the partners collude in order to agree about the individual's negative body image. They might complain about being too heavy or not fit enough or even agree with their partner that their faulty perception of their body is accurate. In other cases, clients with HSD have felt that they accepted their bodies, but their partners managed to find numerous faults with their appearance. We suspect two phenomena may be occurring among these couples. One is that the client with the lack of desire and body dysphoria is truly obsessed with their body and therefore incapable of feeling desire due to the obsessional self-focus. Feelings of depression typically accompany this obsession. The second is that the emphasis on appearance is a red herring or a simple explanation for a deeper, unrecognized problem. Whatever the case, the clinician should keep body image in mind as a risk factor and strive to dissect the real impact this concern has on the lack of desire.

## FUSION OF AFFECTION AND SEX

In the HSD cases we have treated, the interplay between sex and affection have become so fused and confused that it is both a cause and an effect of the sexual problem. The predicament has both stereotypic and idiosyncratic dimensions. Stereotypically, men tend to overvalue sex and undervalue affection. Women tend to do the reverse. What typically happens in a relationship is then a trade. Men are willing to give affection because they expect it will lead to a sexual interaction and women tend to give sex because they expect it will lead to some show of affection. In the minds of both parties, one has to lead to the other or at least one partner may be disappointed, angry, or resentful. This cycle or pattern of behavior persists and can eventually lead to growing resentment and anger that the exchange cannot be honest and mutual. The man begins to resent the fact that he is urged to waste his time on showing such useless and meaningless feelings. Of course, the woman senses that his feelings are not real and feels even emptier that she cannot get these feelings from her partner. She begins to resent the fact that she is urged to have sex that is useless and meaningless to her without the emotional context of affection. What was once perceived as a fair or necessary exchange becomes redefined as a necessary demand in order to get what one should be freely given or what one should freely receive. Eventually, this pattern may escalate to the point that one or both partners are turned off at having to make such an unacceptable exchange.

For those clients experiencing HSD, the problem is a bit more idiosyncratic, because the gender stereotyping begins to break down. The person with the lack of desire wants to avert a sexual interaction. Thus, they try to avoid all contexts in which sex might occur or be expected. Giving or receiving affection is one context in which sex is expected. The client begins to elude affectional encounters even though they might have a desperate need for closeness. They fear that any affectionate encounter is an implicit promise (or tease) for a sexual interaction.

The vast majority of clients with HSD report to us that they have lost the ability to show affection. This inability, in turn, creates even more emotional distance in the relationship. The situation worsens over time. The partner who feels desire is usually sexually frustrated, angry, and engages in strategies to try to get the other partner interested in sex. If that partner shows affection, it is viewed as a manipulation because the partner lacking desire is aware that the partner knows they are not interested. If the partner lacking desire shows some affection, it is interpreted as a manipulation to get affection without giving sex. The partner with the lack of desire continues to fuse the two even more tightly, shutting down affection, and leaving the partner feeling rejected and confused. The relationship deteriorates even further. As we will show in the next major section, the more a relationship diminishes in satisfaction the more likely it is there will be a lack of desire.

## CAREER AND ROLE OVERLOAD

Many of the couples we have treated in our private practices over the years have been in dual-career marriages, in which each partner is committed to employment in a chosen professional or career area. The composition of our practices does not give us an opportunity to adequately compare the dual-career with dual-job marriage. However, a study conducted by Avery-Clark (1986) showed that women in dual-career marriages were more likely to experience a lack of desire than women in dual-job marriages where both worked but were not career oriented. The explanation for their lack of desire is not clear. While women who are in careers may experience more individual life satisfaction, that does not translate into greater sexual satisfaction or desire. Career women are highly committed to their jobs. They may have higher standards, bring more work and worry home, feel their partners do not fully appreciate what they do, and feel the overload that both groups of women feel.

One of our cases illustrates this point aptly. Marge had been married 6 years and was a professional woman. Her husband was also a busy professional man. They presented for therapy 2 years after the birth of their first child. Marge was working full-time, maintaining all the household duties she had performed prior to having the child, and continued to take on more and more responsibilities at work and home. Martin, her husband, was unhappy over the lack of sexual activity and insisted they get some help. Marge explained that she did everything at home. Martin's response was that he did not want to help do anything and they could afford to hire people to take the burden away from Marge. She did not want to bring in outside help. Her response was that she was too tired and busy to think about sex. She also expressed anger that Martin did not want to be more helpful. He was not fitting her expectations of what a husband and father should be.

Perhaps women like Marge are just more likely to identify lack of desire as a problem. A number of women in both groups complain about feeling they have to "do everything" and resent the fact that their husbands are not "more helpful." The resentment towards the spouse can be a powerful inhibitor of sexual desire. The women in the job category were more likely to identify sexual problems other than HSD than those in the career category. We agree with the researchers that much more work needs to be done to determine the causal links between work and sexual problems.

RELATED SEXUAL PROBLEMS

Another possible risk factor is the presence of other sexual problems. Our clinical experience suggests that most cases of lack of sexual desire also involve the presence of other sexual problems. The classic studies conducted by Frank and colleagues (1978) and replicated by Bahr and Weeks (1989) with homosexual couples suggest that the probability of multiple problems within the same individual and couple is high. Our cases have revealed more than a few patterns in how one problem might be related to another, although it is sometimes difficult to tell which was the cause and which was the effect.

Linda and Mary, each in their early 50s, had been in a committed relationship for 20 years. They entered couples therapy to work on improving the sexual intimacy in their relationship. Both partners described a notable decline in desire and sexual avoidance for the last few years. When they occasionally attempted to be sexually intimate, Linda was unable to sustain arousal and she also reported secondary inhibited female orgasm. Additionally, Mary was receiving hormone replacement therapy for the treatment of menopausal symptoms such as vaginal dryness and hot flashes.

An engaged couple, John and Cathy, presented for treatment for her lack of desire. There were several relational issues such as a 22-year age difference (he was 50 and she was 28), her difficulty accepting his children, and many power struggles. They wanted to talk about the relational problems as they felt these had adversely affected sexual intimacy for 4 of their 5 years together. It was discovered that John also suffered from secondary partner-specific HSD. Additionally, Cathy had never experienced an orgasm and declared that she was not interested in correcting this problem.

Mark had been experiencing an erectile problem for several years of his 18-year marriage. Rarely could he successfully complete intercourse. Unlike most spouses we have treated, his wife was not sympathetic to his problem. She criticized him, got angry, and threatened to have an affair. Over a period of years, Mark reported his level of desire began to drop off because he did not want to confront the problem with himself and his wife. He wondered why his wife threatened to have an affair and was so angry with him.

Men with erectile dysfunction experience repeated failures over time, feel more and more performance anxiety, and pressure to succeed. Some of these men eventually feel so much pressure and such a fear of failure that it inhibits their ability to feel desire. Segraves and Segraves (1990) studied 258 men using the multi-axial diagnostic system. They found that 20% of the men with the diagnosis of erectile dysfunction also experienced HSD. This finding would confirm our clinical impression that increased anxiety over performance might begin to interfere with desire. McCarthy (1992) also made the same clinical observation. Likewise, some women who are anorgasmic may begin to worry that they will never be able to have an orgasm for themselves or for their partner. They too begin to feel the same kinds of anxious feelings as the men with an erectile dysfunction. Women with vaginismus or dyspareunia (painful intercourse) will also begin to avoid sex. Women with vaginismus can develop a phobia about penetration sex that is so strong as to inhibit desire. Even those who are not phobic may experience a severe reduction in desire.

The following case example illustrates how it is not uncommon to discover that those women referred for treatment of inhibited female orgasm also suffer from HSD. Many times, an orgasm phase disorder can be a cause (or effect) of a desire phase disorder. One of the authors treated a 28-year-old woman who was referred by her gynecologist after the birth of her second child for treatment of lifelong inhibited female orgasm. This problem occurred globally—with her husband of 10 years and during infrequent attempts at self-pleasuring. Sondra typically avoided sexual relations or tolerated coitus without enjoyment in order to avoid upsetting her husband. Although she lamented the fact that she could not experience orgasm, she had little sexual appetite. Sondra rarely thought about sex, dressed in sexy clothing, read about sex, or otherwise showed an interest in anything of a sexual nature. She somehow expected to experience orgasm without ever "priming the pump" sexually speaking. This trait was consistent with Sondra's tendency to avoid pleasurable activities or engage in behaviors for their intrinsic pleasure. Her presenting problem was reframed by the therapist as HSD and the treatment, therefore, was more comprehensive.

Aside from some of the major sexual dysfunctions mentioned above, many couples with HSD experience so-called minor problems (Frank et al.,

1978). These obstacles could include choosing an inconvenient time for sex on a consistent basis, wanting sexual activities disliked by the partner, or not providing enough foreplay or afterplay. Frank and colleagues actually found these minor dilemmas had a more significant detrimental effect on the level of sexual satisfaction than the so-called major problems, perhaps because they are viewed by the couple as being under volitional control. Thus, when the problem occurs it means the partner has not listened, is not sensitive, or does not care about the other's needs. The end result can elicit a sense of anger, rejection, and not feeling loved or cared for. The lack of skill and sensitivity on the part of one partner can then lead to a reduction or loss of desire in the other. The partner lacking desire antici-pates being unsatisfied and disappointed in the sexual experience.

We have treated couples in which one partner developed a lack of desire and later, the other partner also developed a lack of desire. It appears that in these cases the second partner develops HSD in order to cope with a sexless relationship or to express their anger over not getting what they want. The most common explanation we have heard is that HSD is an attempt to quell the frustration over being in a nonsexual relationship. This situation usually does not occur until many years have passed and the de-sire problem has failed to improve, leaving the partners feeling helpless, hopeless, and demoralized. They want to stay in the marriage, but need to find some way to justify it being a sexless marriage.

Finally, Kaplan (1996) suggested a link between erotic obsessions and HSD. Her article was based on a clinical examination of a number of spe-cific cases involving erotic preoccupation. The individuals were fixated on a specific, limited, sexual/romantic fantasy. The men and women could only be aroused to the fantasy or to someone who appeared to fit their fantasy.

## Psychiatric Factors

A number of psychiatric problems such as anxiety, depression, personality disorders, and sexual orientation conflicts may contribute to a lack of sex-ual desire. The situations discussed represent examples encountered by the authors in clinical practice. The illustrations represent only a few of the numerous situations in which another disorder or conflict contributed to the HSD.

### ANXIETY DISORDER

In the section above, we discussed the role anxiety plays in lack of sexual desire. An obvious extension of this idea is that clients with anxiety disorders may be more prone to lack of sexual desire. For some clients, it is a matter of *generalized* anxiety while in others it is a more *specific* form of anxiety or fear such as a phobia (including sexual aversion) or some form of posttraumatic stress reaction. One client, for example, reported HSD in a time frame that followed a physical assault by a stranger leading to a long medical recovery. She had experienced head trauma, and consequently was fearful about whether she would fully recover and be able to maintain a demanding job when she returned to work. These thoughts constantly occupied her. She had discussed her concerns with her husband who was very supportive. Sometimes she would attempt to initiate sex in the absence of her own genuine sexual desire for her husband because she understood that he was frustrated about the lack of sexual intimacy. In such situations, she was unable to arouse herself. It seemed that the more she tried to feel desire, the more fearful and anxious she became.

Sometimes clients will complain about everyday worries interfering with their ability to feel desire. Katz and Jardine (1999) examined the relationship between worry and lack of sexual desire. Using 138 college students and the Penn State Worry Questionnaire, they were only able to show a weak relationship between the two. This study may or may not be informative because they used such a young and sexually inexperienced age group. Another empirically based study did show a correlation between anxiety and lack of sexual desire. Beck and Bozman (1995) conducted an experimental study using erotic audiotapes that would elicit anxiety. They found that the experimental group that was exposed to anxiety felt significantly less desire than the control group. This experiment would support the idea that anxiety plays a role in reduced sexual desire.

OBSESSIVE-COMPULSIVE PERSONALITY DISORDER

In many cases we have treated, worry appears as a secondary problem to a psychiatric disorder. Individuals who have obsessive-compulsive personality traits or full-blown obsessive-compulsive personality disorder (OCPD) are restricted by their obsessive behavior. When these regimens are not accomplished, they become anxious and worried. In a number of cases, women have talked about starting the day with a checklist and being upset if they cannot complete every task. By late evening, they realize they cannot get it all done and the prospect of having sex is viewed as one more "chore." Men can exhibit a similar pattern, however, it is usually job tasks rather than household chores that they have not completed. One woman put the matter very simply. She said she just never had time for sex because she had too much to do and her husband did not help enough. When we started to examine her list, it was obviously unrealistic and she was attempting to shift some of the blame onto her husband. Another interesting aspect of clients with obsessive-compulsive personalities is their expectation of sex and feelings about various sexual activities. For some, sex has to be "perfect" as they define it. They may also have certain rigid beliefs about what is acceptable and unacceptable. Some will complain that sex is too "messy" referring to bodily fluids. The impression gathered from these individuals is that they want sex to be perfectly patterned or scripted according to their plan and it should be an antiseptic experience physically and emotionally. Additionally, obsessive-compulsive individuals do not like to have their feelings stirred. A sexual interaction has the effect of disturbing feelings; thus, these individuals strive to maintain tight control by avoiding sexual intimacy and any feeling that might lead to a sexual interaction. Moreover, persons with OCPD often strongly dislike the loss of control that accompanies orgasm.

We have also encountered clients, mostly men, who were unable to feel any sexual desire unless their partner satisfied their sexual fetish. In one of these cases, the husband demanded that his wife wear certain items of clothing and bright red lipstick. If she succumbed to these demands, then he felt desire for sex. If she did not comply with his demands, she could do nothing to arouse him. In fact, he would express his anger and frustration over his wife "being so rigid and withholding."

Another couple, married for over 20 years, presented with adjustment problems related to the man's retirement from his employment. The couple typically used her clothing as the fetishistic object during sexual relations. He needed to wear her lingerie in order to become aroused. Since this was an accepted custom for the couple, the treating therapist chose not to address the cross-dressing and dealt with the retirement issues. The treatment was successful. It is the fetish, not the person, which turns on these individuals. Without the fetish in place, they may feel no desire for their partner or anyone else. McCarthy (1994) also noted how men with paraphilias are attracted to their particular fetish and feel that dyadic interaction takes away from their object of attraction unless it can be incorporated in the interaction.

SEXUAL ORIENTATION

Sexual orientation can also be an individual factor for HSD. On rare occasions, we have encountered couples in which one partner was actually a homosexual living in a heterosexual marriage. These individuals may not wish to admit to themselves that they are gay or admit it to the world. One author recently encountered a couple that had been married over 40 years. The wife informed her husband that she was leaving the marriage to live with another woman as a friend. The husband quickly determined this was more than a friendship and then understood why his wife had little interest in sex throughout the marriage. The non-HSD partner does frequently suspect the partner may be gay even though this situation is rare.

Another couple who identified themselves as gay actually reported HSD in the partner who had a more bisexual orientation. She experienced HSD as a defense against her own homoerotic feelings for her partner. She felt unable to accept her "homosexuality" and the avoidance of sexual feelings and activity allowed her to believe that she "wasn't really gay."

PERSONALITY DISORDERS

It can also be the case that personality disorders may affect desire. We have already mentioned OCPD among these. Clients with narcissistic and borderline disorders may exhibit some unusual patterns of desire. The narcissistic individual wants to be loved and desired, but may not love or desire another person. If they allow themselves to have this feeling, they might feel too dependent and too much like everyone else. Their need for superiority and aloofness keeps them emotionally removed from others. In other cases, all of us have experienced the borderline client who loves us one day and hates us the next. They may experience intense desire and neediness and then intense hatred and counterdependence. Sometimes they are like sexual yo-yos—one day on and the next day off. Their personalities are so fragmented and they are so filled with projections that it is difficult to predict where they stand sexually or emotionally from moment to moment.

SEX ADDICTION

Although sex addiction has not yet been identified as a psychiatric diagnosis per se, the authors have worked with many couples in which one or both of the partners engage in sexual activity that is considered to be uncontrollable. The reader is referred to the diagnostic criteria for sex addiction proposed by Carnes (1990) and Goodman (1992, 1993). In general, the sex addict engages in a pattern of compulsive behavior or fantasy that is destructive to the self, the relationship, and/or the family (Turner, 1995). The sex addiction provides a sense of escape or euphoria and often results in feelings of shame and remorse (Carnes, 1991). There exists a wide range of addictive behaviors including those that are considered culturally "acceptable" such as masturbation, pornography, or phone sex. Other acts such as voyeurism, exhibitionism, and obscene phone calls are considered to be illegal "nuisance" behaviors. Nonetheless, in the latter group, there is always a victim.

The most common manifestation of sex addiction in our clinical practices is the rapidly growing epidemic of Internet or Cybersex addiction. Typically, the individual uses the Internet for sexual purposes and engages in solitary masturbation while watching pornographic websites. The behaviors become a preoccupation and often times the Internet addict is "caught" by the suspicious partner who notices that there is a decline or absence in the frequency of dyadic sex. The Internet addict typically experiences partner-specific HSD, which alters the normal pattern of sexual intimacy for the couple. Schneider (2000), who conducted a survey of Cybersex addiction, supports the clinical observations of the authors.

The following examples illustrate actual clinical cases of Internet compulsivity and HSD. A remorseful husband and frightened wife, in their early 30s, married for only a few years, presented in crisis. The husband was discovered spending hours in various pornographic websites. In the initial session, it became obvious that the wife had HSD and therefore avoided sex or engaged in compliant sexual activity with her husband. The husband felt disappointed in her lack of interest, wounded by her rejection of him, sexually frustrated, and angry. He justified his Internet preoccupation as his effort to deal with the marital situation without engaging in extramarital sex. Treatment addressed various issues including conflict resolution, intimacy conflicts, her HSD, and his sexual compulsivity.

In another example, the wife in a 20-year marriage noticed that her spouse had been gradually avoiding sexual relations for the past few years. She discovered an Internet trail of websites involving child pornography. Needless to say, this created a crisis in the marriage that necessitated long-term individual as well as marital therapy. Also, there were onerous legal implications in this case.

Another married couple in their early 30s sought treatment because the husband had been found talking on the telephone with a woman he had met in an Internet chat room. The surprised spouse demanded that the couple enter marital therapy. In this case, the crisis interrupted a situation that was potentially devastating to the partnership. In more than a few cases in our combined practices, one partner decided to leave the marriage in order to live with a person he or she had met on the Internet. Here we will refer the reader to recent articles dealing with the assessment and treatment of virtual adultery and online infidelity.*

---

* See Cooper, Delmonico, and Burg (2000); Orzack and Ross (2000); Shaw (1977); and Young, Griffin-Shelly, Cooper, O'Mara, and Buchanan (2000).

DEPRESSION

Finally, depression is one of the most common psychopathologies we see and it can be one of the most devastating for a person's sexual desire. The clinically depressed client lacks emotional and psychic energy. They view the world and their relationship negatively. Researchers have estimated that 70% of patients with depression lose their libido (Casper et. al., 1985; Matthew, Weinman, & Claghorn, 1980). In our experience, it is quite rare to find a clinically depressed client who has sexual desire. One example is a 30-year-old woman, Laura, who reported feeling only a modicum of desire in the beginning of her courtship. After 2 years of marriage, the couple presented with the symptom of sexual avoidance on the part of the wife. It became immediately apparent to the therapist that her sexual desire, affect, and productivity were blunted. It was an effort for Laura to speak, work, or have sex. Furthermore, she reported the lack of passion in all areas of her life from childhood until the present. Needless to say, the clinical depression was addressed, and she began taking an antidepressant in addition to continuing the psychotherapy. Of course, certain groups of antidepressants are known to inhibit the sexual response, therefore this client was not prescribed an SSRI, a known desire inhibitor. The therapeutic format varied from individual to conjoint sessions in order to deal with the frustration and disappointment of the non-HSD spouse and to substitute joining exercises to interrupt the cycle of sexual avoidance.

Another of our clients, Matt, had a long history of depression. He stated that life was always difficult. It was a chore to get out of bed and decide what he would do during the day. He ran a small business that earned little money. His wife had supported them for years on her salary. He reported he never thought about sex except as a means to keep his marriage together. The idea he shared was that being sexual felt like too much energy would be expended. In fact, he constantly spoke about having to be "careful about conserving" his energy.

One more manifestation of depression is the client who is "acting-out" in a sexual manner through an extramarital affair (EMA) or through hypersexual behavior. For many individuals with depression, anxiety is one of the most significant symptoms, and in situations involving an EMA, it is common to see anxiety as well as an underlying depression. Although the individual may experience sexual desire for the affair partner, there is situational HSD for the marriage or relationship partner. The depression might be a result of engaging in behaviors that are discordant with the individual's value system, resulting in guilt and shame. More frequently, the affair is an attempt to provide a "quick fix" for underlying feelings of loss, or inadequacy. It is not uncommon to find this situation at midlife.

## CONCLUSION

Gaining a better understanding of psychiatric problems and their effects on lack of sexual desire is an important issue. Unfortunately, most psychiatric studies focus little attention on the client's sexuality. We have not mentioned clients who are more severely disturbed to the point of being psychotic or schizoid, for example, these clients have such disorganized personality structures it is difficult to understand the nature of their sexual feelings. Even studies on the effects of medications on sexual functions tend to underemphasize the client's baseline sexual functioning. In the literature, only one study could be located that examined the clients overall level of psychological/psychiatric functioning with sexual desire (Stuart, Hammond, & Pett, 1986). They gave the MMPI to a group of women with HSD and a group without HSD. Basically, they found no significant relationship between psychological functioning and HSD. They suggested that the problem might be rooted in the quality of the relationship rather than any specific symptomology. Certainly, there is some research to show an inverse relationship between desire, anxiety, and depression. More research needs to be done to gain a picture of how various psychopathologies and lack of desire are related.

# 4

## Etiology: Interactional Risk Factors

IN OUR PREVIOUS DISCUSSION OF individual risk factors, we offered an integrative model for purposes of assessment and treatment of HSD. As we have indicated, we believe the therapist must integrate all *three components* of the clinical picture in order to perform a comprehensive treatment plan. The three intersystemic components include individual (psychological and biological), interactional (dyadic), and intergenerational (family-of-origin) factors. Our focus on etiology now turns to the role of *the couple* in the development and maintenance of HSD. The most significant risk factors, especially for *secondary* lack of desire, may be found in the relationship. From an intersystemic perspective, *each partner* is viewed as playing a part in the lack of desire, not solely the "identified patient." In fact, during the assessment process we are always vigilant for the less obvious, yet equally important contributions to the clinical picture from the nonidentified patient.

Clients with secondary HSD have usually enjoyed a sexual appetite for the partner for many years prior to the present relationship and during the first part of their courtship and marriage. During the course of their committed relationship, however, they begin to lose interest. In most instances, the loss of desire is a gradual, insidious process. Without sexual desire, the HSD partner circumvents interactions that could potentially end in sexual relations. By the time the couple seeks treatment, a pernicious cycle of sexual avoidance is usually in place. Moreover, as in other sexual dysfunctions, the couple has attempted to correct the situation unsuccessfully after the pattern of avoidance has set in (Weeks & Gambescia, 2000). They have suffered from the gradual decline and eventual loss of sexual intimacy, the tangible glue in any intimate relationship (Schnarch, 1997). Feelings of resentment often accompany the reduction of intimacy as each partner experiences disappointed expectations of what they hoped the relationship could provide. Further, the couple often feels a sense of hopelessness that the situation can ever improve. Finally, their range of emotional interaction becomes restricted as feelings of congealed anger, frustration, and resentment become more commonplace.

As we mentioned earlier, Masters and Johnson (1970) did not recognize HSD as a sexual disorder. Working from a psycho/biological model, they did not consider the critical role sexual desire played in the sustenance of intimate relationships. Moreover, Masters and Johnson failed to utilize any systemic factors in the etiology or treatment of sexual disorders. In spite of their assertion that there was no such thing as an uninvolved partner, they did not elaborate or pursue this idea anywhere in their volume, except to emphasize how the partner was essentially a "cotherapist" in the homework exercises. Kaplan (1979), on the other hand, recognized how significant the relationship could be in the formation and perpetuation of lack of desire. Although she discussed a number of relational risk factors, she failed to follow through systemically in her treatment approach. Kaplan was thoroughly entrenched in the behavioral/psychodynamic approach to the treatment of HSD. She never made the transition to a systemic format, even though she would sometimes comment on how important it was to treat the clients as a couple. In Kaplan's way of working, the partner was a cotherapist and part of the system needed to *effect* change. The couple would be given behaviorally oriented assignments around sex. Unfortunately, she did not choose to treat the nonsexual aspects of the relationship. Her focus was confined to changing the sexual relationship.

## INDIVIDUAL ISSUES

There are exceptions to the rule when considering relational etiologic risk factors in HSD. Sometimes, an individual issue clouds the relational etiology in one or both of the partners. Moreover, it has been interesting to note that in some cases one partner will assume total responsibility or blame for the problem while the other partner is viewed as playing no role. Of course, when there is an individual difficulty such as drug abuse or severe psychopathology in the partner with HSD, the sexually "interested" partner may not play an active role, but rather, a passive or collusive part in the HSD. For instance, the codependent partner may not manifest the obvious symptoms of drug or alcohol dependency, for insistence, but plays an important position in maintaining the relationship equilibrium. The "interested" partner keeps the level of intimacy to a minimum by passively complying with the agenda of the HSD partner, even though there is much complaining about the symptom. Typically, the "interested" partner does not force the issue or precipitate a crisis if the HSD (or the individual issue) is not addressed. Often times, this collusion is only revealed after the problems in the identified patient are resolved, for example, after the alcoholic has successfully abandoned drinking. Once the desire begins to return in the treated partner, the so-called sexually interested partner begins to find excuses not to have sex. In short, the motivations for the lack of desire are not obvious to the codependent partner.

Another one of our cases illustrates this point quite well. This couple consisted of a professional man and a woman who worked in midmanagement. They were in their mid-50s and had been living together for 4 years. Jonathan and Marsha planned to marry, but only after his problems were resolved. Both partners were in treatment for drug addiction and had met in a recovery meeting. Jonathan had suffered from an erectile problem from the beginning of the relationship. In fact, he had had an erectile problem for many years prior to the relationship. Marsha vacillated between being angry and sympathetic with him. She claimed she was a very sexual person who needed sex every day. Jonathan had lost much of his sexual desire due to his erectile problem. He started a course of Caverject, an injectable treatment for erectile dysfunction, and found that he could now have intercourse.* As soon as he became functional, Marsha started to complain about a lack of genital sensation and attributed it to the fact that his penis was too small. She quickly went from being hypersexual to hyposexual. The therapist attempted to shift the focus onto Marsha, but she persisted in saying the problem was still with Jonathan alone. It was obvious to the therapist and now to Jonathan that Marsha was a part of the problem, but she was unwilling to examine her contribution and dropped out of therapy within two sessions. The therapist continued to work with Jonathan to help him see that he had selected a partner who had pressured him and blamed him for what was in part her problem. A part of the performance anxiety experienced by Jonathan was actually generated by Marsha's unconscious sexual concerns. She projected the blame onto Jonathan. He decided to stay in the relationship temporarily hoping that the situation

* Caverject (Alprostadil) is a self-injectable treatment for erectile dysfunction made by Upjohn.

would improve. Sadly, the therapist informed him that the sexual part of the relationship would probably continue to be problematic as long as Marsha refused treatment.

## DYADIC ADJUSTMENT AND HSD

Our assertion that the relationship is an important factor in the treatment of HSD is supported in the empirical literature. Trudel, Ravart, and Matte (1993) examined the dyadic adjustment in couples with HSD. They examined two groups of 20 couples each. One group of subjects was experiencing HSD and the other did not meet the criteria for this diagnosis. They used the Dyadic Adjustment Scale to assess the level of marital adjustment. The HSD group was significantly less adjusted, according to the criteria designated in the scale. The women in the HSD group perceived less cohesion in the relationship while the men reported less affective expression. Overall, the women in the HSD group were more maritally distressed than the men were. Unfortunately, this study does not tell us whether the HSD was the cause or the effect of the marital discord. It could be argued that the lack of desire produced these effects. However, our clinical experience suggests that the dyadic problems usually predate the loss of desire. It might be useful to remember that the level of overall sexual satisfaction is related to the level of overall marital satisfaction (Frank et al., 1978; Morokoff & Gillilland, 1993). These studies suggest that when couples are happy in their relationships they will rate their sexual satisfaction as being high even though the couple may report a variety of sexual dysfunctions and at a high rate of frequency. It appears that when the marital relationship is poorly rated, couples are more sensitive to their sexual problems. Moreover, they rate their overall sexual relationship as being poor. This is consistent with our clinical experience.

## Marital and Sexual Satisfaction

The relationship between marital and sexual satisfaction is a complex one. It is clear that marital satisfaction is significantly related to higher levels of sexual satisfaction (Frank et al., 1978; Morokoff & Gillilland, 1993). As we stated above, satisfaction does not imply frequency or absence of dysfunction. It is also clear that sexual activity begets sexual activity. For instance, women who masturbate report greater sexual desire, higher self-esteem, greater marital and sexual satisfaction, and required less time to achieve orgasm (Hurlbert & Whittaker, 1991). In this study, married women who masturbate were compared to married women who do not. They found that of the women who masturbate, the frequency was about three times per month. About 54% incorporated masturbating into their dyadic sexual activity with their partner and felt that it was often a precursor to intercourse. From this study, it seems that happily married women derive a good deal of satisfaction from solo sex as well as dyadic sex. This group also reports that oral sex is their most enjoyable way of achieving orgasm (Hurlbert & Whittaker, 1991).

In a follow-up study, Hurlbert and Apt (1994) found that the relationship between overall marital and sexual satisfaction might be more complex than initially realized. In fact, in the second study, women were even more sensitive to the overall level of marital satisfaction, and, hence, sexual satisfaction. Hurlbert and Apt also found that for women, sexual satisfaction was related to a number of factors such as how sex was initiated, their level of physical arousal, and the sexual behaviors that occurred during the interaction. In fact, the authors pointed out the limitations of studying sexual satisfaction in women and stated that a typology of female sexual response is needed that considers a range of specific marital and sexual behaviors in order to better understand desire.

As we stated in Chapter 1, Basson (2000) offers a model for the female sexual response that is sensitive to the issues described by Hurlbert and Apt (1994). For women, sexual desire is often related to nonsexual variables such as trust and comfort in their intimate relationships. Instead of experiencing an overwhelming hunger or an insatiable drive towards physical release, the female sexual appetite is more responsive to factors between herself and her partner. If the relationship is safe, loving, and caring, she can then begin to experience fantasies and feel the bodily sensations that coincide with sexual desire. In essence, sexual appetite is more related to the *expectation* of emotional intimacy than the pressing urge for sexual release (Basson, 2000).

## Gender Differences and HSD

Until recently, there has been very little research about the powerful influence of gender on the experience of sexual desire and lack of desire. In our own clinical experience, we have found that most heterosexual couples report that safety and comfort are preconditions for sexual desire, sexual gratification, and overall relationship satisfaction. However, we have occasionally encountered partners who have ostensibly conflicted and unsatisfying marriages but enjoy "great" sex together. Obviously, some couples are able to compartmentalize sex from the overall relationship. For these individuals, sex can exist in a relationship vacuum as long as certain elements are present sexually. In the ideal relationship, we have found that there is more of a balance of psychological compatibility and good physical/sexual chemistry. This kind of relationship is more companionate although less intense. There are few arguments and these can be resolved with cooperation from each spouse. The relationship is less likely to self-destruct over time through frequent, intense battles. Unfortunately, a number of our clients in marital therapy have reported marrying on the basis of good sexual chemistry even if there is a lack of compatibility.

The reverse can also be true. In the last decade, we have seen many examples of partners who are compatible, but never feel the spark of lust. These relationships can start off with a short period of passion but after months or years, they take on the characteristics of a compatible sibling dyad and remain that way. McCarthy (1997, 1999b) brought attention to the problem of the *nonsexual* marriage, offering assessment and treatment strategies for this multidimensional problem. He distinguishes between partnerships that are viable, in which case they can be *revitalized*, and nonviable partnerships, in which there might be a "hidden" agenda, such as an extramarital affair, which the couple may or may not overtly recognize. Of course, there may be relationships that are asexual by mutual consent and/or unconscious need. Another example is the couple with bilateral HSD in which there has never been a genuine sexual attraction. They married for reasons such as having children or the wish to be cared for by the partner at any cost.

## AN INTIMACY-BASED APPROACH TO DESCRIBING RISK FACTORS

Sexual intimacy is just one form or expression of emotional closeness in a relationship. Defining intimacy has proven to be a difficult task. Schaefer and Olson (1981) were two of the early researchers who tried to clarify this concept. They identified seven areas of intimacy. These included: emotional, social, intellectual, sexual, recreational, spiritual, and aesthetic intimacy. It is our contention that when intimacy is lacking in one or more of these areas, there is often a decline in sexual intimacy. Schaefer and Olson also differentiated between two types of intimacy—an intimate *experience* versus an intimate *relationship*. An intimate *experience* was defined as a feeling of closeness based on sharing a particular type of encounter in one or more of their seven categories of intimacy. An intimate *relationship* is one in which partners consistently share in one or more of several areas and expect that such sharing will continue.

To further our understanding, Sternberg (1986), a theoretically oriented psychologist, developed a model of love based on three interlocking components. He postulated that in an adult loving relationship such as a marriage, three components must exist in about equal measure. These components are: commitment, intimacy, and passion. Sternberg also suggested that difficulty in one area could affect each of the other two areas. Specifically, problems in commitment and/or intimacy could adversely affect passion. In fact, the couple may present for treatment of HSD when in fact an underlying struggle with commitment or intimacy may be the greater issue, such as in an extramarital affair.*

We find that the types of intimacy are linked such that a problem in one area affects another area. For example, many women with HSD complain about a lack of emotional intimacy in their dyadic relationship. They do not expect that they can share their feelings with their partner. Eventually, they begin to feel isolated and abandoned in a relationship that they experience as emotionally barren. Their feelings of anger, frustration, resentment, and their sense of betrayal are often expressed through a lack of desire.

THE CONCEPTUAL FRAMEWORK

Our contention is that when the problem is secondary HSD, one of the contributing factors is *almost always* within the realm of underlying fears of intimacy in the relationship. Before discussing the specific fears we have commonly identified, this section will provide more background regarding how these fears operate. If we think of intimacy in very general terms such as closeness and distance or individuation vs. separateness, then everyone has a certain set point at which they are comfortable. It is like setting the thermostat in the home. Some people like it warmer and some like it cooler. When partners become too close, certain unconscious fears come into play and, conversely, when they become too distant, other fears may come into play. Unfortunately, these fears are not easily recognized except through the acting-out behavior that is used to regulate the distance between the partners. Being sexually cut-off or turned-off is just one way to regulate the distance and quell the underlying fear(s).

We assume that all individuals bring some underlying fears of intimacy to their relationship. In certain partners, these fears are stronger than in others and have a more devastating impact on the relationship. These fears may be personally embedded in one or both partners and constitute what Weingarten (1991) has called the *personal incapacity discourse*. In other words, individuals are limited in their capacity to be intimate. This inadequacy will only be revealed in a relationship where intimacy is expected. In fact, a very interesting phenomenon exists. Initially, the couple may be doing just fine from their own subjective perspective. They may feel they are developing a relationship and growing closer and closer. Without warn-

---

* For an in-depth discussion of intimacy, the reader should consult the newly revised edition of *Couples in Treatment* by Weeks and Treat (2001).

ing, something may happen to disrupt the relationship and create less intimacy. One partner's comfort zone has been violated which resulted in the use of some strategy to create more distance. In many cases we have treated, this phenomenon does not emerge until after marriage. Its appearance can cause the couple to question whether they should be married and whether they really knew or understood the person they were marrying.

Thus far, we have looked at intimacy struggles by discussing the fears in one partner. Relationships are much more complex than the behavior of just the individual. Mate selection is not a random process and much of it operates at an unconscious level. An underlying fear of intimacy in one partner is usually matched in equal measure by an underlying fear of intimacy in the other partner. Relationships are interlocking in many ways and at many levels. The partners may share the same fear or each one may have a different fear. By unconsciously selecting each other, they have made an implicit agreement not to share too much closeness or distance. This fact explains why one partner may complain about a lack of intimacy for years, but never choose to take any steps to resolve the problem. They obtain unconscious secondary gains as in the case mentioned earlier of Jonathan and Marsha.

The therapist can be deceived easily into believing that one partner wants more closeness than the other does. The "complaining" partner will protest the situation and sound utterly convincing that he or she did not get what was expected or that the partner has deceived him or her. The emotionality and pain of the dishonored partner is real, although it betrays a deeper and darker secret. This hypothesis is confirmed when the partner who has been creating distance complies with the overt request of the other and begins to remove the obstacles to intimacy. At that point, the "complaining" partner may begin to do things to unwittingly sabotage getting closer. The classic example is the wife who complains that her husband does not talk to her enough about his feelings. When he does begin to do so she may interrupt, change topics, get angry over his feelings, "over talk" him with her feelings, be angry that it "took him so long," or find excuses to not talk to him. The therapist may need to wait to unmask the fears in the "complaining" partner until the ostensible problems in the other partner are addressed. Exposing the hidden fears in the well-defended partner too soon creates the risk that he or she will drop out of treatment prematurely. It is always critical that the therapist address the presenting problems first even if other issues are suspected. After the therapeutic alliance is established, the therapist can gradually increase the range of intervention.

There are numerous clinical manifestations of couples presenting with HSD in one partner. Many of these situations involve partners who have quietly tolerated (unconsciously accepted) a lack of desire in the other for years. When the person with the overtly recognized HSD begins to change, the other partner may find ways to sabotage being together sexually. Obviously, one partner was gaining from the other's lack of desire. In some instances, the "non-HSD" partner would use the sexual realm of the relationship to gain a position of power and control. The dominant partner implicitly states, "because you won't give me sex, you must be or do the following. . . . " In other situations, the non-HSD partner is chronically angry with the partner who avoids sex, which "excuses" him or her having to make any efforts toward closeness. Additionally, we have treated a number of cases in which both partners appeared to have HSD. In these situations, there typically is a deficiency of sexual desire as well as a lack of intimacy in a number of other areas. These couples will report that they have "grown apart" emotionally, intimately, and companionately.

Relationship homeostasis or equilibrium can be the greatest source of frustration to the therapist. When one partner increases or decreases the tolerated intimacy level, the other partner often modifies the equation to restore the previous level of comfort. David and Mary illustrate this point. Married for 15 years, they had settled into a comfortable yet nonsexual relationship. They requested sex therapy for the treatment of Mary's HSD. David complained that she was sexually inhibited and repressed. In other areas of their relationship, David and Mary shared similar values systems, recreational activities, and generally experienced a nonconflicted style. Overall, they functioned like compatible roommates or siblings. Sadly, they lacked sexual and emotional intimacy. After a year of marital and sex therapy, Mary increased her level of desire for David. She became more proactive sexually, often initiating encounters and discussions. David then retreated stating that "now" he was not interested in her sexually because "he was angry about her sexual avoidance in the past." Mary persisted in her attempts to break through his resistance by assertively expressing her desire for sexual intimacy with David. She did not react personally to his rejections. David remained riveted in his position that he was unable to experience sexual desire for Mary because of his anger. The more she approached David for intimacy, the more he retreated until he became critical of her physical appearance which ultimately wounded Mary so much that she also pulled away emotionally.

## FEARS OF INTIMACY

In the next section, we will identify some of the common underlying fears of intimacy identified in treating HSD. These include:

- fear of anger
- struggles over power and control

- fear of rejection and/or abandonment
- fear of exposure
- fear of feelings
- fear of dependency

This list of fears is by no means exhaustive. It does, however, represent common themes we have seen in our practices. The two most common fears will be discussed first.

## Fear of Anger

Anger is a common emotion that is experienced in every human relationship. Although it is certain to occur periodically, a typical problem for couples is their inability to deal with the anger they feel towards each other (L'Abate & McHenry, 1983). They fear the experience of anger or do not possess the skills to articulate their feelings and come up with a resolution. This problem can manifest itself in different ways. In some couples, a partner commonly withholds anger, fearing that articulating it will be unpleasant or improper. Others express it without appropriate concern for the impact upon the recipient. We have also seen couples that appear to be chronically angry, ready to explode hurtfully or violently with little provocation. When the only options are to suppress the anger, explode, or be chronically angry, it is very likely a desire problem will occur. In most cases we have seen, whatever the manifestation of anger, it is *incompatible* with sexual desire. Thus, the inability to work through the angry feelings is certain to create a barrier to intimacy.

The most common pattern in our experience is for the anger to be withheld. This mechanism is slightly more common in men than women, although we have seen it operate in both genders. Most generally, think of men as being more expressive than women when the issue is anger. This is not always the case. Instead, many men are aware of their anger towards their partner yet they simply store the episode in their memory. Over a period of time, sometimes years, the internalized anger becomes a chronic condition that we call *chronically suppressed anger*. These partners are filled with bitterness or smoldering resentment. The feeling gains in strength and begins to pervade every interaction. A slight transgression on the part of the partner can trigger all the suppressed anger. Suppressed anger becomes the pervasive feeling state and blocks the experience of all other feelings, including sexual desire. These individuals often appear pensive, depressed, anxious, or withdrawn. They are likely to remain emotionally and sexually disengaged from their partners in order to remain quietly angry.

The interactional system that supports the chronically angry partner is likely to be *conflict-avoidant*. The "nonangry" partner unconsciously colludes in *not* dealing with the anger. The unconscious collusion may take many forms. They may pretend not to notice the smoldering anger in their partner or make half-hearted attempts to deal with the issue. They might even overlook or make excuses for the sullen affect in the partner. The anger is never dealt with in earnest. The pattern of avoidance serves to protect the relationship and each partner. The "nonangry" partner may be afraid of any expression of anger, having chosen to marry someone who could not exhibit any anger. This way of dealing with anger may have originated in the family-of-origin. This partner may have learned that the expression of anger was inappropriate or bad. Perhaps parental modeling of problem resolution was based on the myth that anger dissipates if not addressed. Intergenerational factors will be considered in greater depth in the next chapter.

On the other side of this problem is the couple or the partner who is overtly and chronically angry or explosive and intimidating. These individuals express anger in hurtful and vengeful ways. They do not stop to consider the consequences of their expression. For them the best defense is a strong offense. They use anger to keep others at a distance and to control through intimidation. The "nonangry" partner begins to live in a state of fear and dread over saying or doing something "wrong." Obviously, it would be difficult to be emotionally or sexually close to someone who is constantly angry. Of course, the question then arises as to why anyone would choose to stay in such an untenable relationship. The "nonangry" partner may have individual issues such as underlying fears that are served by being with an angry mate. If they do not want or cannot tolerate closeness, this person would be an ideal choice. They can justify their behavior of not being close based on the overtly unacceptable and socially disapproved behavior of their partner. Another possibility is that the "nonangry" partner is so dependent (fears being alone) For example, he or she would accept a relationship on any terms given. Regardless of the underlying etiology within the individual, this couple is guaranteed a relationship with very little sexual desire or intimacy.

A final possibility is when one partner is afraid to express anger because of fear of the consequences. The partner believes if he or she were to ever express the intensity of the anger, it would completely consume them and be devastating to their partner. Partners with this belief have frequently been carrying unresolved anger from childhood into marriage. One female client with a lack of desire illustrates this point. She had never felt desire for her husband. In fact, she was a virgin at the time of marriage and the couple had sex only a few times in 15 years. Her fantasy in high school was to have sex with the biggest football player she could find so she would not injure or kill him. Her husband was a tall, thin, intellectual man. She stated in one session that if she were to have sex with him and let her feelings go, he would spontaneously ignite from the intensity of her rage. Her rage could be traced back to two very controlling parents. Marrying a man who was overcontrolling further exacerbated it.

## Struggles over Power and Control

Every couple must deal with issues around power and control in their relationship. This involves a delicate balance of negotiating and maintaining the relationship equilibrium while each partner enjoys an appropriate degree of power. In many relationships, this issue has not been successfully negotiated. An imbalance may exist in which one partner assumes too much control (*overcontrol*) while the other assumes too little control (*undercontrol*). In other dyads, both partners might be *overcontrolling* or *undercontrolling*. A large percentage of our HSD cases involve couples where the husband is overcontrolling and the wife is undercontrolling resulting in a lack of sexual desire in the woman. Issues of power and control are manifested at two levels. The first involves behavioral control over another in which compliance is expected and the second, the more insidious, entails actually "defining" the other person.

The first level of the power/control conflict is overt and requires a partner who is "in charge" and a colluding partner who conforms to sometimes unreasonable, arbitrary, and rigid expectations. In some of these couples, the spouse simply does what he or she is told, promoting a kind of stable instability. In other couples, there is ongoing instability manifested in frequent power struggles over who is "in charge" of the relationship. These couples often fight over trivial matters as if the bickering determined life or death. The therapist can be easily distracted by the details of the heated arguments and by the relentlessness of the couple while engaged in battle. Actually, these couples are exhausting to work with because they do not accept redirection very easily. Nonetheless, it is essential to see the greater issue, which is always the underlying struggle over control. For those couples where both are *overcontrolling*, there is an obvious or manifest conflict. Thus, each partner wants to control the other in every situation, including sexually. They cannot work together because they are constantly in competition for control, giving up control would be too great a loss for each partner. If one wants something, the other doesn't. How could they ever agree on anything including when and how to have sex?

The reverse situation of the first power/control problem category is one in which both partners are *undercontrolling*; each wants the other person to be in charge. Paradoxically, each possesses deep-seated dependency needs that are so great that they expect *not* to be taken care of adequately. Relationships cannot possibly provide the kind of safety and intimacy these individuals require because their needs are so great. In fact, by not taking charge, the undercontrolling partner hopes to be taken care of yet expects that this *cannot* happen. Thus, they cannot become too needy or ask for too much or they will feel let down once again. In sexual terms, the person is expecting that they will not be taken care of, therefore they do not desire sexual intimacy for fear of disappointment.

The second or deeper level of the problem of control and power is more complex and difficult to perceive or measure. At this level, authority is exerted by actually trying to define the other person. It is not the same as telling them *what* to do, but, rather, *how they should be*. This issue takes us to the heart of how partners are able to remain self-differentiated or seek autonomy in a relationship. L'Abate (1976) developed a model of *self-differentiation*. The *self-differentiated* partner defines the self as being both similar to and different from others. They are *self-determining*; they have sufficient ego-strength to know themselves, who they are, and what they want. Their self-image is positive, and they can maintain a sense of separateness, yet closeness in a relationship. The *undifferentiated partner*, on the other hand, defines the self in terms of being either the same or diametrically opposed to the other. Their behavior is reactive and fused rather than autonomous. Typically, this partner tends to position him or herself at the extreme position of conformity or rebellion.

Elisa was a classic representation of this problem. She had been married for 12 years to a physician and worked as a manager in an insurance company. Each partner was successful in his or her respective careers. They came to therapy due to her lack of interest in sex. She claimed she never felt like having sex although she acquiesced to the sexual requests of her husband, Richard, once or twice a week. Several sessions into the therapy, Elisa raised an issue about his parents, complaining that they "practically lived" at their home. She revealed that she had been disturbed by their ongoing involvement in the couple's lives. Richard's retired father had been a contractor, and both parents were very involved in the current remodeling of Richard and Elisa's home. Richard would call his parents several times each day and see them in the morning and at night. It was clear that at an emotional level, he had never fully separated from his parents. Elisa, on the other hand, had a rather detached relationship with her parents. She held the expectation that she would be so close to her husband that they would be almost fused. During their courtship and later in their marriage, she had constantly pursued him but he distanced himself from her. Because she did not believe she had any control in the marriage, Elisa tried to define herself according to standards set up by Richard. If she could be more like him, perhaps he would permit the fusion she so ardently desired. Unfortunately, he was not emotionally available for her. Moreover, Elisa failed to define a set of standards, values, likes, and dislikes that were representative of herself as an individual. In terms of a partnership, she had little autonomy and self-esteem. Eventually, she grew to resent Richard and his parents, feeling isolated in a family system that seemed to function without her input.

In our culture, we have a strong belief that we have certain rights over our bodies. These rights are especially strong in the sexual area. Most people claim ownership over their sexuality; it belongs only to them and to no one else. Control over one's sexuality is a given. Control over one's feelings is also a given. We may be told what to do and we may do it, but most adults draw the line over being told *how* to feel, think, or be. The inability to resolve issues of control and power is often played out in the area of sex or sexual desire. For instance, a spouse could insist on having sex and have it because the partner complies. However, a partner cannot force the other to have sexual desire or arousal. Feeling a lack of sexual desire and withholding sex is an indirect way of taking control. Of course, this is an unconscious process. What is sometimes ironic about this situation is that the partner who is overcontrolling will sometimes comment on how the other partner has complete control over sex. It is clear to them at some superficial level what the other partner has been able to achieve.

Some of the couples we have treated engage in a sort of magical thinking regarding their power struggles. The HSD partner often automatically assumes that if they acquiesce to have sex, the overcontrolling partner has "won the battle." It is not just a sexual victory, but also some part of this person's sense of self has been taken because the partner has gotten what they wanted. If one wins, the other loses. These partners are so prone to lose themselves in the relationship or to fuse with each other that they must maintain some distance. Sometimes sex is chosen as the area of the relationship to maintain separateness. The individual who is undifferentiated and expresses it through "oppositeness" feels he or she has "won" at some level by *not* giving in to their partner's desire for sex.

Like Elisa and Richard, we have noticed many couples in which the wife enters the marriage in order to fuse with her spouse. We have also worked with couples who unwittingly collude to fuse with each other until the wife or husband at some later date is able to begin differentiating. Unfortunately, this spouse may go to the extreme and move to the position of "oppositeness." These situations may have worked sexually during the initial phase of the relationship, but then crumble when one partner wants to change the underlying dynamic or contract of the relationship.

Schnarch (1991; 1997) offers another approach to the role of differentiation in sexual desire. Sometimes it can appear that individuals with HSD are isolated or withdrawn when in fact they are often fused or poorly differentiated from their partner. Instead of relying on the self, poorly differentiated persons look to their partners for important functions such as validation, comfort, and definition (Schnarch, 1991). They are dependent on, hypersensitive to, and, often extremely reactive to the feelings and responses of their partner. Moreover, they do not respect themselves nor do they respect their partner for loving them.

Somehow, individuals choose partners who will provide a level of intimacy that is tolerable within an intimate relationship. When HSD is at issue, the high-desire partner is often the one who complains about the low sexual frequency. The low-desire partner, however, determines the frequency of sexual intimacy and the various sexual behaviors that are acceptable. HSD is a reflection of an individual's low tolerance for sexual intimacy according to Schnarch (1991). The couple system in which there is an HSD partner is filled with hurt feelings, blaming, giving up, pressuring the HSD partner, or giving in to the high-desire partner. All of these strategies insure a low level of intimacy. In addition, the bickering and struggles over sex keep the individuals fused by hurt and angry feelings.

Obviously, the goal of treatment is to increase the intimacy tolerance level and the level of differentiation in the couple, enabling each partner the power to enjoy a clear sense of self, to comfort and soothe oneself, and to be nonreactive to others (Schnarch, 1997). Differentiation increases the individual's tolerance for intimacy and is fundamental to sustaining sexual desire, particularly in long-standing relationships.

## Fear of Rejection and/or Abandonment

This particular fear is deeply and historically rooted in most partners during the formative years of childhood. There may have been a rejection by a parent(s) through circumstances such as desertion, divorce, or possibly death. Others have been emotionally abandoned or rejected by a parent who was detached, mentally ill, unsuitable to be a parent, or did not want the child for one reason or another. Sometimes the fear has a basis in an adult experience such as being rejected by a lover or marital partner. Some partners who have experienced these feelings will maintain a defensive posture in a relationship. They do not wish to become too intimate or close for fear that they may be terribly hurt if the relationship were to come to an end. One of our cases illustrates this fear quite vividly. A 26-year-old woman presented for the treatment of HSD and a resultant inability to orgasm. She had never had these problems prior to the sudden, traumatic ending of an intimate relationship. She was engaged, and the couple had agreed to postpone intercourse until they were approaching the date of their marriage. When the couple decided to have sex for the first time, it was wonderful according to the client's report. Without warning, the man she was to marry disappeared and was never heard from again. This experience was devastating in several ways. A few months later, she met another man and they started dating. She could tell she was afraid a similar situation might occur again. Nonetheless, she decided to engage in sexual relations with him. She was too apprehensive to be sexually desirous of her partner and could not have an orgasm with him due to fear and lack of desire. During sex, she felt the fear most intensely. She expressed concern in the session if she could ever be close to or trust a man again.

## Fear of Exposure

The fear of exposure is rarely recognized in the couples therapy literature. It is a manifestation of the imposter syndrome in the couple. These persons believe they have tricked or fooled their partners into believing they are likeable and lovable. Inherently, they assume they are defective and unlovable. They believe they have created a disguise and the partner has fallen in love with the façade rather than the person within. In order to maintain the relationship, they must create emotional distance from the partner. They can't let anyone know their horrible secret. In fact, they try to hide the secret from themselves by overachieving or being unemotional. Feelings of self-loathing and disgust are at the core of their defensive strategy.

Robert, 58, was a very successful executive who felt his success was all luck. As a high school student, his parents told him he was not smart enough to go to college and he should just find some simple job he could do well. His parents "forgot" to attend both his college and graduate school graduation ceremonies. He was clearly an overachiever, always striving to do things perfectly and to be the most successful at what he did. His perfectionism masked a profound emotional void as well as a conviction that he was a charlatan. His wife had never heard Robert describe himself in this way. She experienced him as constantly preoccupied with work and extremely nonemotional. Robert's interest in sex was low because he felt he would not be able to perform perfectly in order to please his partner. He also needed to maintain his emotional distance from his wife, fearing that she might get some glimpse of how he actually felt about himself.

## Fear of Feelings

Sexual desire is a feeling. Some partners are fearful of experiencing their feelings in intimate relationships. They fear that the intensity of the feelings might cause them to be out of control. Perhaps they fear experiencing vulnerability or exposure as mentioned above. Commonly, individuals who fear feelings engage in elaborate efforts to circumvent or avoid experiencing affect. Invariably, their defensive strategies keep the partner at bay. Some individuals defend against feelings by thinking too much. They may even be diagnosed with obsessive-compulsive personality disorders. This type of personality disorder leads to overfunctioning in the cognitive realm and underfunctioning in the emotional realm. These individuals also like things to be ordered, patterned, clean, neat, nonmessy—all the things sex is not.

Individuals who cannot tolerate affect also assiduously circumvent other feelings such as anger, depression, or grief. Unfortunately, in order to turn off or control one feeling an individual tends to suppress all feelings. This defensive mechanism can be very disconcerting for the partner. Moreover, it creates an impediment to intimacy. Some individuals are even afraid of the pleasure they will feel from sexual intimacy. They might say that if they were to let themselves go sexually, they would never be able to regain control or they would become like animals. One young wife with HSD was raised in a sexually repressive home. She had been taught that sex was bad, sinful, and dirty. She tried to constrain her sexual thoughts, behaviors, and feelings to live in a manner consistent with her upbringing. She commented that if she were to let go she would appear animalistic and be consumed by wanting to have sex all the time. Her fear was that of losing all emotional control. This complaint is not unusual in our practices, particularly among women from sexually repressed or extremely religious families.

## Fear of Dependency

In order to be in a relationship, an individual must strike a balance between being dependent and independent. A relationship is characterized by *interdependency*. Each partner depends upon the other to take care of various tasks and for love and sex. Some individuals who lack desire have an underlying fear of dependency or are counterdependent. The counterdependent partner goes to the extreme to prove that he or she does not need anyone. This partner acts in self-sufficient ways and is emotionally isolated and insulated from others. In some cases, the counterdependent partner will select a partner who is quite dependent so that person may carry or express his or her needs for the other. This process of *projective identification* however, has the unfortunate consequence of the counterdependent partner criticizing the dependent partner for his or her neediness. The dependent partners do not have to look at themselves because they are occupied with taking care of their partners who cannot take care of themselves. The partner with an underlying fear of dependency does not ask for much, is not aware of needing much, and remains emotionally aloof.

Men are more prone to experience this fear than women. For some men, being dependent is the same as being weak, vulnerable, and less of a man. After all, they think strong men are able to take care of themselves and others without being taken care of. A number of these men report being trained to be self-sufficient and competitive. They received little parental support and guidance, except to be told to "tough it out" and "act like a man."

One partner in a middle-aged couple presented with a lack of desire and a problem of committing to his partner. As a child, he was told that whenever he cried he was being a baby and would be physically punished and criticized whenever he showed any emotional weakness. He stated that if he were to ask his partner for anything, it would represent that he was a "nothing." Occasionally, he would begin to feel a need to ask for something and would be overcome with a sense of panic that was so strong he had been diagnosed with a panic disorder. Although he had some understanding regarding why he was so distant and could not let himself feel desire, he was not able to work through the problem without lengthy therapy.

Another case was perhaps one of the most fascinating. A couple in their early 40s entered therapy with the stated complaint that the wife lacked desire. Her desire for sex was low but it was quickly determined that her desire was based on his sexual desire and problems. The husband in this case was quite successful in his profession and saw himself as being problem free. He would project all the difficulties of the relationship onto his wife. This man had an interesting history. His mother had died at childbirth and a nanny reared him. His father was wealthy, lived in a mansion, and always had several women living in the house. The father's ideal was to be like Hugh Hefner, the Playboy mogul. The son remembered that as a small boy his father would play a game called "bending toes." The father would bend his toes until he cried at which point the father would tell him he was being a baby and he would continue to bend his toes more until he stopped crying. Later on, his father told him the world was a cold and cruel place and this game was designed to make him tough enough to survive. At the age of 16, the father asked his son if he was still a virgin. The son replied that he was. A couple of hours later, his father returned with a much older woman, told him she was a whore, and was going to teach him about sex. He was to go upstairs to begin his lessons. The prostitute was impatient and critical of him for not knowing what to do. He felt it was a disaster and was ashamed that he did not know much about what to do sexually.

Through a combination of early experiences, he internalized the beliefs that women exist there to serve men and that men should never have to ask for anything. A real man will never cry or show his needs. Men should be successful. If men are truly successful, women will automatically know what they want and please them. Unlike his father, he did not become a womanizer, but was faithful to his wife of 12 years. As a result, he remained distanced from her and never asked for anything. There were many times when he felt disappointed, angry, and resentful that she did not fulfill his wishes and needs. In his mind, to feel desire was a weakness because it meant he had a need he could not fulfill by himself. His wife stayed in the marriage because she feared being rejected and alone.

## CONCLUSION

In the vast majority of HSD cases we have treated, the lack of desire is a product of multiple factors. In cases of secondary HSD, relationship concerns or the underlying intimacy fears described above are almost always present. These factors have been overlooked or underemphasized in virtually all of the clinical literature on HSD because the writers were not systemic in their theoretical orientation nor were they trained in couple therapy. Assessing the desire of both partners is essential even when it appears the HSD is a unilateral problem. More will be said about the assessment of these fears and how to treat them in the treatment chapters, especially Chapter 9. Next, we will discuss the role of the intergenerational factors in the development and persistence of HSD.

# 5

# Etiology: Intergenerational Risk Factors

WE HAVE DISCUSSED THE ETIOLOGY OF HSD in Chapters 3 and 4, concentrating first on the *individual* and then on the interactions of the *couple*. We now turn our attention to the *intergenerational* or "family-of-origin" risk factors. Although mentioned last, this category is another significant area of the three components of the Intersystems Model. Information about sexuality is learned primarily within the family-of-origin and augmented by outside sources such as peers and schools. Although many of our clients contend that sex was never discussed in the home, we find that sexual scripts and directives from generations before are strongly ingrained in the sexual information that is transmitted within the family. Innumerable beliefs and assumptions about sexuality are acquired, sometimes without the use of language, yet they are deeply imbedded into the value system of the individual. Families also tend to perpetuate sexual mythology by passing on misinformation that is not open to questioning by outside sources. Through culture, race, and ethnicity, sexual scripts are preserved even though they might be loaded with inaccuracies and stereotypes. Consider the image of the traditional man; strong, potent, and rigid. Such beliefs are accepted without question, and maintained through blind allegiance to the family's moral, ethical, or spiritual systems. Additionally, in more instances than we wish to believe, we find the presence of another intergenerational risk

71

factor in family histories—sexual trauma. The most common presentations include incest (Maltz, 1988; Talmadge & Wallace, 1991) and covert incest (Adams, 1991). However, inappropriate execution of family boundaries, culminating in the family's failure to protect the sexual development of the child, often contributes to HSD. A notable example of boundary problems is the parentification of the child; a phenomenon that we often notice in our sex therapy clients. This chapter will address the intergenerational risk factors of: sexual secrecy, sexual ignorance, parentification, and sexual traumatization.

In the field of marital and family therapy, "family-of-origin" theories have been very influential. However, the available literature pertaining to HSD has not followed suit. This research literature fails to recognize the importance of intergenerational factors on the lack of desire. Nevertheless, clinicians dealing with the assessment of HSD and other sexual dysfunctions are aware of the important connection. Perhaps, one of the reasons for this absence is the fact that it is more difficult to demonstrate a causal link between something that happened in one's childhood or during the teen years and one's adult behavior. For example, the term "intergenerational" is absent from the index of Leiblum and Rosen's (1988) edited volume on disorders of sexual desire. This is also true of Kaplan's (1995) second text on sexual desire disorders. While she recognizes the importance of family-of-origin factors in the development of HSD, these etiologic factors might not necessarily be addressed in psychotherapy unless the behavioral treatment fails. Clearly, Kaplan does not utilize an integrated or systemic approach in the assessment of etiologic factors contributing to HSD.

We believe that *all three* areas of the system, including the family-of-origin, must be addressed when treating HSD. In fact, the senior author has highlighted the intergenerational factor in connection to sexual dysfunction in several prior works (Weeks & Hof, 1987; Weeks, 1989; Weeks & Gambescia, 2000) and more recently in a book on focused genograms (DeMaria, Weeks, & Hof, 1999). One way of incorporating sexual information family-of-origin into the Intersystems assessment is through the use of the sexual genogram. The traditional genogram format is adopted, but the scope is narrowed to focus on sexual scripts learned within the family-of-origin and carried through the generations of each partner (DeMaria et al., 1999). Myths, legacies, secrets, and conflicts are noted during the assessment and recalled later in the therapy as the connection is made to adult sexual beliefs and concerns such as HSD. Hof and Berman (1986) and Berman and Hof (1987) were among the first to describe the use of the sexual genogram. As colleagues of ours, they helped us to extend our thinking into this area.

## THE SEXUAL GENOGRAM

### Sexual Secrecy

The sexual genogram is an invaluable learning tool for therapists in training as well as in our clinical population. Clients and students often report that the exercise of examining intergenerational sexual messages was the most difficult yet most rewarding task they have ever encountered. The goal is to *begin* to uncover the connections between adult sexual functioning and implicit and explicit sexual messages that were exposed within the family-of-origin. The process of understanding and gaining insight into sexual family dynamics is not an easy task, yet it is fundamental to the development of a more sound adult sexuality. Many of our students and clients realize that family "discussions" about sexuality were brought about in a circuitous, uncomfortable manner or sometimes without the employment of language. For instance, instead of using accurate anatomical terms to identify the genitals, some families avoided applying labels at all, leaving the child with the task of constructing a name of their own or continuing to evade any discussion of the sexual organs.

The strongest sexual mandates and beliefs are disseminated from generation to generation covertly or through secrecy. Sometimes the most powerful covert message is in what the parent *fails* to say or expresses with a look of disdain or disgust. Many children are reared in families where sexual talk is frankly prohibited or somehow confined to a certain context such as religious or spiritual in which euphemisms are used. The message transmitted is often the message received; sex is so negative and frightening that words cannot be used to discuss it! The mind of the child can be critical in its interpretation of such nonlanguage by superimposing harsh judgments that anything related to sex is *bad* or *wrong*. It is difficult to quickly expunge such negative introjects, therefore the first step of the sexual genogram journey is to recognize their presence.

Families often protect sexual secrets such as out-of-wedlock pregnancies, abortions, extramarital affairs, and stillbirths. We often hear about how particular events are accepted, but unquestioned from generation to generation. For example, a client reported that at age 50, only when he asked family members directly, did he discover that his maternal grandmother was never married to his maternal grandfather. Another client shared that when she was 3 years of age, her mother disappeared after a full-term pregnancy. Magically, the mother returned six months later without the baby, and no explanation was ever given to the family. Through her genogram work, this client discovered that her mother was psychiatrically hospitalized after delivering a stillborn child. One more client, a male who engaged in multiple extramarital sexual liaisons, reported that he thought

his parents separated when he was 5 years old. He presumed the separation
was about an affair, but he was not certain. He attempted to learn more
about the separation by breaking the barrier of silence with his family.
Consequently, while in therapy, he discovered that his father had been a
philanderer during the entire duration of his parents' marriage.

Unquestionably, an obvious outcome of sexual secrecy is the promulga-
tion of sexual ignorance. We will discuss this in greater detail in the next
section. However, the worst form of sexual secrecy is that which occurs in
situations of overt incest. One of our cases illustrates the sexual trauma
that can occur through secrecy. A couple in their 20s presented for marital
therapy for the treatment of HSD in the female partner. The couple was
married for one year and she was extremely fearful of penetration and
was uncomfortable in any sexual situation, although she was otherwise
compatible with her spouse. She typically avoided sexual intimacy by pro-
claiming she was "not interested." The therapist suspected sexual abuse
could have been a factor due to the woman's fear of penetration and the
presence of HSD. Through exploration of intergenerational factors, the
woman was eventually able to share that she had been molested regularly
by her father from puberty until she left the family home for college, two
years prior to marriage. Furthermore, many instances of the abuse occurred
while her mother was in the home. We will discuss the devastating impact
of sexual trauma on the adult sexual response later in this chapter.

## Sexual Ignorance

Theoretically, the family is responsible for providing and clarifying accurate information about sexuality. Unfortunately, parental acceptance
of this responsibility is rarely the case. Instead, families tend to generate
and perpetuate a *lack of knowledge* about sexuality, which contributes to
sexual ignorance and anxiety in the adult. Families also tend to breed sexual misinformation and mythology that conforms to religious, moral, eth-
nic, and psychological tolerances of its members. Even in otherwise
enlightened families, the sexual intelligence quotient is not necessarily on a
par with its overall intellectual propensity. Legacies of sexual fear and
avoidance are perpetuated from their respective families of origin. Also,
because sex is within the domain of emotional functioning, it cannot easily
be approached with the clarity of other more logical issues with which a
family contends on a daily basis. Regardless of the cause, a lack of knowledge contributes to sexual anxiety in the child and fosters sexual dissatisfaction in the adult.

The language of sexuality is replete with terms and phrases that encourage and perpetuate sexual ignorance. The terms used by many individuals

are extremely subjective and do not necessarily describe a universally recognized set of behaviors. In fact, when our clients use slang to describe sexual acts, we ask that they operationally define the term and agree about the meaning. Often, it is initially impossible to determine if the euphemism is descriptive of coitus or another sexual activity. Clarification is always required. Consider how the following terms add to the ambiguity and confusion involved in sexual communication. For example, genital anatomy is sometimes called, "down there," and intercourse is often described through the use of familiar euphemistic terms such as, "sleep with" and "doing it." Such indirect terms assuredly leave a lot to the imagination.

We often ask our clients to recall milestones in their development throughout the life cycle. It is not unusual to hear that they were frightened or unprepared for normal physiologic occurrences such as nocturnal emissions or the menarche. Consequently, they experienced fear or shame instead of excitement about entering the next phase of life. Frequently, we hear stories about how our clients were told they were about to have "the talk" (about sex) with a parent. The imminent sex talk instilled so much dread that when it finally occurred, they were in a state of severe anticipatory anxiety, only to be amazed that very little was actually discussed. Some parents avoided any discussion by handing the uninformed adolescent a book about menstruation or sexual intercourse in order for our clients to fend for themselves during this vulnerable time.

Other individuals have reported experiencing shame and anxiety as a young child due to the punitive treatment of bedwetting or other accidents involving the genitourinary system. Another practice that engenders fear and perpetuates sexual ignorance is the mislabeling and/or expressing disgust at the sight of the genitals. Anxiety and ignorance set up a breeding ground for the acceptance of sexual myths and the later development of sexual dysfunctions. It is no surprise that a woman with HSD learns to ignore her intrinsic sexual feelings after a lifetime of being told that these feelings are unthinkable, wrong, nasty, or otherwise undesirable. Likewise, in cases of secondary HSD (those who have felt desire, but have lost the feeling), many of our male clients have unwittingly followed the example of their parents who demonstrated a *lack of interest* as a coping strategy. They learn to disconnect their feelings, especially sexual feelings, when they are displeased with their partner.

With regard to the risk factor of sexual ignorance and HSD, we believe that information reduces anxiety and combats sexual ignorance. Consequently, part of our therapeutic role is to provide accurate data designed to increase the sexual IQ of our clients. Furthermore, our students and clients learn to interrupt the practice of blindly perpetuating sexual beliefs and practices that cause sexual discontent.

## Parentification

Another pattern we have noted in our sex therapy practices is that of parentification or being the "parental child." We view it as a risk factor for HSD because it is a reflection of the lack of appropriate intergenerational boundaries within the family-of-origin. When parentification occurs, the child is not being properly nurtured or protected. In the existent marital/family literature, this pattern is referred to as a "parent-child" or "caretaking" relationship. Sauber, L'Abate, Weeks, and Buchanan (1993) contend that the child is implicitly asked to take on parent-like responsibilities such as attending to a parent's feelings of unhappiness or depression, assuming decision-making authority, and acting as a confidant to a parent(s).

In our experience, parentification is much more likely to occur in single parent homes where the principal caretaker, usually the mother, is feeling depressed and lost over a recent divorce. The parentified child willingly assumes this role in order to help and protect the parent. If the parent is strengthened, potentially the child will be nurtured. As time goes on, the dynamic between the parent and child may become more and more exacerbated. The child begins to act like the parent and the parent begins to act like the needy child. These children eventually develop a sense of omnipotence and underlying rage that their parent is not able to take care of them as they see their childhood disappear relative to what other children are receiving.

The long-term effects of parentification on the sexual response have not been discussed anywhere in the marital or family therapy literature. What happens is quite simple and predictable. When the child becomes an adult, he or she is programmed to take care of others. Hence, he or she selects a mate who is in need of help. Initially, this relationship works until the parentified adult begins to feel empty, burned out, and rageful that the partner is not able to do more for him or herself. As these feelings begin to emerge or be acted out, the parentified adult perceives the partner as a child and no longer wishes to play the role of parent. The partner becomes unattractive and the parentified adult begins to lose sexual interest. Unfortunately, there has been no connection in the literature between the intergenerational phenomenon of parentification and the development of HSD in the adult. This clinical observation awaits empirical verification.

## Sexual Trauma

As therapists, we seek to uncover the sexual values that operated within the family-of-origin of our clients. In HSD cases, family beliefs concerning sexuality and sexual intimacy are often negative and therefore potentially traumatic. The implicit family messages may have been as innocuous as the notion that sex is only for procreation and not for the enjoyment of the woman. Interestingly, some of our clients have developed HSD only after the birth of their last child, when the couple decided not to have any more children. One bewildered husband could not understand why his wife rejected him sexually after the birth of their third child. He assumed she did not love him any more. This could not have been further from the truth. In therapy, they traced the presence of strong religious messages from her family-of-origin linking sex to procreation.

In other cases, the negative messages were of a more traumatic nature. Some of our clients were surreptitiously instructed that sex is nasty, dirty, wicked, and sinful. In fact, a number of the women we have treated for HSD have reported that their mothers complained that sex was "disgusting" to them, but it was one of the "necessary evils" of marriage. Some of our female clients have had to endure their mothers' itemized depictions of unpleasant sexual encounters with their fathers. Discussions of this nature obviously violate the intergenerational boundaries between the child and adult and give rise to disgust and fear of sexual intimacy in the child. Additionally, children may internalize a distorted idea about sexual intimacy from a variety of notions learned in the family, which link sexual intimacy with danger. For instance, we have heard from our clients the ideas that "sex is dangerous," "you can't trust men," "men only want sex," and that sex is a form of "abuse" that a woman must silently endure.

Another variation of sexual trauma, although not overtly destructive, is the presence of covert incest in the family-of-origin. We have noticed a connection between the blurring of intergenerational boundaries through covert incest and HSD in several of our clients. The child becomes the surrogate spouse of the opposite sex parent by acting as a confidant or otherwise assuming a privileged position in the family (Adams, 1991). The parent develops an extreme dependency on the child that overlooks the emotional needs of the child. As we stated above, covert incest can be reflected through the parentification of the child. The child is unable to meet his or her own emotional needs without fearing the loss of the parent. As an adult, he or she may enter partnerships that are sexually neutral or nondemanding or hold the expectation of not becoming sexually intimate with their partner.

In other instances, we have learned that sexual trauma occurred by virtue of observation of sexual events that were performed indiscriminately in the presence of the children. For example, we sometimes hear that the mother was inappropriately dressed in sexually revealing attire or that she allowed herself to be seen without clothing by her pubescent son. In one family, the parents had sex in full view of the children, and when the children looked uncomfortable with this behavior, the parents expressed their belief that something was wrong with the children's reactions. Plainly, such situations create confusion about sexual feelings in the child. As adults, they report having had feelings of voyeuristic stimulation or perhaps disgust. In some instances, the traumatic events caused the child to view the mother as someone who allowed herself to be sexually used and abused. It is not difficult to imagine how such instances of inappropriate sexual activity in the presence of children can distort or destroy the development of sexual desire in the adult.

Sexual abuse in the child has been clinically or empirically linked to a lack of desire in the adult. Courtois (1988) wrote a landmark book detailing the long-lasting implications of sexual abuse on adult sexual functioning. She pointed out how sexual abuse may contribute to any number of sexual dysfunctions and specific dislikes, including HSD, if not phobic reactions. Some of the adverse responses can be traced directly to the sexual abuse. For example, girls who were forced to have oral sex may have an aversion to oral sex or may even develop a phobia about it. Other women report that certain types of touching create flashbacks and unpleasant feelings. For instance, one woman could not tolerate the approach of her husband if she was not facing him. She gave an example of how she became panicked when he kissed her on the back of her neck while she was preparing dinner at the kitchen counter. Her surprised husband felt rejected by her response until he understood that this behavior was a "trigger" for the memory of sexual abuse that occurred throughout adolescence. During a 10-year period at family holiday functions, her older cousin would force her to an isolated area of the house and have rear-entry intercourse with her.

Other ramifications of childhood sexual abuse in the adult are demonstrated through a variety of negative reactions to adult sexual relations within an intimate and loving context. Some examples include the experience of guilt related to sex, a fearful feeling of losing control, or a sense of being abused in some way. A more severe reaction is that of dissociation or a "numbing out," during a sexual interaction. The formerly abused partner will report that he or she feels nothing during sex. Sometimes, no memory is present of the adult sexual interaction. In one of our cases, a woman reported a neighborhood boy had sexually abused her for several years. When asked why she did not tell her parents, she responded that she could never talk to her mother, especially about things that troubled her. She thought her only option was to accept the abuse. The experience of being abused left her with a feeling of mistrust of men and a fear of getting physically and sexually close. She chose to marry a gentle, kind man who was sexually nondemanding. Their relationship was more like that of brother and sister, and she had little sexual desire for him. In a somewhat similar case, the female partner's brother was the childhood sexual abuser. She believed that her rigid and cold parents did not seem to care about her, therefore, she accepted her brother's sexual advances as a sign of his love. He did appear to treat her well otherwise and would talk to her rather than ignore her like her parents did. When she engaged in sexual relations with her spouse, this woman often felt "nothing."

We do not want to suggest that everyone who has been sexually abused will develop a lack of desire, or that everyone with HSD has been sexually abused. It is a factor that should be examined and ruled out during the assessment of anyone presenting with problems with sexual desire. Much more research needs to be done to establish links between sexual abuse and sexual problems, including lack of desire. Sexual abuse is a cross-cultural problem that is difficult to investigate or measure. In fact, within the last two decades, the research literature on sexual abuse has been inconsistent with respect to frequency in the general population. Finkelhor (1994) reviewed studies from 19 countries, including 10 national probability samples. He found that the rates ranged from 7% to 36% for women and 3% to 29% for men. Females were 1.5 to 3 times more likely to be abused than males. In our clinical experience, we have found that covert or overt incest has been a factor in many of our sex therapy cases. The sexual abuse history might not be revealed upon initial assessment. As we reported previously (Weeks & Gambescia, 2000), many times, a level of trust needs to be established between the therapist and the client before the painful experience can be discussed.

While it is beyond the scope of this book, we feel it is imperative to remind the clinician to inquire about domestic violence in the family-of-origin as well as the possibility of partner abuse in the current relationship. The two are often correlated (McKibben, De Vos, & Newberger, 1989). In both instances, acts of violence, threats, intimidation, and psychological abuse are used to establish power and control over the child and/or female partner. In the case of partner abuse, unwanted or forced sexual relations or penetration occurs (Russell, 1990). Women who are raped by their husbands or intimate partners are likely to experience multiple assaults (Mahoney & Williams, 1998). Like the child who is abused, these women live with the covert and ongoing threat of another assault by someone they live with. (Randall & Haskell, 1995; Resnick, Kilpatrick, Walsh, & Vernonen, 1991). The long-term physical results (Campbell & Alford, 1989) and psychological consequences (Bergen, 1996; Widom, 1999) are significant. The aftereffects are often far greater than the complaint of HSD, yet the sexual symptom can be the tip of the iceberg.

In addition to making historical inquiries about child abuse in the family-of-origin, the therapist must ask directly about physical threats, injuries, or forced sexual relations from the intimate partner. Another way of initiating the discussion is to ask if she is ever afraid of her partner.

Kinzl, Traweger, and Biebl (1995) conducted a study using 202 female college students in order to examine the relationship between sexual abuse and sexual dysfunctions. Two findings are relevant to the current discussion.

1. Women who reported multiple incidents of sexual abuse were more likely to experience a lack of desire than those who reported a single incident or no incidents. Thirty-one percent of the women with multiple-incidents reported a sexual desire or arousal disorder. About 11% to 12% with no incident or a single incident reported a sexual desire or arousal problem. It would make sense that women who had been abused multiple times would be more likely to experience greater sexual difficulty.

2. Women who reported a negative parental relationship were more likely to experience desire problems. The research tool used to measure the quality of the parental relationship consisted of eight independent variables. The variables that predicted a lack of sexual desire were not reported.

Kinzl, Mangweth, Traweger, and Biebl (1996) further investigated the significance of the two factors mentioned in the prior study. They wanted to know which of the two factors, sexual abuse or negative familial experience, was most predictive of sexual dysfunction in adulthood. They studied a sample of 301 males. The most common problems discovered were lack of sexual desire (10.4%) followed by premature ejaculation (9.8%). The results of their study suggest a gender difference. For males, having a negative parental relationship was more significant than sexual abuse, and for women it was the reverse. In both sexes, each factor played a role, but men and women reported different sexual outcomes. One possible reason mentioned by the researchers for this difference is that men tend to report more single-incident assaults that were less violent than those experienced by the women.

These two studies suggest that growing up in a dysfunctional family places a child at risk for developing a sexual dysfunction later in life. Within this context, sexual abuse may occur partly due to the family dysfunction, and, when it does occur, the family fails to help the child deal with it. Thus, sexual abuse as a risk factor is important but is not the whole picture. The clinician must examine the entire family context as a risk factor, especially in men. In our experience, male clients are often reluctant to talk about their families and do not see how there could be any connection with their present problems and "things that happened 20 years ago."

For the more psychoanalytically oriented, Radin (1989) published a theory describing pre-oedipal factors in HSD. The fundamental fact of this theory is that when children are not able to experience the normal attachment or bonding process, they begin to turn inward in order to seek gratification of their needs through a fantasy bond or emotional fusion with a "good" parent. The immediate consequence of this situation is to feel shame, rage, rejection, annihilation, or pain associated with emotional connection. The long-term consequence is the formation of a negative self-concept and a sense of not being loveable. Ultimately, this individual learns to turn inward creating emotional distance from both the self and others. Viewing oneself as unlovable and wanting to be loved would be contradictory. Having sexual desire would motivate a person to have a connection with another that could revive the painful early memories. Whether one subscribes to an analytic hypothesis or not, this and related theories strongly suggest that adult attachments, including sexual attachment, are historically grounded in the family-of-origin.

We sometimes recommend the following books to our clients to assist in the understanding of the effects of sexual trauma on the sexual response:

- Adams, K. (1991). *Silently seduced: When parents make their children partners: Understanding covert incest.* Deerfield Beach, FL: Health Communications, Inc.
- Maltz, W. (1995). *The sexual healing journey: A guide for survivors of sexual abuse.* New York: Harper Collins.

## CONCLUSION

The number of risk factors associated with HSD, including the intergenerational risk factors, appears to be overwhelming. A thorough appraisal is time consuming and tedious. In the assessment and treatment chapters to follow, we will further describe a systematic process for uncovering these factors as quickly as possible. Typically, the initial assessment requires a few sessions with continued assessment as treatment is implemented. HSD is a multifactorial problem, therefore, the clinician must be careful not to preclude the presence of additional risk factors once one or two conditions have been identified. Throughout treatment, supplementary risk factors may appear, as the client is able to recall these events with the help of the therapist's support and encouragement.

# 6

## Medical Aspects of HSD

THE THERAPIST WITH TRADITIONAL TRAINING in marital, family, and sex therapy is challenged by the abundance of new medical data that is available for the treatment of sexual dysfunctions. Most sex therapists are not practicing physicians, yet they are required to become familiar with the current medical tests and remedies and to integrate this information into the sex therapy format. As we discussed in our text about erectile dysfunction, the role of the therapist is rapidly expanding to include a working knowledge of procedures, devices, and medications such as sidenafil (Viagra) (Weeks & Gambescia, 2000). The evaluation of HSD incorporates the medical history as well as the psychological risk factors within the individual and the couple. Often, a medical evaluation is necessary. Treatment options are now more varied than ever and often require the collaborative effort of the client, the sex therapist, and the physician.

Frequently, the symptoms of HSD are similar to those of other disorders such as depression or androgen (male hormone) deficiency. Many therapists are unfamiliar with the medical conditions that could affect sexual desire or feel uncomfortable asking questions about the client's medical history. Nonetheless, they understand that organic or psychiatric factors could contribute to or predispose an individual to HSD. In fact, often the etiology is a mixture of organic, psychogenic, and relational factors. The sex therapist needs to know if a referral to a physician is necessary, how to integrate the medical data into the treatment of the individual or couple, and how to work collaboratively with physicians.

In this chapter, we will discuss the prevailing medical risk factors that can contribute to diminished sexual desire such as hormone deficiencies, chronic disease states, and certain medications. Then, some of the medical treatments for HSD will be reviewed in addition to antidotes for medicines that can cause HSD. Also, we will examine certain current non-prescription and alternative prosexual treatments and devices.

The following case example represents a common clinical presentation of HSD with mixed etiology. The case of Sandie and Mark illustrates the complexity of an *initial* assessment and the departure from the typical marital/sex therapy process involving a couple. A 51-year-old highly functioning schoolteacher suffered from HSD and was afraid she was "falling out of love" with her husband. She had been seeing a psychiatrist for dysthymia who felt she was ready to work on the sexual aspects of her treatment. Sandie had been taking a maintenance dose of an SSRI for several years and had a family history of depression. She was in a 31-year marriage with a loving and considerate spouse. They did not appear to have overt relational obstacles that contributed to her HSD. The couple had three children who ranged in age from mid to late 20s. For the first 20 years of their marriage, Sandie had a robust sexual appetite and was orgasmic with sexual intercourse with her husband. She believed that her sexual appetite decreased gradually after the birth of their last child. They agreed that she was more tired when the children were younger and that she never really recovered her sexual interest. Mark recounts a more precipitous decline in her interest after the birth of the last child, a slightly different view of Sandies story. Their sexual frequency had decreased to once a week or every other week over the last 10 years. Sandie would comply with Mark's requests for sex although she was seldom in the mood and never initiated. Mark was saddened and distressed with her disinterest and avoidance of sex. Finally, he became so concerned that he urged Sandie to seek help for her lack of desire. She made the initial phone call after being referred for sex therapy by her psychiatrist.

At the initial interview it was apparent that Sandie was not under the care of a gynecologist, therefore a recommendation was made for her to set up an appointment immediately. She appeared to have symptoms of menopause such as hot flashes and menstrual irregularities. The therapist recommended a gynecologist since Sandie did not know one and a letter was sent (with her consent) reviewing her sexual symptoms and requesting hormonal and gynecologic assessments. Next, Sandie gave permission for a consultation with her psychiatrist. In the first of many conversations, we discussed her psychiatric status and the possibility of using alternative or additional antidepressants, such as bupropion hydrochloride SR (Wellbutrin SR), which can be less offensive to the sexual response (Crenshaw & Goldberg, 1996). The couple was assigned sensate focus exercises in order to interrupt the avoidance of intimacy and to reduce the anticipatory anxiety that was now a precursor to sex for Mark as well as Sandie. In addition, bibliotherapy was recommended in order to increase their fund of knowledge and lessen the anxiety about sex. They were instructed to read the first chapter of *For Each Other* by Barbach (1982) and to underline significant passages each using different color markers. We planned to meet conjointly for several weeks initially and to begin discussing their reactions to the book in the next session.

After the initial interview with Sandie and Mark, the therapist was busy with "behind the scenes" work such as talking with the psychiatrist and gynecologist. The gynecologist conducted hormonal studies and a thorough medical examination. (Interestingly, in a communication after her initial visit, the gynecologist commented that Sandie appeared sad, and that she definitely had noticeable symptoms of menopause). In the next session, the couple discussed their reactions to the book. They were relieved and encouraged to be "working on the problem." The homework assignments helped the couple to become proactive and interrupted their sense of hopelessness. During each session, we discussed their reactions to the sensual massage exercises, which they performed enthusiastically. The therapist explained that Sandie's HSD could be a result of several factors such as menopause, depression, and her own psychological issues. The therapist hinted that there could be more to the story regarding Sandie's loss of desire after the couple decided to have no more children. (Sandie is from a Catholic family-of-origin and she associates sex with procreation.) Also, the therapist inquired into the possibility of more covert relationship issues such as unspoken disappointments or resentments. Despite the suspected presence of psychological etiologic factors, we agreed that perhaps hormonal deficiencies might also be contributing to her lack of desire.

Inquiring about medical conditions, medications, alternate medications such as herbs, exercise, recreational drugs, alcohol, and other medical treatments is part of the sex therapist's role. Also, talking to physicians about treatments and reading medical reports is sometimes necessary. Questions about medical issues can easily be integrated into the Intersystems Model. Furthermore, we find it beneficial to use a conjoint format in order to promote a systemic process especially during the assessment phase of therapy. The partner is helpful in providing support as well as correcting or embellishing information. Later in the treatment process, the format can become more flexible, allowing for individual sessions with either partner if indicated. Once a therapeutic alliance is established, either partner will feel comfortable with occasional individual sessions.

## SEXUAL PHYSIOLOGY: THE SEXUAL RESPONSE CYCLE

The human sexual response can be understood as a cycle with three distinct phases, each with unique characteristics according to Kaplan's triphasic model (Kaplan, 1979). The phases include *desire*, *arousal* (or excitement), and *orgasm*. The first stage is primarily psychological, and the next two involve genital and extragenital physical processes. If the cycle is not interrupted or inhibited, one phase will flow smoothly into the next. The initial phase, sexual desire, is a state of mind that reflects lust or an appetite for sex. The individual is driven to think about, yearn for, want, seek, and need sexual gratification. Most notably, sexual desire is fueled and maintained by fantasies, mental images, cognitions, and feelings related to sex. It is described in many ways, such as being "in the mood" or "interested in" dyadic or solo sex. Also, emotional considerations are involved, such as a sense of deserving or being entitled to feel sexual pleasure and a willingness to experience intimacy and closeness with a partner.

As Kaplan (1995) explains, however, the sexual drive is not purely an emotional condition. It is a biologically based appetite requiring adequate amounts of bioavailable testosterone in order to function normally. Thus, the sex drive requires the presence of a well- functioning hormonal system and the absence of debilitating or chronic disease. Sexual desire sets the stage for arousal or excitement, which triggers a series of physical responses facilitating erection in men and lubrication in women. If the physical and psychological processes of sexual desire and arousal remain uninterrupted, orgasm will occur, relieving the physical vasocongestion and providing a feeling of satiety.

## THE PHYSIOLOGY OF SEXUAL DESIRE

The intersystem conditions discussed earlier interface with the physiologic components of the sexual system in a delicate balance, which promotes and maintains the sexual appetite. A disruption or deficiency in the structure or functioning of the sexual system such as injury, hormonal imbalance, chronic illness, surgery, some of the normative changes of aging, or the lack of a partner may negatively impact sexual desire. Medications, prescribed or recreational, can also interfere with libido or sexual desire. In this chapter, we will discuss the organic etiologic factors that are commonly associated with an absence or lack of sexual desire. These include *hormonal deficiency, chronic conditions,* and *medications* that can cause or contribute to HSD. An in-depth discussion of sexual physiology is beyond the scope of this book; therefore, we recommend the following texts: *Sexual Pharmacology* by Crenshaw and Goldberg (1996) and *The Sexual Desire Disorders* by Kaplan (1995).

## THE PHYSIOLOGY OF HSD

### Hormonal Deficiencies

The endocrine system works in conjunction with the central nervous system to promote equilibrium among all body systems. Endocrine glands (such as the testes, ovaries, pituitary, thyroid, pancreas, and adrenals) produce *hormones.* These chemical hormones communicate messages from one organ to another. Hormone imbalance is the most common organic cause of HSD. Although numerous endocrine conditions can cause hormonal imbalance and affect sexual desire, only a few occur frequently. These include the following conditions that need to be considered in the assessment conducted by the sex therapist according to Kaplan (1995):

1. testosterone deficiency in men and women
2. postmenopausal estrogen deficiency in women
3. hyperprolactinemia (excess prolactin in the bloodstream)

While diabetes and thyroid deficiency are hormone deficiencies that cause low libido, they do so less commonly. We will discuss them later under the heading of chronic conditions causing HSD.

### Testosterone and Sexual Desire

Testosterone is considered the libido hormone in men and women. However, different body chemicals such as DHEA (dehydroepiandrosterone), estrogen, progesterone, and other unidentified substances interact with testosterone to promote sexual desire (Crenshaw & Goldberg, 1996). Testosterone influences the development of the male sex organs as well as secondary sex characteristics such as pubic, facial, and underarm hair. In both genders, it acts directly on brain centers responsible for sexual interest and appetite. Moreover, testosterone helps maintain muscle mass, mood stability, bone density, and overall strength and well being throughout the life span (Winters, 1999). Thus, testosterone stimulates the sexual appetite and promotes the physical strength and vigor necessary for sexual functioning. In both men and women, testosterone levels fluctuate in response to emotional factors, aging, time of day, and season of the year. According to Crenshaw and Goldberg (1996), circulating levels of testosterone are highest in the morning and in the fall season.

Testosterone circulates in the blood in three forms, two of which are *bound* to protein. The third form, called *free* testosterone, has the greatest impact on the body's tissues because it circulates freely in the bloodstream and is not attached to protein (Davis, 1998a). Only about 2% of the body's testosterone is considered to be free. The measurement of total testosterone (sum of the free and bound levels) alone does not give enough information about problems with production or insufficiency of this hormone. Accurate determination of testosterone levels in men and women involves assessing all three forms. Furthermore, precise measurement of the free and bound levels is difficult using current assessment measures available to most physicians.

TESTOSTERONE AND MEN

Testosterone levels in men are 10 to 20 times higher than in women (Crenshaw & Goldberg, 1996). Most of the testosterone production in men occurs within the testes, although additional amounts are secreted by the adrenals, located above the kidneys. Normally, testosterone levels peak during adolescence and decline slowly through the life of the man with a more noticeable drop after the age of 40. The surge during adolescence is associated with an increase in sexual appetite and development of the genitals and secondary sex characteristics. Also, testosterone maintains sperm production; therefore, spermatogenesis gradually ebbs throughout life but never ceases entirely. Although total testosterone remains relatively stable throughout life, the level of free testosterone declines at a rate of about 1% per year in men (Lund, Bever-Stille, & Perry, 1999). This natural decline with age in men, called andropause, produces subtle changes in the sexual appetite. The orgasm-focused adolescent and young adult will mature into an adult who is more composed and patient, sexually speaking.

TESTOSTERONE DEFICIENCY IN MEN

Age-associated diseases, medical treatments, or any organic condition in which the testes fail to produce customary levels of testosterone can cause testosterone deficiency (also called androgen deficiency). Examples include testicular injury, inflammation, tumor, radiation, or surgical removal. Viruses that invade the body such as HIV and the resulting AIDS and also some genetic conditions can cause testosterone deficiency. Symptoms are dependent on the age of onset and severity of the disorder. In adults, HSD is often the first indication of such an organic problem. Since the sex centers in the brain are exquisitely sensitive to fluctuations in sex hormones, sexual desire can diminish before it is reflected in other body structures (Kaplan, 1995). Other symptoms of testosterone deficiency may include depression, decreased energy, body hair, muscle mass, bone density, erectile capacity, and fertility.*

TESTOSTERONE REPLACEMENT IN MEN

Ideally, replacement of normal testosterone levels will correct many of the conditions that occur as a result of deficiency of this hormone, and prolong the quality of life among older men (Brodsky, Balagopal, & Nair, 1996; Burris, Banks, Carter, Davidson, & Sherins, 1992; Katznelson et al., 1996; Tenover, 1999). The sex therapist should be aware that a variety of preparations are available in the United States, each with advantages and disadvantages to the individual client. Also, the side effects associated with each modality can vary from benign to significant. We will mention a few of these preparations along with references for additional information.

1. *Oral medications* containing testosterone derivatives are convenient to take but have been associated with liver abnormalities in some recipients (Maurice, 1999; Westaby, Ogle, Paradinas, Randall, & Murry-Lyon, 1977). See Winters (1999) for a current review of current forms of testosterone replacement in men.

2. Weekly *intramuscular injections* of testosterone are a widely used form of replacement according to Mackey, Conway, and Handelsman (1995). Although the authors noted few serious side effects, this method of replacement is often inconvenient and uncomfortable.

3. *Transdermal scrotal patches* containing testosterone (Testoderm by ALZA Corporation) are applied directly to the shaved skin of the scrotum each day. Testosterone is released through the scrotal skin into the bloodstream. See Jordan (1997).

4. *Transdermal skin patches* containing testosterone (Androderm by Smith, Kline & Beecham in the U.S.; Testoderm TTS by ALZA Corporation) are applied to the skin of the upper arms, thighs, back, or abdomen. Two patches are used in different areas each day. Testosterone is released through the skin and into the bloodstream. See Parker and Armitage (1999) and Confrancesco and Dobbs (1996) for a discussion of the advantages of transdermal testosterone.

---

* For a more detailed discussion of the role of testosterone production in health as well as androgen deficiency, we recommend the book *Sexual Pharmacology* by Crenshaw and Goldberg (1996).

5. A clear, colorless *testosterone gel* (AndroGel by Unimed Pharmaceuticals, Inc.) is applied topically to the skin of the trunk of the body. Used daily, it is slowly absorbed through the skin into the systemic circulation. It was approved by the Food and Drug Administration in February 2000 for the treatment of testosterone deficiency in men.

6. Currently, Columbia Laboratories is testing another form of testosterone delivery for men. It is a small pill that dissolves in the buccal cavity between the gums and the cheek and is absorbed into the body. It is called the Progressive Hydration Buccal Tablet (PHBT).

TESTOSTERONE AND WOMEN

Once considered the *male* hormone, testosterone is now recognized as an important component of the sexual appetite in women. Unfortunately, this fact is often overlooked in the routine medical attention to women's health issues. Testosterone promotes sexual desire, curiosity, fantasy, interest, and behavior. Also, it enhances sensitivity in the nipples and clitoris, promoting sexual pleasure (Crenshaw & Goldberg, 1996). Produced in the ovaries and the adrenal glands throughout the life of the woman, the amount of circulating testosterone peaks during adolescence and gradually declines during peri-menopause (Zumoff, Strain, Miller, & Rosner, 1995). A deficiency in testosterone can become more pronounced during and after menopause as ovarian and adrenal production drop (Buckler, Robertson, & Wu, 1998). Surgically induced menopause (with removal of the ovaries) causes a more dramatic reduction in testosterone production although small amounts continue to be secreted by the adrenals. The actual circulating blood levels of testosterone are difficult to measure because of the normal hourly fluctuations, differences among women, and the insensitivity of most laboratory instruments to the various indices such as free and bound types. Research evaluating the role of testosterone on sexual desire in women is based primarily on self-reports of the frequency of sexual thoughts, fantasies, and masturbation rather than laboratory studies alone. Thus, the diagnosis of testosterone deficiency in women is based predominantly on the women's report of her levels of sexual desire before and after menopause and is confirmed by laboratory studies (Basson, 1999).

There is a growing body of research concentrating on the previously underreported connection between the hormone testosterone and sexual desire in women (Sands & Studd, 1995). Earlier studies of this nature examined the correlation between sexual *activity* and levels of testosterone. Two early investigations in particular noted the correlation between mid-cycle elevations in female testosterone levels and increased sexual *activity*

(Bancroft, Sanders, Davidson, & Warner, 1983; Persky, Lief, Strauss, Miller, & O'Brient, 1978). Another study conducted by Sherwin and Gelfand (1987) positively related blood levels of testosterone to sexual *desire*, *fantasy*, and *arousal* in their female subjects.

More novel explorations on the role of testosterone on sexual desire in women examined the *differences* between women with and without sexual desire. An interesting study performed in England employed a sample of women between the ages of 18 and 45 years (Riley & Riley, 2000). They compared a group of 15 women with lifelong HSD to a control group, matched for age, weight, and number of pregnancies. The HSD group reported the absence of sexual desire or fantasies for a 2-year duration. The control group consisted of women who enjoyed sexual activity and fantasies. Each participant completed a diary each day for one month recording the following parameters:

- feelings of sexual desire, using a 5-point scale ranging from *absent* to *strong*
- feelings of sexual need
- sexual thoughts and feelings
- initiation of sexual intercourse
- the actual experience of sexual intercourse
- frequency of masturbation
- frequency of orgasm

In addition, a single midcycle blood sample was taken from each subject measuring various indices of sex hormones such as testosterone.

The level of *free* testosterone was found to be significantly lower in the HSD group. Free testosterone is positively correlated with sexual desire (Davis, 1998a). As predicted, the control group reported significantly more frequency than the HSD group in *all* of the sexual variables mentioned above. Note that the first three of the above mentioned items represent *subjective* experiences of sexual desire rather than actual behaviors. Frequency of sexual behavior alone cannot accurately indicate sexual desire because, as mentioned in Chapter 2, individuals sometimes engage in sexual behavior in the absence of sexual need or desire, often in order to please their partner (Shortland & Hunter, 1995; Sprecher et al., 1994). Interestingly, Riley and Riley (2000) also reported that in both groups, sexual frequency occurred more often than sex was desired, supporting the assumption that sexual desire cannot be inferred from the frequency of sexual behaviors. Also, as testosterone levels decline, some women agree to have sex in the absence of desire because they anticipate that the stages of arousal and orgasm will be pleasurable. Thus, once actual stimulation commences, feelings of desire can emerge. Moreover, as Basson (2000) suggests, in menopausal women, the emotional satisfaction gained from an intimate and loving sexual encounter often replaces the yearning for sex experienced previously. The therapist is reminded to inquire about *fantasy* rather than *frequency* when assessing sexual desire.

TESTOSTERONE DEFICIENCY IN WOMEN

Roughly one third of the women in the United States suffer from HSD (Laumann, Paik, & Rosen, 1999). For most women who are premenopausal, the etiology of HSD is usually psychogenic. Individual factors (such as stress and depression) or relationship discord are common precipitants. As women age, however, they are more likely to develop an organic etiology, such as estrogen or testosterone insufficiency, which may exacerbate the more psychogenic issues or it may act alone to cause HSD (Davis, 1999a, 1999b). After menopause, many women report fewer sexual thoughts and fantasies (Davis, 1998a). In fact, the decline in testosterone production in women negatively affects responsiveness at all three phases of the sexual response: desire, arousal, and orgasm (Bartlik & Kaplan, 1999). In addition to sexual symptoms, testosterone deficiency can contribute to more generalized symptoms, such as reduced bone density and muscle mass and an elevation in LDL (bad) cholesterol. Nevertheless, determining the cause of low desire in women of any age is not always simple because of the many emotional factors that can affect the sex drive. In fact, female sexual dysfunction involves a combination of biological, psychological, and interpersonal determinants (Basson, Berman, Burnett, Derogatis, & Ferguson et al., 2001). According to Rako (1996), the most obvious signs of testosterone deficiency in women are as follows:

• a decrease in sexual desire and fantasy
• diminished energy and sense of well-being
• decreased sensitivity to nipple and clitoral stimulation
• decreased capacity for sexual arousal and orgasm
• thinning of the pubic hair in some women

Low levels of free testosterone often accompany the subjective reports of fatigue and low sexual desire in actual cases of testosterone deficiency (Davis, 1999b). Moreover, these women report that they need more than the usual amount of stimulation to experience arousal. They are saddened by the lack of erotic response in their nipples and clitoris, and often lament that having sex is just not worth the effort. In addition, they recount that orgasms are reduced in intensity. Their motivation to have sex is thwarted by the amount of time and effort required to experience only a fraction of their former robust sexual response. The change to a diminished sexual response is usually insidious and gradual, often becoming undeniable during menopause. In cases of surgical or chemically induced menopause, the shift is more dramatic. Some testosterone-deprived women continue to enjoy cuddling and kissing, while others become "turned off" by their neutral response to stimulation. Partners are often dismayed and concerned by the deterioration in sexual responsiveness of their formerly amenable lover.

In order to demonstrate the relationship between testosterone levels and sexual desire, researchers often study women who have a deficiency of testosterone caused by natural or surgically induced menopause. In these women, sexual desire is often significantly lower than prior to menopause. This decline in testosterone production has been associated with secondary HSD in menopausal women (Basson, 1999; Davis, 1998b). The reader is reminded that estrogen deficiency at menopause can also contribute to sexual disinterest due to vaginal atrophy and lack of adequate lubrication. These genital changes can affect sexual enjoyment *indirectly* by making sex uncomfortable or even painful (Sherwin & Gelfand, 1987). Often, women are given estrogen in conjunction with progesterone to replace the deficiency, thus relieving the estrogen-deficiency symptoms of menopause that make sex difficult, such as vaginal atrophy, insomnia, or vasomotor instability (hot flashes). Women with a genuine testosterone deficiency report that sex is less painful after hormone replacement therapy (HRT) yet they still feel sexually "dead" or neutral in terms of sexual desire.

In some investigations, the relationship between testosterone production and sexual desire is examined by replacing testosterone in women who have a testosterone deficiency due to menopause. In two such studies, the subjects received the usual menopausal HRT with estrogen and progesterone. They were given supplemental doses of testosterone *in addition to* the HRT typically used to treat menopausal symptoms. Testosterone replacement is not normally a component of HRT, although the combined use of estrogen and androgens is gaining favor (Everard & Laan, 2000). Theoretically, adding testosterone to the HRT regimen should increase sexual desire.

Shifren and colleagues (2000) used a sample of 75 women with surgically induced menopause over a period of 36 weeks. All of the women had below-average age-appropriate testosterone levels prior to the administration of the testosterone. The subjects were given testosterone *transdermal* skin patches in addition to HRT to replace the deficiency caused by the surgical removal of the ovaries. Warnock, Bundren, and Morris (2000) also conducted a similar preliminary investigation of a small sample of women with surgically induced menopause. The subjects were given testosterone replacement in the form of a compound taken *orally*. In both studies, sexual desire, fantasies, and activity increased significantly as a result of the addition of *testosterone* replacement in conjunction with HRT. Thus, in women who have had surgical removal of their ovaries, adding testosterone to their HRT regimen could restore sexual desire. Gelfand (1999) and Sherwin and Gelfand (1987) also reported similar results, particularly for younger women. More frequently, researchers and clinicians are recognizing the advantages of combining the use of estrogen and testosterone for HRT regimens (Sarrel, 1999; Sherwin, 1998).*

TESTOSTERONE REPLACEMENT IN WOMEN

For men with testosterone deficiency, there is an established replacement regimen that now includes the more convenient transdermal patch and gel in addition to the oral and injectable forms that were widely used in the past. To date, there are fewer replacement options for women despite the obvious need to restore sexual desire as well as the overall quality of life (Warnock, Bundren, & Morris, 1997). Currently, there is insufficient research and less available information about appropriate doses or methods of testosterone replacement in women (Buckler, Robertson, & Wu, 1998). Nonetheless, there are a variety of delivery systems under investigation, which are producing encouraging results in preliminary studies.

1. Tuiten and colleagues (2000) have tested a *sublingual* form of testosterone with promising results.
2. Also, a small (6mm) *vaginal tablet* that is used twice a week is currently undergoing clinical trials. It is the progressive hydration vaginal tablet (PHVT) by Columbia Laboratories, Inc.
3. The *transdermal skin patch* has been found to effectively restore sexual desire in preliminary studies on women by Shifren and colleagues (2000) and Buckler and colleagues (1998). These researchers recommend the more convenient transdermal patch because it produces predictable blood levels with little variation.
4. *Transdermal gels* containing testosterone are currently undergoing clinical trials for use in women. We will discuss two gel products later in the chapter. The transdermal skin patch and gel are not marketed yet or

---

* For a comprehensive exploration of this subject, we recommend the book *The Hormone of Desire* by Susan Rako (1996).

FDA approved for use in women. It is hoped that the transdermal delivery systems will become a safe option for women when the doses and side effects are regulated. Theoretically, the transdermal delivery method bypasses the liver and is absorbed without the problems associated with oral administration.

5. Subcutaneous *implants* such as those used in Europe are not considered to be a safe method of replacement because they cause testosterone levels to rise and fall in an unpredictable manner (Buckler et al., 1998).

6. Intramuscular *injections* of testosterone, even at low doses, are often unpredictably absorbed and cause blood levels to be too high for women, according to a study comparing testosterone delivery systems conducted by Buckler and colleagues (1998).

7. *Oral* preparations marketed for replacement in women such as Estratest by Solvay Pharmaceuticals, actually combine testosterone with estrogen. The amount of testosterone needed by most women is much lower than the dose contained in the pill. In addition, the portion of estrogen needed may be different or greater than what is in the pill. Rako (1996) warns that the two hormones need to be given separately in order to more precisely effect replacement. Moreover, the oral route of administration is less desirable because of the potential harmful effects on the liver (Maurice, 1999).

Testosterone may be prepared by a pharmacist who "compounds" the hormone by mixing it with gels, creams, and other agents for oral, vaginal, and transdermal absorption. The dose is adjusted to meet the specific needs of the woman. Of course, there are no established guidelines for compounding because of the lack of controlled clinical studies utilizing this method. Rako (1996) discusses in detail the advantages and disadvantages of this and various replacement modalities.

Adverse effects of testosterone replacement are uncommon in the low doses used by women (Davis, 1998b). Some commonly noted adverse effects include the presence of male secondary sex characteristics such as facial hair and a deep voice, liver damage, reduced high density (good) cholesterol, acne, and irritability (Warnock et al., 1997).

## Postmenopausal Estrogen Deficiency

Until recently, there has been little research interest on the effect of menopause on sexuality. For many women the hormonal alterations of menopause do not induce sexual desire problems (Sommer et al., 1999). Estrogen has no direct effect on sexual desire (Sherwin & Gelfand, 1987).

However, the gradual decline in circulating estrogen has been associated with body changes that can cause discomfort during sex. As women age, they will inevitably experience sexual symptoms if the natural estrogen deficiency is not corrected by hormone replacement therapy. Symptoms such as dryness, loss of elasticity, or shrinkage of the vaginal tissues can contribute to a reduction in sexual desire *indirectly* by making sexual activity uncomfortable or even painful.

Commonly known as the female hormone, estrogen is produced in the ovaries and to a lesser degree in the testes in men. The production peaks during adolescence and begins to decline gradually at perimenopause, continuing to decline throughout life. Estrogen affects virtually all body organs consequently, a deficiency of this hormone is certain to impact physical and emotional health. For instance, estrogen promotes bone density, tissue growth, skin elasticity, reproductive cycles, and the integrity of blood vessels and organs. It affects mood, concentration, memory, and facilitates a sense of well being. Estrogen also preserves physical "attractiveness" by reducing appetite and maintaining feminizing characteristics such as skin and hair softness. Estrogen proves critical to sexual health as it promotes lubrication, muscle tone, and integrity of the delicate vaginal tissues.

Many women are given estrogen replacement to correct the sexual symptoms of menopause. Estrogen also helps with generalized problems such as "hot flashes." reduced bone density, elevated low-density (bad) cholesterol, insomnia, and concentration difficulties (Grodstein et al., 1997). Of course, the decision to use hormone replacement therapy (HRT) (with or without progesterone) must be made judiciously as there is an increased risk of certain cancers in some women. Furthermore, the estrogen in standard HRT can actually contribute to or worsen a lack of desire by reducing or inactivating free testosterone in some women (Rako, 1996).

Estrogen replacement is now available in many forms including the transdermal patch, oral medication, vaginal cream, and a ring that is inserted into the posterior portion of the vagina and remains in place for 3 months.

## Hyperprolactinemia

The pituitary gland, located deep within the brain, secretes the hormone, prolactin. An elevated serum prolactin level is an indication that the pituitary is not functioning properly. The term hyperprolactinemia describes an elevation in circulating prolactin levels above the normal range. A number of medical conditions, which affect the pituitary, including a benign tumor, can cause hyperprolactinemia (Kaplan, 1995). Sometimes HSD is the first and only symptom of such an unusual medical condition. The sex therapist is not expected to make such a complex medical diagnosis. However, it is always prudent to recommend a physical evaluation to rule out the presence of an organic condition of this sort. This is particularly necessary if our clients have not undergone a routine annual examination or if the HSD is global and follows a period of normal functioning.

## CHRONIC CONDITIONS

Of the three phases of the sexual response cycle, the stages of *arousal* and *orgasm* are quite vulnerable to the many vascular and central nervous system conditions that could potentially interrupt the vascular and nerve supply to the genitals needed for erection and lubrication. This is not necessarily the case for the stage of sexual *desire*, which can endure in the presence of vascular or neurological conditions, such as coronary artery disease or paralysis. Indeed, if the individual is unable to experience arousal or orgasm, the natural appetite for sexual intimacy often continues, allowing the individual to think about or long for sex.

In some instances, however, the person is simply too depleted by chronic illness to think about sex very often. The fatigue, discomfort, and general debilitating effects of unceasing illness eventually can short-circuit the sexual appetite. Some chronic disease states involve degeneration or failure of the lungs, liver, and kidneys. Others may include arthritis, severe infections, advanced-stage cancer, congestive heart failure, chronic obstructive pulmonary disease, HIV infection.

Thyroid deficiency and diabetes are two endocrine conditions that can contribute to HSD either directly or indirectly. Diabetes is related to insulin deficiency of the pancreas. Although the thyroid gland and the pancreas are parts of the hormonal system, they were not included in the above-mentioned discussion because they are less likely to directly cause HSD than testosterone deficiency. In diabetes, blood sugar levels can be unstable, making the individual too weary to be interested in sex (LeMone, 1996; Schreiner-Engel, Schiavi, Victorisz, & Smith, 1987). In the more advanced forms of diabetes, damage to the nerve endings of the genitals can obstruct the enjoyment of physical sensations thereby indirectly contributing to HSD and erectile dysfunction. The endocrine disorder, hypothyroidism, alters the synthesis of testosterone, directly contributing to a lack of desire (Kolodny, Masters, & Johnson, 1979). Moreover, the decreased energy associated with chronic thyroid disease can contribute indirectly to a lack of desire in men and women.

Regardless of the etiology, any sexual dysfunction that occurs persistently at the latter two phases of the sexual response cycle could *indirectly* inhibit desire. The individual anticipates difficulty or pain with sex and learns to negatively anticipate sexual relations. For instance, in the case of premature ejaculation, the man can become so performance focused and anxiety charged that he eventually avoids the pleasurable anticipation of sex. Instead of enjoying erotic fantasies, he anticipates the next failure. The same is true for conditions such as Peyronie's disease, a structural abnormality of the penis. In women, vulvar vestibulitis and vulvodynia are syndromes of unexplained pain, itching, rawness, and burning around the vulvar area surrounding the opening of the vagina (Baggish & Miklos, 1995; Davis & Hutchinson, 1999; Maurice, 1999). These and other chronically painful disorders often adversely affect sexual desire. The pairing of sexual pleasure and physical pain can eventually lead to the avoidance of positive sexual anticipation altogether. Thus, a sexual dysfunction that occurs during arousal or orgasm can *precede* and *degenerate* to HSD.

## MEDICATIONS

### Drugs that Can Diminish Sexual Desire

Many prescription, nonprescription, or recreational drugs can cause sexual side effects through the direct action of the drug on the body, or indirectly through nonsexual side effects, such as nausea, that make the individual feel sick. Any or all three stages of the sexual response cycle can be affected. According to Crenshaw and Goldberg (1996), however, diminished sexual desire is the most common of the sexual side effects of medications although it probably is underreported because the reason for the lack of desire is usually explained by situational factors such as stress or fatigue.

Commonly used prescription medications that may decrease sexual desire fall into five general categories. These include the following groups: antiandrogen, psychotropic, cardiac, drugs that bind with testosterone, and miscellaneous medications. We will consider psychotropic drugs in the following paragraphs.* It is essential that the therapist know all medications the client is taking and the condition for which the medication is being used. Ask for a list of the medications, dose, and length of time that the client has been taking the medication(s). Consider the following:

- Is the change in sexual function a desire phase problem or perhaps a loss of desire due to another sexual dysfunction such as erectile dysfunction?
- Does the timing of the HSD coincide with the new medication?
- Sometimes, sexual side effects occur after a period of time on a medication.

* For a more detailed discussion of the other groups that may cause HSD, we recommend *Sexual Medicine in Primary Care* by Maurice (1999).

- Could the sexual side effects be dose-related?
- Is the sexual symptom global or situational?
- Ask directly about nonprescription drugs such as cold or sleep aids that can be used without consideration of the side effects or interactional effects with other medications.
- Inquire about *how often* the client uses alcohol, marijuana, or recreational drugs.

The spouse or partner is often helpful in verifying the client's recollection of quantity, frequency, and reasons for taking medications or recreational drugs. Using a *Physicians' Desk Reference* (PDR) or other reliable sources, review the mechanism of action, classification, and side effects of each drug. Psychiatrists, physicians, and pharmacists are extremely helpful with medication information.

## Medications for Medical and Psychiatric Conditions

It is common for our clients to tell us that they are taking prescription medications for a variety of medical problems, from mild to severe. Some of these organic conditions are commonly associated with HSD, while others are not. The same is true for medications used to treat the various conditions reported by our clients. Some diseases, however, are commonly associated with reduced libido, and the clinician should be alerted to the possibility that the actual disease or medications for the treatment of the disease often cause HSD in the following conditions: hypertension, heart disease, prostate cancer, chronic pain, endometriosis, and other forms of cancer.

Many types of psychotropic medications have been associated with disturbances in sexual functioning, particularly diminished desire. These medications include antipsychotics, sedatives, narcotics, mood stabilizers, and the various groups of antidepressants such as the tricyclics, monoamine oxidase inhibitors, and selective serotonin reuptake inhibitors (SSRIs) (Salerian et al., 2000). The iatrogenic sexual side effects of the psychotropic drugs can contribute to noncompliance or adversely affect intimate relationships as well as the overall quality of life. In fact, the sexual side effects in particular have been found to be a leading cause of noncompliance (Ferguson et al., 2001).

### ANTIDEPRESSANT-INDUCED SEXUAL DYSFUNCTION

The lack of sexual desire is a common symptom of depression. Perhaps this side effect is frequently reported because the other features of depression might be given less importance than the sexual ones, or the client notices the change in sexual functioning first (Basson, 2000). Also, HSD is an established side effect associated with many antidepressants (Ballon, 1999; Rosen, Lane, & Menza, 1999). Sometimes it is difficult to determine the degree to which the lack of desire is due to the depression or the antidepressant.

Of the numerous antidepressant groups, the SSRIs are used frequently because they are relatively safe and effective. Unfortunately, they are associated with dysfunction at all stages of the sexual response cycle, most notably desire and orgasm (Woodrum & Brown, 1998). The actual incidence of SSRI-induced sexual dysfunction varies with the specific drug and may be underreported, yet some investigators have found an incidence of roughly 50% (Montejo-González et al., 1997). The sexual side effects of the SSRI group usually do not remit over time if untreated with antidotes (Ashton & Rosen, 1998). The depressed individual is often forced to tolerate a reduction in libido or inhibited orgasm during the course of treatment unless antidotes are explored and the treatment plan changed.

ANTIDOTES FOR ANTIDEPRESSANT-INDUCED SEXUAL DYSFUNCTION

Treatment strategies for overcoming the sexual side effects of antidepressants include waiting to see if the symptoms remit, lowering the dose, substituting another antidepressant, or adding a supplementary medicine to act as an antidote (Fava, 2000). Some psychiatrists recommend the idea of a drug "holiday" over a weekend or during a time when sexual relations are anticipated. There are two major disadvantages associated with this strategy. First, the long half-life of some medications does not allow for an absolute window of no sexual side effects. Second, such holidays can encourage noncompliance. The coadministration of sildenafil (Viagra) or bupropion hydrochloride-SR (Wellbutrin SR) to the existing SSRI regimen has been effective in some of our clients. A thorough explanation of treatment strategies along with a comprehensive listing of antidotes is offered by Rosen, Lane, and Menza (1999) and Ashton, Hamer, and Rosen (1997).

Currently, sildenafil (Viagra) is recognized as an effective *antidote* for antidepressant-induced sexual dysfunction. According to recent studies by Fava, Rankin, Alpert, Nierenberg, and Worthington (1998), Ballon (1999) and Nurnberg, Lauriello, Hensley, Parker, and Keith (1999), sildenafil (Viagra) restored sexual satisfaction in men and women whose sexual response deteriorated as a result of taking SSRIs for depression. Moreover, sildenafil (Viagra) has helped to reverse the sexual side effects in men and women using *many* types of psychotropic medications, including the SSRIs (Salerian et al., 2000).

Sustained-release bupropion hydrochloride SR (Wellbutrin SR) is FDA-approved for the treatment of depression. It is often used as a single agent or an add-on medication in cases of refractory depression (Rosen, Lane, &

Menza, 1999). It does not affect the reuptake of serotonin, therefore, it is not associated with the sexual side effects of the SSRI antidepressant group (Segraves et al., 2000). It acts by enhancing the brain's production of nor-epinephrine and dopamine. These two neurotransmitters are linked to sexual desire.

Recently, bupropion hydrochloride SR (Wellbutrin SR) has been used as an add-on drug for clients who experience the sexual side effects of SSRIs such as decreased sexual desire. There is little actual research available about adding or substituting bupropion hydrochloride-SR (Wellbutrin SR) for SSRI-induced sexual dysfunction and the findings to date about the sexual effects of bupropion hydrochloride SR (Wellbutrin SR) are mixed. One study by Modell, May and Katholi (2000) reported that 70% of their sample of nondepressed men and women improved sexual functioning at all phases of the sexual response cycle on bupropion hydrochloride SR (Wellbutrin SR). In another study by Michelson, Bancroft, Targum, Kim, and Tepner (2000), bupropion hydrochloride SR (Wellbutrin SR) was found to be no more effective than placebo in reversing SSRI-induced sexual dysfunction. Anecdotal reports by colleagues have touted the prosexual properties of bupropion hydrochloride SR (Wellbutrin SR) when used in conjunction with many SSRIs and also when used alone in the treatment of HSD. Ongoing research is needed.

Because information about medications and side effects changes rapidly, the therapist must remain informed of the latest drug-related data.

## Drugs that Promote or Restore Sexual Desire

HORMONES

As discussed earlier, in cases of androgen deficiency, replacement of *testosterone* can restore sexual desire in many men and women. Replacement of deficient levels of *estrogen* can reverse some of the age-related changes in the female genitals that make sex uncomfortable, thereby enhancing sexual desire indirectly. While the replacement options for testosterone are more diverse for men, currently safe and reliable replacement regiments for women are being investigated. Three forms of testosterone replacement therapy for women are undergoing clinical trials and hopefully will be released within the next year or two.

1. Transdermal skin patches, similar to that used by men but with much smaller doses

   • Androderm by Smith, Kline and Beecham, Inc.
   • Testidern TTS by ALZA Corporation

2. Transdermal gels similar to the kind used by men
  - AndroGel by Unimed Pharmaceuticals, Inc., is now marketed solely for men should theoretically be effective for women in smaller doses.
  - Tostrelle by Cellegy Pharmaceuticals, Inc.
3. Vaginal tablet
  - Progressive Hydration Vaginal Tablet (PHVT) by Columbia Laboratories is inserted into the vagina and absorbed gradually.

VASODILATORS

Sildenafil (Viagra) is not an aphrodisiac, therefore, it has no direct effect on sexual *desire*. However, this vasoactive drug was found to enhance the male sexual response by targeting and intensifying *arousal* (Goldstein et al., 1998). Sildenafil (Viagra) increases the blood supply to the genitals, thereby promoting erections in men. Restoring erections can indirectly promote sexual desire because of the positive anticipation of sexual arousal and erections that remain operative throughout the duration of sexual activity. Theoretically, sildenafil (Viagra) could also facilitate overall sexual satisfaction in women by increasing the blood supply to the clitoris and genitals. Could sildenafil (Viagra) enhance or "jump-start" sexual desire in women *indirectly* by promoting the swelling and lubrication of the genitals? If difficulty in attaining or sustaining sexual arousal is removed, is the woman more likely to become more interested in having sex? In addition, could the anticipation of an uninterrupted sexual response replete with orgasm increase the sexual appetite?

In a preliminary investigation of the effect of sildenafil (Viagra) on the sexual response of women, Kaplan et al. (1999) studied a small number (33) of postmenopausal women with "sexual dysfunction." In this study, dysfunction was defined in numerous ways, involving all stages of the sexual response cycle: desire, arousal, and orgasm. Unfortunately, fewer than 20% of these postmenopausal women reported improvement in sexual function after taking sildenafil (Viagra) for 3 months. Moreover, *none* of the subjects experienced an increase in sexual desire. Although the vasoactive nature of sildenafil (Viagra) might have promoted increased clitoral sensitivity and vaginal lubrication in some of the subjects, this effect did not enhance libido or augment arousal or orgasm. While these results are disappointing, we are reminded that the experience of sexual desire and excitement for women is dependent upon many factors, and genital engorgement is not necessarily one of them. In fact, even in the presence of genital swelling and lubrication, many women do not realize that they are sexually aroused (Laan, Everaerd, van der Velde, & Geer, 1995).

Currently there is continuing ongoing research on sildenafil (Viagra) and the sexual response of women. Basson conducted a placebo-controlled study of over 500 women with sexual dysfunctions at all stages of the sexual response cycle.* Although sildenafil (Viagra) was found to be safe for use in women, it was only as effective as a placebo in improving the sexual response. Yet, Berman noted an improvement in sexual functioning in a small group of women who had undergone a hysterectomy.†

Numerous vasodilators are proposed for the treatment of "female sexual dysfunction." None of these products target the desire phase of the sexual response cycle. Instead, they promote vasodilation of the female genitals, hoping that the physical engorgement can promote arousal, even if desire is not present. We will discuss a few of these products because our clients often ask about them, but their effectiveness in treating HSD is questionable.

Two products undergoing clinical study are Femprox (TM) by NexMed, Inc. and ALISTA by Vivus, Inc. These transdermal creams contain alprostadil (prostaglandin E1), a vasodilator, which promotes arousal and erection in men. Applied to and absorbed by the tissues of the clitoris and genitals, they enhance the physiologic aspects of sexual arousal in women. Intranasal Apomorphine Chloride by Nastech Pharmaceutical Company Inc., undergoing clinical trials, is a nasal spray that contains apomorphine, which works on the central nervous system by activating chemicals associated with sexual arousal.

## ALTERNATIVE TREATMENTS

Men and women seeking to enhance or restore libido often turn to the Internet, health food stores, or alternate sources in search of aphrodisiacs and other remedies. The products available often contain herbs and other products that are reputed to improve the sexual appetite. Sometimes, well-intentioned physicians and other health professionals recommend alternative remedies based on their clinical experience or as a first step in the treatment of low libido. In most instances, these remedies have not been studied empirically and they are prescribed solely on the basis of anecdotal evidence. Furthermore, many contain ingredients that can cause serious side effects. An Internet search or literature review under the heading, "aphrodisiac," will turn up volumes of substances known for their prosexual properties. We will discuss some of the more commonly mentioned alternative remedies.

* The results of this unpublished study were reported to the American College of Obstetricians and Gynecologists in 2000.
† The results of the unpublished preliminary study were presented to the American Urological Association in 2000.

Yohimbine is derived from the bark of the West African yohimbe tree and is reputed to be a potent aphrodisiac. Unfortunately, there are few controlled studies on the effect of yohimbine (or the synthetic formulations such as Yocon) on sexual desire. In fact, one study found that it is not helpful in promoting the sexual appetite of women (Piletz et al., 1988). Yohimbine can be dangerous, as it is associated with many side effects such as agitation, elevated blood pressure, mania, and depression (Crenshaw & Goldberg, 1996).

Ginkgo biloba is an extract derived from the leaf of the Chinese ginkgo tree. It has been reported to be an effective antidote for antidepressant-induced sexual dysfunction at all three stages of the sexual response cycle (Cohen & Bartlik, 1998). Its effectiveness in promoting sexual desire in nonclinical samples is yet unproven.

Ginseng, a Chinese perennial herb, may promote desire due to its overall effect on energy levels, yet this assumption is not validated through research on sexual desire specifically.

DHEA (dehydroepiandrosterone), a potent adrenal hormone, facilitates the body's production of testosterone, thereby promoting sexual desire. DHEA levels gradually decline with age. In one small group of women with adrenal failure, improved sexual functioning was reported at all stages of the response cycle with synthetic DHEA (Casson et al., 1996). Others have found that DHEA replacement does not restore sexual desire in older men or women (Morales, Nolan, Nelson, & Yen, 1994). Synthetic DHEA may prove to be an effective treatment for HSD although its safety and efficacy are unknown.

Some nonprescription products contain L-arginine, an amino acid that promotes arousal in men. An example is Natural Sensation (TM) by Strategic Science and Technologies, Inc., marketed as a "natural" alternative for the treatment of female sexual dysfunction. It is a transdermal cream that theoretically enhances arousal and promotes more "intense" orgasms. It is understandable that such a compelling promotion might give hope to the many frustrated women who seek to regain their sex drive. Other nonprescription remedies contain herbs that claim to have an aphrodisiac effect. One such product, Ascend, is a pill made in formulations for men and women. It contains *Avina sativa*, an extract derived from oats that is purported to enhance the sexual appetite. Ascend can easily be found on the Internet under the heading, aphrodisiac.

DEVICES

The EROS-CTD by UroMetrics, Inc. is a hand-held, battery-powered clitoral vacuum device. It creates the same effect as sildenafil (Viagra) for women without the necessity of taking a systemic medication. By applying the EROS-CTD to the genitals, gentle suction promotes increased blood flow to the clitoris, theoretically enhancing genital stimulation and lubrication. It is marketed for treatment of "female sexual arousal disorder," which is a generic term describing difficulties at all phases of the sexual response cycle. If used in the absence of desire, it potentially could "jump-start" the sexual response, although there are no published studies on the efficacy of this apparatus. It requires a prescription and was FDA approved for home use in 2000. Currently, the cost is $359.00.

Inquiry into the use of alternate remedies attempted by our clients has yielded some interesting results. We have heard stories of ordering prescription and nonprescription medications over the Internet without the approval of a physician. A few of our clients have tried sildenafil (Viagra), while others have experimented with herbal remedies. When we ask about what efforts our clients have made to correct the situation prior to treatment, we usually hear descriptions of behavioral efforts that have failed. It is useful to follow-up with questions about nonprescription drugs, herbs, and devices.

## CONCLUSION

One of the traps for the sex therapist is to think of etiology as falling into discrete categories such as either hormonal or psychogenic. Sometimes the new medical advances can be so exciting for the therapist that the clinical picture is seen as more organic than it actually is. For instance, not every menopausal woman complaining of diminished desire needs testosterone replacement. In the majority of cases of HSD, the cause is related to the psychogenic risk factors within the individual or the relationship. The organic risk factors, if present, will require attention, as they are a part of a clinical picture with a mixed etiology. Treatment therefore needs to address the medical, individual, and relational issues that contribute to or result from the HSD.

# 7

## The Comprehensive Assessment

THE ASSESSMENT OF HSD must be time efficient and practical. The partners are often frustrated and pessimistic by the time they seek help from the sex therapist. Frequently, they have been disappointed by other treatments that might have circumvented the HSD or focused on more global individual or relational concerns. Very few practitioners are skilled and comfortable in treating sexual problems, particularly HSD, and the couple might have been a casualty of well-intentioned yet, ill-prepared therapists.

### THE INITIAL TELEPHONE CALL

The initial telephone call with the clients can be critical in deciding whether they will actually begin treatment. It is important to convey a sense of hope by assuring them that they are calling the right therapist. The best way to accomplish this goal is to let them know you are familiar with the problem and to ask some pertinent questions that deal specifically with the HSD.

Some clients request an appointment immediately, while others are calling to "shop." The ones who intend to set an appointment are aware of the therapist's reputation for treating sexual problems. Nonetheless, it is always useful to ask the potential client how they found your name. If a friend or a professional referred them, then they will probably want to make an appointment with a minimum of questions since they already know something about the therapist. Typical concerns such as fee, insurance, appointment times, and who needs to come to the sessions may be briefly discussed.

On the other hand, some potential clients may have heard a lecture or found your name in the telephone book or in a professional directory. Asking about the source of the referral tells the therapist about the kind of help that is needed. For instance, a couple called for an appointment stating that they learned about the therapist on the Web site of a professional organization which deals specifically with sexual problems. Without hesitation, the therapist was able to ask about the kind of sexual problem with which the couple was struggling.

Issues such as fee, location, insurance, and available times are often discussed with clients who are shopping for the right therapist. The therapist should view this initial discussion as an opportunity to educate the HSD couple about the kind of therapist they need. The therapist should be:

- familiar with the problem,
- able to combine individual, couple, and sex therapy,
- able to develop a comprehensive and flexible treatment plan, and
- willing to spend time on the telephone answering questions.

Clients may be informed about the fact that sex therapy is a specialty and that few therapists are trained in this modality. Provide some background about your own training and experience. Basically, what the therapist is trying to do is to inspire confidence and convey a sense of accessibility.

One of the most difficult tasks of the initial telephone call is to get the partner involved. From our prior discussion of etiology, it should be clear that the partner is often instrumental in getting the problem resolved. The therapist may begin the discussion by simply saying that a sexual relationship takes two people and for that reason the spouse or partner should be involved. The therapist can explain that therapy sessions are often educational and it is best if both partners hear the information together. Also, remind the couple that therapy will require assignments to be performed together at home. Homework needs to be emphasized as a key part of the therapy. Finally, suggest that the partner is a necessary part of the treatment. (Of course, it might not always be judicious to state in the initial contact that the partner is also a part of the problem.)

In some cases, the person calling is the "identified client." They might not believe the problem is all theirs, but their partner is refusing to attend sessions. In order to get the "higher desire" partner into therapy, all therapists must be *absolutely committed* to the belief that conjoint treatment is essential. We often sabotage ourselves by lacking in this undertaking. Unless we entrust ourselves to this position, we will give up prematurely and accept the identified client's statement that getting the spouse to attend is a hopeless task.

The therapist will want to ask about the partner's reluctance to participate in therapy. Listen carefully to the reasons and then try to find some positive way to reframe the partner coming to therapy. Many of the reluctant partners anticipate being blamed, told what to do, or have some other negative notions about therapy. The identified client can be instructed in how to counter these beliefs and to offer some positive rationale to their partner. The therapist might instruct the HSD client to say to the partner:

- The therapist really needs *your* insights and understanding about this problem.
- We will need to do homework so the level of desire can get better. The therapist wants you there to help with the homework.
- The therapist thinks our relationship is strong except in this one area and we need *your* help.
- The therapist says that individual treatment is in most cases not useful, but working with us as a couple usually leads to a good result.
- The therapist knows *you* must be frustrated and thinks that you believe nothing will work, but he or she has had good success when the couples work together.

Specific resistances on the part of the unwilling partner to enter therapy can be identified and the spouse coached on dealing with these resistances over the telephone and in the first couple of sessions. If the HSD partner has tried and failed, ask whether it is acceptable for the therapist to call to discuss participation with the reluctant partner or ask that they come to *one* session. The therapist is looking for an opportunity to interest the reluctant partner in therapy. Obviously, this individual *should be* interested in having a sexual relationship. If they refuse to come to treatment, this assumption may also be questioned. Perhaps the resistant partner really is not interested in having a sexual relationship, and this is the reason for nonparticipation. Later, once the therapist has established a therapeutic alliance, this point could be restated.

Another situation should also be mentioned at this point. As we said earlier, some partners *lack desire for desire*. They are "dragged" into therapy by frustrated partners who are threatening to leave, divorce them, or have an affair. In these cases, it is usually the non-HSD client who calls for an appointment. The HSD partner might attend the therapy sessions, but *does not want to be there*. Since they have no interest in generating or improving sexual desire, they see no point in treating a nonexistent problem. We will discuss this presentation later when considering contraindications for couple therapy.

## PRELIMINARY ASSESSMENT

The preliminary assessment occurs during the initial telephone call and the first interview. It is the therapist's first opportunity to gather data and to begin to formulate systemic hypotheses that may later be confirmed or disconfirmed. The following types of information are obtained.

1. *Initial impressions and reactions.* A concrete description of the presenting problem(s) is obtained. This includes information about four components: *who*, *when*, *how*, and *where* the problem manifests itself. In HSD cases, the lack of desire is usually embedded in other issues. Two questions need to be answered at this juncture. What is each partner's view of the problem? How is the problem systemically maintained? The second question immediately sets up conditions for a systemic hypothesis. We will return to this topic later when discussing the Rapid Assessment Technique.

2. *History of the problem.* Next, the history of the problem is obtained by asking the following questions: When did the problem begin? What were the conditions at that time? How has it changed over time?

3. *Recent significant changes in the client's life.* Life stressors and life-cycle changes may be adversely affecting one or both of the partners. These might include transitions such as the birth of a child, a new job, midlife concerns, relocation, death, marital conflict, a child leaving home, or retirement.

4. *Changes sought by the partners.* The therapist then asks about what the partners wish to change. The therapist must be careful not to superimpose his or her own expectations and desires. It is critical to ask about what the partners hope to gain from therapy in order to provide education and adjust unrealistic expectations.

## PRELIMINARY INTERSYSTEMIC ASSESSMENT

The intersystemic assessment is our unique contribution to the field of sex therapy and we believe it provides a thorough assessment tool for HSD since the disorder is multidimensional. This model includes assessment of individual, couple, and intergenerational risk factors mentioned previously. Our clients often mention pieces of the intersystemic assessment during the initial telephone conversation. Take note of these factors and return to this aspect of the assessment in the next few sessions.

1. *The individual.* A detailed psychological assessment of the intrapsychic components of each partner is undertaken based on the material provided in Chapter 3. The therapist would evaluate for cognitive distortions, irrational beliefs, and ego-defense mechanisms such as denial and projection using the Axis I and II diagnostic categories of the *DSM-IV* (1994).

2. *The couple.* This dyadic assessment would include such concepts discussed in Chapter 4 such as the partner's emotional contracts, styles of communication, conflict resolution style, and ways of defining problems. It would also focus on each partner's capacity for intimacy.

3. *The intergenerational system.* The intergenerational factors mentioned in Chapter 5 are assessed through the use of a genogram (DeMaria et al., 1999), which examines different aspects of familial functioning. This tool provides the general context of each partner's personal development as well as contexts relevant to the problem at hand. The clinician evaluates for incest, parentification, triangulation, and other dysfunctional patterns of familial relating that could have an impact on intimacy and sexuality.

## THE RAPID ASSESSMENT TECHNIQUE

The next part of the assessment phase targets the HSD. The couple is assessed in five different areas:

- frequency of sex
- frequency of sexual desire
- degree of sexual interest
- context of sexual desire
- presence of other sexual dysfunctions and difficulties

The couple should be prepared for a 3- to 4-session assessment phase. During this time, the therapist will continue to organize information from the preliminary and intersystemic assessments. The couple is told that a number of questions will be asked during this phase and that some of the questions will be given to them to take home in order to give them more time to think about them. They should also be told that they would each be given some individual time to discuss matters that might concern them.

During the assessment phase, bibliotherapy and other homework may be given to the couple to initiate the feeling that treatment has begun.

## Frequency of Sex

The frequency of sex is a behavioral question referring to how often sexual activity actually occurs. The definition of *sexual activity* is specific to each couple; therefore, the clinician and the couple must first define what they mean by *sex*. We usually start by working from the present to the past. For example, begin by asking, "How often have you had sex during the last six months?" Proceed to the last year, 2 years, and work back to the beginning of the relationship asking about the frequency before the marriage or commited relationship began and the frequency just after. These questions will give the clinician a baseline from which to assess the problem. It also helps in differentiating between primary and secondary HSD.

Along with this question, the clinician can ask about which partner usually has initiated sex over the duration of the relationship. Couples will sometimes disagree about frequency and how often each one has initiated sex. Note the difference without making it an issue. We frequently normalize this difference by pointing out that couples rarely agree. Frequency by itself does not tell us about regularity. We also want to know whether sexual activity has been on and off and whether they are giving us an average. Some couples go through cycles of greater activity and then long dry spells. It is important to know under what circumstance sex is more likely to occur, such as during weekends or vacations.

The therapist will also want to focus on when each one perceived a reduction in sexual activity in order to assess whether the process was sudden or gradual. In general, this is the area where couples tend to disagree the most. One reason is because they are often trying to remember something that changed several years ago. Secondly, there may be memory distortions based on unconscious factors. Once the period of time is identified during which desire started to diminish, the clinician can begin to explore the circumstantial changes during that timeframe.

Finally, the therapist will want to obtain a history of sexual activity of each partner prior to the current relationship, asking the same types of questions. For most couples, this is best accomplished in individual sessions. Most spouses do not like to hear about prior sexual activity, especially when the current sexual relationship is "dead."

## Frequency of Sexual Desire

The second series of questions are much like the first except that they pertain to desire rather than actual behaviors. We explain that sexual desire is like a hunger or an appetite for sex, or perhaps a yearning or longing to be sexual with oneself or one's partner. The clinician then assesses the level of sexual desire by asking about how often the partner thinks about sex, fantasizes, daydreams, has sexual dreams, or masturbates within a given time-frame. We often introduce the topic by normalizing the concept of sexual fantasy and coming up with a definition that the partners and therapist can agree upon. Sometimes, it is best to ask these questions in the private sessions because many individuals have not discussed masturbation with each other and they are embarrassed to do so in the conjoint format. Of course, the issue of embarrassment about masturbation would need to be addressed. Again, we ask about how often the individual acts on the urge to masturbate, whether they self-pleasure in the absence of desire, and the reasons for each. It is important to ask about changes in sexual appetite over time and across conditions that may be favorable or unfavorable for sexual desire.

Additionally, we inquire about how often the low-desire partner had sex without feeling desire, whether they ever initiated sex when they did feel desire, and how sexual desire would be communicated to the partner. As stated in Chapter 2, it is not unusual to sometimes have sex without feeling sexual desire in order to please the partner. Sometimes, the low-desire partner hopes that sexual desire will emerge once sexual activity commences. Seek information about how often this situation has occurred and about the feelings of the low-desire partner when sexual activity happened in the absence of desire. Conversely, did the high-desire partner notice the lack of desire and what was his or her response to the partner's lack of this feeling? Sometimes desire is present, but the individual will not initiate activity. This issue needs to be explored. In our experience, women for a variety of reasons are less likely to initiate sex even when they feel desire. It is important to ask about her reasons. Of course, this fact would lead to a discussion of giving permission for either partner to initiate when sex is desired. However, one of the most interesting reasons for not initiating is the belief that if he or she initiates sex once, it now sends a signal that the lack of desire has disappeared. Hypoactive sexual desire clients do not want their partner to be misled into thinking that they have more desire than they do because they would rather not be in a position of constantly saying no to sex or having sex when they are not in the mood. A pervasive tendency on the part of HSD clients is sexual avoidance. Eventually, this avoidance can become contagious and even the high-desire partner avoids initiation or at least anything that resembles a direct initiation.

## Degree of Sexual Interest

It is relatively easy to get an objective measure of a behavior but much more difficult to get a measure of a feeling. It is useful to know just how intense the sexual feelings are in a variety of situations. We suggest that the couple imagine a scale ranging from minus-10 to plus-10. Plus-10 represents the most anyone could ever feel sexually aroused psychologically. It would represent 2 variables; feeling a strong motivation for a sexual encounter and feeling aroused throughout the experience. Minus-10 represents sexual disgust, aversion, and repulsion to the point of having a negative bodily reaction, such as feeling pained or nausea. Zero would represent feeling sexually neutral. We then ask a number of questions depending on what has been learned thus far. These questions could include:

- Where would you generally place yourself/your partner on this scale?
- Where would you place yourself/your partner just prior to sex?
- Where would you place yourself/your partner when your partner initiates any sexual activity?
- Where would you place yourself/your partner during the day when you recall/imagine having sex?
- Where would you place yourself/your partner during the act of sex?
- Where would you place yourself/your partner when your relationship is working?
- Where would you place yourself/your partner when your relationship is not working?
- Where would you place yourself prior to and during self-pleasuring?

These questions can also be asked from an historical perspective in order to get a better picture about the intensity of desire over time. The key time points would be:

- prior to a committed relationship or marriage,
- just after a committed relationship or marriage,
- when desire stared to decrease, and
- the last few months.

During the individual session, the therapist may ask about different sexual partners, assuming there were other partners. Although we ask about intensity of desire in the conjoint session, we return to it in the individual session to avoid hurting the partner's feelings when there is a strong aversion to sex. This information gives us another baseline, a sense about whether the HSD is a primary or secondary problem, and some idea about prognosis. In general terms, most of our clients place themselves in the minus-2 to minus-5 range, most of the time, and during sex some may feel they actually move into the positive range. The more negative the sexual feeling, the more difficult the treatment. The clients who are very negative may be experiencing a sexual aversion disorder rather than HSD and need to be treated appropriately (Kaplan, 1979). Those who are very negative may also lack the motivation to have the desire. Determine if this is the case. Also, ask if they can recall sexual desire as a pleasant feeling and whether they want it back *for themselves*. Some partners want to have the feeling just to please the partner or to be "normal." On the other hand, others cannot remember the feeling nor do they care about feeling sexual desire again. They are in treatment because the partner has insisted on getting help. Those partners who lack the desire for sexual desire will need special attention at the beginning of treatment in order to find some motivation to restoring or finding sexual desire for the first time.

## Context of Sexual Desire

Some HSD partners never feel sexual desire under any circumstances. Nothing in their experience is sexually stimulating. Fortunately, these cases are not the norm. Most clients with HSD report feeling desire in certain contexts. When assessing the context in which the partner is likely to experience or have trouble sustaining sexual desire, we continue to use the simple formula mentioned in the preliminary assessment. This context involves four parts: *who, when, how,* and *where.* Also included are persons or events that precipitate the loss of desire. In order to answer the first part of the context issue, *who,* we recommend starting with the following questions:

- Do you feel desire for your partner?
- Do you feel desire for anyone else that you know?
- Do you feel desire for people you do not know such as television characters or characters in books?
- Do you sometimes just feel desire without it being attached to anything or any person?

The timing of sexual desire adds another dimension to the context in which it is expressed or inhibited. For the *when,* we recommend asking:

- Are there times when you do feel desire? How much?
- Do you tend to feel desire at a particular time of day?
- Are weekends better for you?
- What about vacations?
- Are there times when you feel desire and then suddenly lose it?

- What happens to trigger the loss of your desire?
- What do you think just before you lose interest in sex?
- Is it the same thought each time?
- How do you feel just before you lose desire?

The answers to the last questions related to the loss of sexual desire are the most significant. As the client with the HSD monitors their desire, they will be able to identify the conditions and the cognitions that trigger the loss of desire. Once these conditions have been identified, they can be treated. The irrational notion that sexual desire is beyond their control is questioned through the use of context questions. Some clients will report feeling a rather high level of sexual desire but then find they lose it and/or become disinterested when certain events occur. These events are typically the partner suggesting some form of sexual activity, being in a context where sex can occur such as getting ready for bed, undressing, or taking a shower, or the mere appearance of the partner. Interestingly, some clients will feel desire in the absence of the partner, but not when the partner is actually present.

The *how* part of the context relates to the person's own responsibility for creating and sustaining sexual desire. We recommend starting with the following questions:

- Are you aware of how you help create sexual feelings in yourself?
- Do you enjoy particular thoughts or fantasies?
- Do you have a routine or ritual you use when getting in the mood for sex?
- What are some of the ways that help you get in the mood?
- What are some of the things your partner does to help you get in the mood?
- Do you set aside time for yourself or for your partner to help you get relaxed and in the mood?

The reverse of these questions can also be asked. These questions would focus on ways in which the client becomes turned off:

- Do you have a thought or fantasy that causes you to lose interest in sex?
- Does your partner do or say anything that turns you off?
- Do you get distracted when you are feeling sexual?
- Are there certain physical or emotional states that cause you to feel sexually disinterested?

Inquiries about the physical surroundings that facilitate relaxation, intimacy, and eroticism are an important part of the context assessment. The *where* component investigates the couple's responsibility to create an intimate, private environment that allows for sexual intimacy. The following questions address the last piece of the context for sexual desire, the *where*:

- Do you tend to relate certain places to your ease in experiencing sexual desire?
- Are these places easily accessible to you and your partner?
- Can you create an environment that is quiet and stress free?
- Do you have privacy?
- What measures have you taken to ensure privacy?
- Have you created an intimate environment that lends itself to relaxation and eroticism?

We have occasionally found that some partners can only function when they are on vacation or out of the house. When they are home, they feel too distracted with getting through their perfunctory tasks. More frequently, we notice that couples have stopped setting aside time for sexual intimacy. It becomes a chore like other household duties and finds its place at the bottom of a long list of nonintimate tasks. Moreover, the romantic activities that were often a part of the couple's dating behaviors have somehow been removed over time. Instead, they hurry through sex without giving it the time and preparation it requires.

## Presence of Other Sexual Dysfunctions and Difficulties

This area in the rapid assessment involves 1) the overall level of sexual satisfaction and 2) the presence of other sexual dysfunctions in the HSD client or the partner. As we discussed in Chapter 1, many couples report that they are satisfied with sexual relations even in the presence of dysfunction in one or both partners (Frank, Anderson, & Rubinstein, 1978). Sometimes satisfaction is judged by parameters, such as frequency or the quality of sexual intimacy, thus it is highly subjective. The therapist will need to directly ask the couple to comment on how satisfied or dissatisfied they are with their overall sexual relationship. Typically, their responses are initially overly positive. The therapist will then ask specific questions in order to obtain more accurate information.

- Are you happy with how often you have sex?
- Are you pleased with the way you make love?

- Do you devote a satisfactory amount of time during lovemaking?
- What is most pleasurable?
- Do you wish your lovemaking could be different?
- In what ways?
- Is there something about your sexual response that concerns you?
- Does your partner seem to enjoy sex?
- Do you have concerns or worries about you or your partner sexually speaking?

Next, inquire about the presence of other sexual dysfunctions in the HSD partner, especially difficulties that may have predated the lack of desire. Sometimes the problem may have started with inhibited orgasm, for instance, and over time degenerated into a situational or global lack of desire. In our experience, there is often a sexual dysfunction in the nonidentified client. If the clinician is mindful of the sexual response cycle, questions can be asked about dysfunctions at the desire, arousal, and orgasm stages. Include an assessment of sexual pain disorders in either partner.

For the male, we often ask the following:

- How would you describe your level of sexual desire over the course of your relationship?
- Do you have any trouble getting or keeping an erection long enough to successfully have intercourse?
- Do you find there are times when you are unable to have an orgasm during intercourse?
- Are you able to control when you want to ejaculate?
- Do you have any pain with intercourse?

For the female, these are a few of our typical questions:

- How often are you in the mood to have sex?
- Is this different from the beginning of your relationship?
- Do you have trouble staying focused once you begin to have sex?
- Do you have any trouble getting lubricated?
- Are you able to have an orgasm when you desire to have one?
- Do you have any pain with intercourse?

## PRESENCE OF MEDICAL PROBLEMS

As discussed in Chapter 6, there are many medical risk factors that can contribute to or underlie the lack of sexual desire. Ask directly about age, medical conditions, surgeries, recreational drug and alcohol use, diet, exercise, smoking, and any other factors that the clinician should consider when assessing for HSD. We often ask our clients to supply a list of any prescription or nonprescription medication they take regularly, doses, duration, and the reason for taking the medication. This is an opportunity to inquire about psychotropic medications. This task helps them to remember substances that they might have otherwise forgotten or considered to be noncontributory. In addition, if the client has not had a routine physical or gynecologic examination in the past year, we take this opportunity to request that they do so.

## LACK OF SEXUAL DESIRE: DIAGNOSTIC QUESTIONS

Prior to the rapid assessment, we give an assignment. The couple is to take home 15 questions *to think about* before the therapist begins to ask questions in session. The 15 questions cover all areas of the rapid assessment. Giving this assignment allows them to prepare what they want to say in session. Moreover, the questions create a mindset for the therapeutic process that will require the couple to answer a number of questions that might be difficult for them to discuss. The 15-question "take home" list is as follows:

1. How often do you *actually* have sex? In a week, month, or year?
2. How often do you *feel like* having sex?
3. Do you believe *your* level of desire is too low?
4. When did you first notice losing your desire for sex?
5. What was happening at that time?
6. Did you lose the desire rapidly or slowly?
7. What was your level of sexual desire earlier in your relationship?
8. What medications are you taking now/since losing your desire?
9. Any changes in your health?
10. On a scale from −10 to +10, how much desire do you feel?
    - in general
    - prior to sex
    - during sex

11. If you feel desire, is it *suddenly* lost? If so, under what conditions?

12. Are you having specific sexual problems, such as loss of interest in sex; difficulty getting aroused; lack of lubrication; erectile problems; difficulty having orgasm; or pain with intercourse? Is your partner having any sexual problems?

13. Do you just feel a lack of desire for your partner or is it for anyone?

14. To what extent does your lack of desire distress you/your partner?

15. What is your explanation for your lack of desire?

## COGNITIVE ASSESSMENT

Cognitive therapy has traditionally been considered an *individual* approach to treatment (Beck, 1976). Weeks and Hof (1987, 1994) were the first to suggest that when applying cognitive therapy to dealing with lack of sexual desire, a *systemic* approach needed to be used. Very often, couples develop interlocking sets of beliefs that perpetuate sexual problems, and these beliefs need to be explored and changed conjointly. A man with HSD might think, "I'm just not interested in sex." His partner might also think, "He isn't interested in sex, so why initiate anything?" These two interlocking thoughts help to perpetuate sexual avoidance. Because couples usually have such interlocking thoughts, it is necessary that they both examine their negative cognitions. The therapist can then deal with the thoughts in each partner that tend to reinforce those in the other.

For the reader who is unfamiliar with cognitive therapy, it involves changing the person's thoughts or cognitions. The irrational or unproductive thought is identified, and, with the therapist's assistance, it is replaced with one that works better, helps the person feel better, and/or helps the person to act more appropriately or effectively. The client must then monitor his or her thoughts or behaviors in order to determine when the nonproductive thought has started again. It is stopped and consciously replaced with a productive thought. With repeated experience, the old thoughts are replaced with the new thoughts and they become the unconscious or automatic thoughts.

Part of the purpose of the cognitive assessment is diagnostic and part is therapeutic. In a prior text (Weeks & Gambescia, 2000), we emphasized the fact that assessment and treatment often overlap. The diagnostic part consists of having the client capture as many of the underlying or unconscious sexual/relational cognitions as possible. Our theory is that a major *immediate* factor contributing to HSD is the presence of negative cognitions in several different areas. We also believe that the individual who is able to experience sexual desire is actually *having* sexual thoughts whereas the individual who lacks desire has an absence of sexual thoughts or has a number of negative sexual thoughts. Our approach incorporates tenets suggested by Firestone's (1990) "voice therapy" approach. She maintains that negative cognitions interfere with the natural flow of desire and excitement. She describes "voices" *prior* to sex which emphasize the dangers of sex to the individual. The voices *during* sex often involve negative thoughts about one's body, sexual performance, and partner-based stereotypes. Voices *following* sex can devalue the experience. In general, we are often unaware of what we are thinking. For instance, when we get in our cars to drive, we do not stop to think about every manipulation we must make. The behavior seems to be automatic. When we decide to go to our favorite eatery, we do not stop to think about everything that will happen when we are there. We do begin to notice that we are hungry, that we might taste a favorite food for which we have a certain craving, or that time passes slowly because we would like to be in the restaurant already.

This cognitive mental mechanism is powerful. We may not be able to directly observe it much of the time, but it has strong behavioral consequences. If we are thinking about a sexual encounter or the opportunity for an encounter, then we may begin to have more frequent positive thoughts. As these thoughts increase, so does desire. In fact, many clients have reported that they actually feel sexier or hornier right after having had a pleasant sexual encounter. They are mentally rehearsing or replaying the encounter. This mental process creates a state of positive anticipation for the next experience. Eventually, our therapeutic goal is to create a state of positive sexual anticipation, one that we call sexual desire.

## Categories of Negative Cognitions

The first step in this part of the diagnostic process is to identify as many of the negative thoughts as possible. We suggest that the partners divide the negative thoughts into four categories:

1. about the self
2. about the partner
3. about the relationship and
4  those from the family-of-origin

This assignment could begin in the session, but we usually suggest that it be done at home. We ask each partner to set aside two or three short periods of time to write down his or her negative thoughts. We ask that they try to identify as many sexually negative thoughts as possible and any other thoughts they think about frequently or believe might have a negative impact on being able to experience desire. This exercise is specifically targeted toward the client with the HSD. We also ask the partner to do the same exercise because we may discover a lack of desire or negative thoughts in this partner. For example, a common thought might be, "my husband/wife/partner never wants to have sex, so why should I ask?" This thought leads to sexual avoidance that is detrimental for both partners. Another common negative thought in either partner is that of no longer being attractive to the other due to weight or age for example. Sometimes a partner's thoughts may reinforce what the HSD partner is thinking.

A similar technique is used for those clients who sometimes feel "turned-on," but then *suddenly* lose desire. We use a therapeutic reframe, suggesting that when this happens a learning opportunity has presented itself. The negative cognitions have come into play and have shut off the sexual feelings. As soon as they notice this change in mood, they should stop what they were doing and think about *what they were thinking*. Another variation of this cognitive assessment technique is to pay attention to the thoughts during the physical, sensual, or sexual homework assignments. Some of the thoughts will not be recognized until the client is in a context that triggers the thought or allows it to surface.

The couple is told that these thoughts will be examined in the next session and if they would rather their partner not hear some of the cognitions, individual session time will be set aside. Next, the therapist explains these cognitions will be explored in two ways: (1) to determine which of the negative thoughts can be changed through cognitive therapy or just in the client's mind and (2) to assess other problems in the relationship that need to change through couple therapy. For example, if the partners say they are always angry and fighting, they are probably not in the mood to make love. The relational issue will need to be addressed.

A few samples of the HSD partner's initial cognitions regarding sex and their relationship will be provided. The reader will note that most couples focus on the sexual aspect of their relationship rather than the relationship in general.

## Couple 1

This couple was in their early 30s. The husband presented with HSD. He had never recovered from being jilted by his first girlfriend. Below, we have listed some of his negative cognitions about himself, his partner, and the relationship.

*Self*
- I am too thin and therefore sexually undesirable.
- I fantasize too much about sexual things other than my wife.
- I think about other women too much.

*Partner*
- My wife has gained a lot of weight and isn't as attractive.
- I constantly think I should be with a more attractive woman.
- I don't think she cares enough about me sometimes.

*Relationship*
- I'm still in love with my old girlfriend.
- I think my old girlfriend had the perfect body.
- I compare my wife to my old girlfriend.
- I want my wife to look like my old girlfriend.

## Couple 2

A professional couple in their early 40s presented with the wife having HSD. This case had multiple issues, including those originating in her family-of-origin.

*Self*
- My breasts are too small.
- I rarely feel sexually attractive.
- Not much turns me on.
- I get distracted easily.
- I'm not a good lover.
- I'm not a good kisser.

*Partner*
- He has gained a lot of weight.
- I don't find him physically attractive
- He has to control everything.
- He criticizes the way I make love, everything about it.

*Relationship*
- We don't agree on anything.
- We can't agree on anything.
- He is still married to his family. They live at our house twelve hours a day.
- We can't do anything without his parent's approval.
- I can't talk to him about his parents.

*Family-of-origin*

- My parents never talked about sex.
- I got the idea there was something bad about sex.
- My mother told me sex was a woman's duty and not something to be enjoyed.
- I got in trouble once for some sex play with another boy when I was very young.

## Couple 3

This couple was in their early 50s, and the husband presented with HSD. His cognitions clearly show the combined effect of negative cognitions in every area of his life.

*Self*

- I have a skin disorder that makes me ugly and unattractive.
- I always come too fast.
- My penis is too small.
- I'm always worried about my business.
- I was a virgin when I met my wife.
- I still don't know much about sex.
- I don't know how to please a woman.
- I am looking old.

*Partner*

- My wife is always comparing me to her former lovers.
- She had a lot of sexual experience before we got married.
- Every time we make love, my wife tells me I have the smallest penis she has ever seen.
- She is always criticizing me.
- I can't do anything right for her.
- She is overweight, aging, and nonathletic.
- She is insecure.
- She isn't willing to do things on her own.
- She doesn't like any of my friends.

*Relationship*

- We don't know how to fight.

- We stop communicating for days.
- The anger and resentment builds up between us.

*Family-of-origin*
- I married my mother.
- My wife is helpless like my mother.
- My father was unhappy in his marriage.
- I thought it would be different for me.
- I am stuck like my parents.

The illustrations given above demonstrate a number of points. First, some items could be placed under several headings. It is not that important where the client chooses to place the item. Secondly, some items are much more important than others. Certain items are central to the level of desire improving, while others are used to justify the lack of desire. For example, a client may complain about a weight gain in the spouse, but this may not be the real or central issue. It is an easy and understandable way to justify the loss of desire when the real or unconscious reason is unknown. Finally, the examples serve as a point of departure in the therapy session. Further examination of each item gives the therapist a much better sense about the factors producing the lack of sexual desire. Once this assessment has been completed, the therapist may move on to treatment.

The examples listed above show how some of the issues are individual and can be treated cognitively at the beginning while others are relational. The therapist helps the couple identify the major risk factors and suggests a plan of treatment. The therapist may choose to focus on the negative cognitions initially or to combine the cognitive work with marital/couple work, or just work on the relationship, depending upon the results of the assessment.

Assuming the therapist begins to work on the negative cognitions first, he or she explores those ideas that have no basis in reality, that are residual thoughts from the past and are no longer true, or that are exaggerations of reality-based perceptions. We utilize a 3-column written procedure in beginning the cognitive work. The first column is to list the negative thoughts, and this process occurs throughout therapy. The second column is to develop thoughts to counteract the negative thoughts. In fact, we suggest creating several positive thoughts for each negative thought to neutralize the negative thoughts.* The third column is the

---

* This approach to cognitive work has been described in some detail in *Couples in Treatment* by Weeks & Treat (2001).

opposite of the first and involves thinking of as many unconditionally positive thoughts as possible.

In the last set of negative cognitions listed in Couple 3 above, the therapy took an extended length of time. Many individual, couple, and family issues were involved in this case. The husband was instructed to work on developing counterideas to the negative cognitions that did not have any basis in reality and to write out unconditionally positive ideas about himself. This process was slow and tedious for him. He had difficulty developing any positive ideas. With the help of the therapist and his wife, a number of favorable attributes were pointed out and he was able to begin to repeat those ideas to himself at least daily. He was informed that at first he probably would not believe any of these ideas and think that it was just some mechanical exercise for him to do. Over a period of time, he could see that he felt better about himself and that his wife and others were responding to him differently. At the same time, unlike pure cognitive therapy, we worked to trace the origins of his thoughts. It was important for him to understand why he thought the way he did. Having parents who appeared to be emotionally distant and unhappily married had a profound impact. Understanding the origin of his negative cognitions and relearning to think differently raised his self-esteem, desire for sex, and his sexual performance.

## FAVORABLE CONDITIONS FOR THERAPY

The final part of the comprehensive assessment involves making a decision about whether the couple is an appropriate candidate for sex and relationship therapy. We use guidelines similar to those presented in an earlier volume on the treatment of erectile dysfunction (Weeks & Gambescia, 2000).

1. The client is experiencing response anxiety. This type of anxiety is a type of pressure to feel desire and perform ideally in sexual situations. It is both a cause and effect of HSD. We will discuss response anxiety in greater detail in chapter 8. Anxiety from other sources can also interfere with sexual desire and can be successfully treated within the context of the couple in some cases.
2. Both partners are relatively free of psychiatric problems.
3. The partners have positive sex beliefs and want to experience desire again.
4. The HSD partner is unable to break the cycle of negative sexual cognitions and obsessive thoughts that interfere with building sexual desire.
5. The HSD client has been carrying a secret such as sexual abuse, physical abuse, or emotional abuse that needs to be shared with the partner.

6. The client or the partner is experiencing a real or imagined loss of health. The negative anticipation produces anxiety and fear that is unknown to the partner.

7. Couples who do not understand the physiological changes resulting from aging can impose the same set of sexual expectations as when they were in their early years. These expectations set them up to perceive failure, increasing anxiety, producing even more failure.

8. The person with the HSD is going through a divorce or significant life stressor. Divorce or loss of a spouse due to death creates a unique adjustment problem because of the societal pressures to be sexual.

9. The couple or partner has a high level of sex-related guilt and negative sexual attitudes based on religious beliefs. Guilt and lack of internalized permission to experience sexual enjoyment and pleasure can inhibit sexual desire.

10. The couple experiences difficulties with power, control, and attachment.

11. The couple's sexual script has not been successfully negotiated. The partners may have different preferences, ease of arousal, and expectations regarding orgasm.

12. The partners are not sexually attracted to each other, but have favorable compatibility. They see themselves as friends, but lack passion.

13. The HSD is embedded in other sexual difficulties such as erectile dysfunction, inhibited female orgasm, or vaginismus.

14. There is *treatable* discord in other areas of the relationship, such as ineffective communication, anger resolution, and expectations (Weeks & Treat, 2001).

15. The HSD is a symptom of a lack of intimacy or an underlying fear of intimacy. These risk factors were described earlier and constitute a major risk factor for secondary HSD.

16. The partners have internalized negative parental sexual messages or are still enmeshed in a dysfunctional family system. The partner may also still be trying to emotionally recover from a dysfunctional family system without realizing the effects their childrearing had on them.

Virtually any risk factor described earlier is amenable to treatment in sex/couple therapy. In some cases, the presence of medical conditions directly contributes to the HSD. Nonetheless, sex/couple therapy can be used in conjunction with the medical treatment. The medical factor(s) should be treated first, and the results closely monitored. In many instances, sexual desire has been missing for a long time, and it is difficult for couples to get started again. The therapist can facilitate the couple relearning how to be sexual with each other and can assess for and treat other risk factors. In virtually every case, response anxiety will play a role because of the anxieties associated with expected lack of sexual arousal (see Chapter 8). It is similar to the phenomena seen in men with organic erectile dysfunction. Viagra helps to produce an erection, but the men still felt tremendous performance anxiety in spite of having taken Viagra (Weeks & Gambescia, 2000).

## CONTRAINDICATIONS

There are several conditions under which beginning treatment is ill advised.

1. The partner *does not* have any desire for desire or has sexual aversion. When one feels so negatively about sex, it is pointless to begin the usual course of sex therapy. First, treat the individual for the aversion and the lack of motivation for sex therapy. Partners are usually reluctant to let each other know just how negatively they feel about being sexual. They will most often "soft-peddle" this feeling when asked in a conjoint session. One of the reasons we routinely split couples during the assessment phase is to allow them to say those things they do not want their partners to hear.

2. The partner has no interest in sex therapy because they see the problem as residing *solely* in the HSD partner. In the field of couple therapy, we are frequently challenged with the idea that the problem exists within one person. The spouse externalizes any responsibility for the problem or for being able to help solve the problem. This may be a generalized defensive posture stemming from lack of ego-strength ("something is wrong with me, and I don't want anyone to find out").

3. The partner of the HSD client has no interest in sex. Often, this individual would rather use the HSD client as a foil for their problem. The partner is actually attempting to sabotage the treatment before it begins by not agreeing to participate. In some cases, the noncompliant partner may have other sexual problems that are too embarrassing to discuss, such as an erectile dysfunction or vaginismus. In other cases, the partner may be experiencing a sexual addiction, fetish, sexual compulsion, transvestitism, or other sexual orientation and not want anyone to learn about their sexuality.

4. The partner of the HSD client is unwilling to participate in therapy. If the partner is unwilling to seek help, there is little we can do. When the partner refuses to participate, and some of the major risk factors are in the relationship, it will be impossible to solve those problems

which stand in the way. Additionally, the partner must help with some of the individual exercises, making sex therapy difficult or impossible without their help.

5. There is significant psychopathology in the couple's relationship. When the level of marital or couple pathology is high, the couple will not be able to work together in session or on the homework assignments. Hostility, anger, and externalization make sex therapy virtually impossible and lead to a slow start to the couple therapy.

6. Of the couples we have seen for HSD, many have high levels of discord over a number of issues and do not want to work together cooperatively. They are more interested in proving the other person is wrong or sick. The partner with the HSD can then be labeled as sick, and the other partner feels they are right.

7. In order to conduct treatment of any sexual problem, the couple's relationship must be healthy enough to allow them to work together on solving some difficult problems, some individual and some relational. Although some couples may be able to "bypass" (Kaplan, 1979) their relationship problems, meaning, they simply do not deal with them, the vast majority in our experience will not be successful in overcoming the lack of desire unless the relationship issues are an integral part of the treatment plan. One of the ways couples try to bypass their relationship problems in this area is to try some questionable medical or herbal remedy. Men and women will take Viagra hoping that it will increase their libido in spite of the fact that it has no direct affect on desire. Both sexes are willing to undergo hormone therapy or try an herbal remedy they found in an advertisement or on the Internet that purports to increase desire. Efforts such as these indicate an *unwillingness* to confront the problem from a psychological and relational view.

8. Significant psychopathology in the client or the partner makes couple/ sex therapy highly problematic. An Axis I diagnosis must usually be treated first before beginning sex therapy.

9. When both partners are narcissistically vulnerable and trade projections, the slightest comment can cause one to feel wounded and/or distance him or herself from and criticize the other. Weeks and Treat (2001) have written a chapter describing the treatment of this most difficult problem. These partners are so sensitive to each other that they tend to demonize or idealize the other person. The treatment of choice initially is individual therapy. Seen together, they are a volatile combination.

10. An affair on the part of one or both partners, whether revealed or hidden, presents an impediment for conjoint therapy. An active affair

creates emotional distance and when revealed or found out, emotional havoc ensues for a couple. Treating the affair takes priority over all other issues. Couples will not be able to proceed to any other issue until some progress has been made in this area. In fact, if this issue *is* dealt with, there may be no couple to treat, as many of these couples separate or divorce.

11. When one or both partners are in an active addiction, it is senseless to conduct couples therapy. Addictions take priority in treatment, since the addictive behavior is the central focus of the addict's life. No real therapeutic progress will be made until the addiction is under control. Some addicts create an illusion of change while they are still engaging in the addictive behavior in order to keep the enabling relationship going. We have seen an increasing number of women in long-term marriages and relationships with partners who were active sex addicts. In these codependent relationships, the sexual frequency was very low. The addict had HSD for the partner while engaging in sex with prostitutes or on the Internet. For example, the partner often complains about the low sexual frequency but does not bring the issue to a crisis point until the addict is discovered. In one case, the addict excused his actions, stating that his partner was not "really interested in sex."

12. When one or both partners are not committed to the relationship, couples therapy is difficult. For most partners sexual intimacy is an expression of commitment. When the partners are unsure about their commitment, it is difficult to keep reaffirming commitment through sex. In some cases, HSD is the symptom used to express the underlying lack of commitment. Individual or couple therapy may need to precede the sex therapy.

## CONCLUSION

The comprehensive assessment for HSD addresses the problem directly, efficiently, and judiciously. The couple is immediately relieved that their sexual concerns are taken seriously. Moreover, they can begin to feel optimistic about finding a solution for a problem that they previously believed was insurmountable. Since it is a relational concern, the partners are empowered to become a part of their own treatment. In the next chapter, we will discuss the basic techniques of treatment.

# 8

## Basic Principles and Strategies of Therapy

Most of the sex therapy literature on HSD focuses on *treatment techniques* rather than the general principles and strategies employed when working with couples (Masters & Johnson, 1970; Kaplan, 1979; Leiblum & Rosen, 1988; and, Winzce & Carey, 1991). These treatment techniques typically arise from clinically based models of treatment. Thus, clinical practice often runs ahead of research. One exception is Schnarch (1991, 1997), who begins with theory as a way of guiding various treatment strategies in therapy. Regardless, the clinical literature has not yet provided us with an approach that is effective. For instance, Leiblum and Rosen's (1988) edited book demonstrates that clinicians tend to take an unduly simplified view of HSD. An elementary explanation for etiology is offered that considers a single or a few factors. Moreover, it is assumed that one model of treatment is comprehensive enough to be effective with all cases. Our experience and the literature on the risk factors demonstrate that not all HSD cases are alike; therefore, they cannot be reduced to a single causative factor. In most cases, several factors are linked together in a complex fashion, and each couple must be considered within a unique context. Any therapy that is to be effective with this type of intricate problem must be flexible, comprehensive, focused enough to address the presenting problem, yet broad enough to deal with the myriad of contextual problems. The principles and strategies we propose are based on the Intersystem Approach described earlier, and therefore are viewed as highly integrative (Weeks, 1995). In this and the subsequent chapters, we will outline a treatment approach we believe fits these criteria.

## THE RESEARCH LITERATURE AND HSD

The research literature on HSD also has many shortcomings. In a review of controlled psychotherapy studies on sexual desire disorders, O'Carroll (1991) brought to light the paucity of adequate treatment studies. In two of the controlled studies discussed in the O'Carroll review, the subjects used were not limited to those with HSD alone. Instead, couples experiencing a variety of sexual problems *including* HSD were grouped together, seriously limiting treatment options *specifically* for HSD (Crowe, Gillian, & Golombok, 1981; Zimmer, 1987). O'Carroll also reviewed controlled drug/hormone studies and studies combining psychotherapy with drugs/hormones. As a whole, the only finding noteworthy *for the treatment of HSD* is that testosterone replacement may be useful for men with abnormally low levels of testosterone. O'Carroll concluded that no effective treatment options for HSD could be generated from the research available at the time.

Segraves and Althof (1998) published another review of the effective treatments for sexual dysfunctions using less stringent criteria than the reviewers did in the aforementioned investigations. The studies included in this meta-analysis generally had small sample sizes and received brief sex therapy based on Masters and Johnson's (1970) behavioral approach. Segraves and Althof summarized the psychotherapeutic treatment results for HSD by stating that 50% to 70% of couples reported moderate gains at the end of treatment, but half also reported they did not maintain their desire 3 years post-follow-up. All of the couples noted that their sexual satisfaction had not changed over time (DeAmicus, Goldgerg, LoPiccolo, Friedman, & Davies, 1985; Hawton & Catalan, 1986; Hawton, 1995).

A few other studies are also noteworthy. Two suggest that orgasm consistency training may help to increase desire for those women with HSD who also complain about lack of orgasm (Hurlbert, 1993; Hurlbert, White, Powell, & Apt, 1993). *Couples* were treated in both studies. One study compared couples and women-only groups for therapeutic effectiveness. The couples groups produced better results. Hurlbert also noted that the women with HSD reported a number of relationship concerns, especially the lack of affection from the partner (90%). These two studies lend support to the idea that couple issues are a significant risk factor for partners developing HSD.

Another study investigated 49 couples in which the women were experiencing HSD. (MacPhee, Johnson, & Van er Veer, 1995). The couples in this study received emotionally focused therapy (EFT), which did not significantly improve the overall level of sexual desire. This finding was perplexing because EFT has been shown to improve couples functioning within a short period of time (Johnson & Greenberg, 1985). Furthermore, marital therapy with couples experiencing sexual problems usually does lead to improved marital satisfaction (Bennun, Rust, & Golombok, 1985). The researchers speculated extensively about the lack of improvement suggesting that 10 sessions of treatment was insufficient for improvement and that the symptoms of HSD are so distressing for the relationship as a whole that short-term marital therapy would not improve the relationship. They also mentioned that 24% of the women in the HSD group reported sexual trauma, whereas 6% did in the non-HSD group. What this study may tell us is that marital therapy alone without the benefit of focused sex therapy is ineffective in treating HSD.

Heiman and Meston (1997) published a review of all the research that empirically validated treatments for sexual dysfunctions. They used the research criteria established by the American Psychological Association Task Force (1995) for treatments that were well established and probably efficacious. They found that there were no controlled studies to demonstrate the effective treatment of HSD. This statement should be viewed in perspective, as they applied rigorous standards in evaluating the research. A number of studies have been conducted that fall short of their standards.

While the treatment strategies for HSD found in the clinical and research literature may have influenced our treatment principles and strategies, we have developed the following guidelines based on extensive experience in working with couples experiencing HSD in one or both partners. The issues covered in this chapter have been overlooked in other publications because they appear generic or overly simplistic. The assumption might be that any well-trained therapist should automatically know these techniques. However, we find that even the advanced students we have trained do not know how to apply these principles and strategies, especially when applied to treating lack of sexual desire. In the following discussion, we recommend specific principles and strategies of sex therapy which we consider essential to the treatment of HSD.

## OVERCOMING PESSIMISM AND SKEPTICISM

We have often mentioned that couples approach sex therapy with a sense of pessimism and skepticism because they cannot imagine how talking about a sexual problem could possibly alleviate it. Often, they have attempted to change the HSD on their own, have failed, and then have resigned themselves to a passionless relationship. While some clients have tried years of therapy without any success, others delay entering psychotherapy (and exacerbate the problem) by believing that the situation is hopeless and that they are helpless.

Lack of sexual desire is a complex phenomenon and difficult for a person to change. The couple's failed attempts need to be normalized by explaining that pessimism is a natural response to a difficult situation. Support them for their efforts to correct the problem even if these strategies have failed. Often, couples try to *force* themselves to feel desire, and this has made the problem more severe. Explain that most partners have tried this strategy. Do not blame them for their efforts to help themselves. The HSD client has, in fact, *learned* to be helpless, pessimistic, and skeptical. Their partners do not see any point in beginning something that will only have failure as an outcome. It is essential for the couple to understand this reaction. Otherwise, they will prematurely predict failure and be unconvinced that any measure, including therapy, can help. Furthermore, they do not understand what treatment requires of them. Educating the partners early in the process can interrupt pessimism. They need to know that the therapist cannot *make them* change or feel desire, but that they must *work with* the therapist to make changes within themselves.

We believe it is important to be honest from the outset of therapy. Clients need to be given informed consent. We are optimistic that most couples can be helped, if given enough time. We inform clients that there is both good and bad news. The good news is that the majority of couples will find an increase in desire, but that the time required could be from 6 months to 2 years, depending upon the number of risk factors at work. Further, couples are told that at the end of the assessment phase of 3 to 4 sessions, the therapist will have a better idea of whether the timeframe may be shorter or longer. A discussion should then follow regarding the length of treatment allowing the couple to express their frustrations and to ask questions. The simplest way to reassure the couple is to tell them that ultimately they are the judges of whether the therapy is working. They can be encouraged that they will experience incremental improvements during the course of treatment, although they might not expect to reach their anticipated goal for at least several months. Couples know whether they are dealing with the right issues and whether any progress is being made. As long as they see progressive improvement, the length of therapy becomes much less important. The therapist can also explain that sometimes gains are followed by setbacks. These will provide information for the therapist, because setbacks represent another problem or an underlying risk factor. The therapist also needs to remain positive and optimistic, in spite of setbacks. The therapist must view these periods as informative rather than resistances to treatment, because the client is trying to communicate some-thing, cannot articulate it with words, but expresses it through actions.

Finally, commitment is an important factor in overcoming skepticism and pessimism. Ideally, the couple will be committed to each other. If not, then commitment becomes an immediate issue. Assuming the partners are committed to each other, they must also be willing to commit to the process of therapy. This means not giving up during regressive periods and encouraging each other when a partner is feeling hopeless, when progress is slow, or when the issues become painful and the tendency is to drop out of treatment. If the therapist *predicts* that these things will happen, then the couple can have a discussion about what they will do when it does happen. The couple has been inoculated to these occurrences and given an antidote.

## LOWERING RESPONSE ANXIETY

One of the first general tasks of treating HSD is to lower response anxiety. The reader will recall this concept was first described by Apfelbaum (1988) to describe a phenomenon similar to performance anxiety (Masters & Johnson, 1970). Response anxiety is the feeling the individual creates when they try to *force themselves* to feel sexual desire. The client may try to force this feeling because they truly want to feel desire, they want to feel "nor-mal," or they hope to become more sexually compatible with their partner. Whatever the reason, this type of anxiety has been observed in every case we have treated with the exception of those individuals who have no desire to feel desire.

Response anxiety is both a cause and an effect of HSD. Once the clients begin to experience themselves as lacking in desire, they begin to feel anx-ious over not having the feeling. The more anxious they become, the less likely it is that they will experience sexual desire. Response anxiety can also be created by thinking that one *should* feel more turned on than one does, should feel turned on more rapidly within or without a sexual con-text, should reach an orgasm more quickly, and so on. The cause of the anxiety may be independent of the effect, but once the effect has been experienced, it usually becomes a causative or risk factor.

The experience of response anxiety is similar to performance anxiety in that the HSD client "spectators" or monitors his or her reactions, especially in certain situations where they think sensual or sexual feelings should oc-cur. Although Masters and Johnson (1970) are generally credited with the "discovery" of the concept of spectatoring, it is clear that Viktor Frankl (1952) described it much earlier. He used the term, "hyperreflection," to refer to watching and monitoring oneself, and "hyperintentionality" to refer to trying to force oneself or will oneself to make something that occurs spontaneously to happen willfully. Sexual desire is normally a naturally occurring state that is transparent. It just seems to happen. Of course, we are all aware that certain situations and behavioral interactions are more likely to help create this feeling. When the lack of desire is constantly noted, and the client attempts to force the feeling, the feeling will not occur. Response anxiety is all but universal in the cases we have treated.

## Techniques to Lower Response Anxiety

### EDUCATION ABOUT RESPONSE ANXIETY

The clinician can use several strategies to stop this process. The first is to educate the clients and suggest that they observe for response anxiety and to note when it happens and ways in which they force themselves to feel anything except what they feel. This is a bit like saying to go with the flow and feel whatever you feel naturally.

### THOUGHT STOPPING

A cognitive technique is used in which the client would need to say to self, "Stop trying to force feeling turned on."

### PARADOXICAL INTENTION

The third technique, developed by Frankl (1952), is called paradoxical intention (PI). The therapist prescribes the hyperintentionality usually using some humor. The client might be told that they are to try to force themselves to become as turned on as they can imagine. In order for PI to work, the therapist would need to have some sense of what the client would find humorous. We generally describe the principle to the client and ask them to develop a prescription for themselves that they would find funny. We explain that the more they find the image humorous, the more difficult it is to feel anxious. Imagine your partner ripping your clothes off and attacking you like an animal in heat. You keep your body absolutely still, and do not register feelings. You strive to keep yourself as turned off as possible, even though your partner expresses great passion. If they can break the cycle of feeling anxious, then they may be able to feel more desire than in the past. We also caution them that if they feel some desire, it will probably be very little at first (Weeks & L'Abate, 1982).

### ELIMINATING IDEAS THAT FOSTER RESPONSE ANXIETY

One way to accomplish this goal is to help the couple to broaden the definition of the meaning of sex. For many couples, sex is equated with intercourse. Yet, many other couples are able to enjoy an active sex life with a extensive range of sexual behaviors that may or may not always include coital activity. The couple also needs to move away from goal-oriented sex. The anticipated goal could include intercourse, orgasm, erection, and lubrication, for example. Couples tend to fixate on one or two behaviors as being the goals of their sexual interaction. Sexual desire itself can become an object of fixation. There is no rule that says you must hit 7 on a scale of 10 of sexual desire during every sexual or sensual encounter. Additionally, the couple is taught to separate intimacy, affection, sensuality, and sex. For most couples, these ideas are fused together; thus, one must lead to or be linked with the other. All of these concepts help the couple redefine their sexuality and their definition of sexual desire.

MANIPULATING THE ENVIRONMENT

The final strategy is to instruct the client about ways to become more aroused by environmental factors. First, this means educating the couple about how to create a sexual environment and a working relationship. We will elaborate on this point later in this and subsequent chapters, because it is a critical factor in treatment.

## REFRAMING THE HYPOACTIVE SEXUAL DESIRE

Couples almost always think of HSD as a problem in *one* partner because one wants to have more sex and the other has a lower level of desire or no desire. When a couple presents for treatment of HSD, it is usually only one partner who is the symptom bearer because he or she does not want to have sex and feels pressure to *want to* have sexual desire. Generally, the symptom bearer wishes they had more desire or the same level of desire as their partner in order to please *the partner*. The higher desire partner is never quite sure why the therapist has invited them to the first session. Rarely does the partner understand the role he or she plays in the other partner's lack of sexual desire.

In order to get the higher-desire partner fully involved in the process of therapy the client must accept the responsibility of participating for two reasons: First, his or her support is essential for the HSD partner. Then, the higher-desire partner must see that the HSD is a *relationship* problem. The process for creating this conceptual understanding in the couple is known as reframing. Reframing is one of the most widely used techniques in couples and family therapy (Weeks & Treat, 2001). It is a strategy that is difficult for a therapist to master because it is often misunderstood. Reframing is not something a therapist does *to* a client or a couple. A therapist does not unilaterally develop a reframe and then announce it to the couple, expecting that they will readily accept the therapist's frame. Reframing is a *gradual* process, involving eliciting bits of information from the clients. The primary goal of the reframe is to help each partner see his or her involvement in the problem. There are usually secondary goals, such as changing the conceptual framework from medical to psychological, moral to psychological, negative to positive.

First, the therapist asks highly focused questions that become more and more directed. By so doing, the therapist is able to elicit information that is fed back into the couple system. As the partners begin to hear their own answers, they start to get a different picture of what is happening, a viewpoint that is more systemic than individual. Eventually, they will reframe their own behavior and the role of the symptom bearer will be discarded. If the clients can see the situation differently, they can fully accept the reframe without questioning the therapist's veracity. It is an "explanation" that makes sense to them.

## Therapeutic Reframes

There are three possible reframes involved in treating HSD. The first has to do with the phenomenon of *response anxiety* described earlier. Two factors cause response anxiety in the HSD client. First, one partner has a higher level of sexual desire than the other. Next, the partner with lower desire wants to please the other partner. As much as the higher desire partner tries to "back off" and not put pressure on the other partner for sex, the fact that both know one wants sex more than the other is a problem. The partners frame this part of the problem by pretending that it is acceptable for the HSD partner not to have desire. They try to minimize the problem and avoid talking about it. The first reframe is that the problem *affects them both* in certain predictable ways, as described above, and *they* need a way to talk about how they are feeling. This reframe has the effect of normalizing the problem in terms of how each partner is likely to feel about it.

The second reframe is designed to show how the HSD is a symptom of the couple's *relationship*. The therapist should not hasten to make this reframe, particularly with those non-HSD partners who would like to believe they are *not* a part of the problem. Remember that the non-HSD partner does not usually see the role he or she plays in the lack of desire. This reframe has much more "depth" in the psychodynamic sense, because it relates to the underlying fears of intimacy and other relationship problems such as anger, which always represents an obstacle to intimacy. The reframe would suggest to the couple that the lack of sexual desire is a way to maintain their distance from each other in order to avoid triggering the underlying fears of intimacy. The following example illustrates this point. Both John and Martha entered therapy with an underlying fear of abandonment. Although they cherished each other, they did not expect their marriage to last. They were vigilantly reading into what the other's words and actions meant, fearing and anticipating that "the end was near." Their sexual relationship had always been problematic. They seemed to be "on and off" sexually. Neither one had much sexual desire and both would joke that they were just too busy to think about sex. Each partner's personal history fueled his or her fears. John's father had died when he was young, and his mother was emotionally unavailable. He said he was the "poster" latchkey kid. Martha's first husband had unexpectedly divorced her when he announced one day that he did not love her and had found someone else. Being sexually intimate exposed John and Martha to their underlying fear of abandonment. The sexual union was a symbol of commitment and increasing psychological involvement with each other, conditions that carried great risk to their survival in the relationship. Because they highly valued their relationship, they relegated sex to mean something unimportant to them both.

The third reframe pertains to the possibility of sexual dysfunctions in the other partner. In a number of cases, the other partner is experiencing a sexual dysfunction or paraphilia that they do not want to discuss or confront. It is much easier for them to focus outwardly on the HSD of the partner than to examine their own sexual problems. Questions about the sexual functioning of the partner may eventually reveal these problems, and then the therapist can comment on how much each partner may be alike sexually. For example, the couple may come to the conclusion that her lack of sexual desire helped him avoid dealing with his erectile dysfunction and accompanying loss of desire and anxiety, or with his sexual addiction and acting-out with prostitutes that he justified by her lack of desire.

There is not a formula for creating a reframe. It is guided by a general principle, the therapist's hypothesis about the meaning of the loss of desire, and the information provided by the couple. We have found some of the following questions useful in helping us reframe HSD:

*To both partners*
- How would you compare your levels of sexual desire?
- How often do you have some kind of sensual/affectional encounter?
- How often do you have sex?
- How often would you like to have sex?

- What is your theory about the lack of desire?
- How do you feel when you do have sex/when you don't have sex?
- Can you think of any ways this problem has helped you?
- What are some of the other sexual problems you have?
- Are there secrets you keep from each other about sex?
- How much closeness do you like?
- How do you use sex to get closer?
- How do you use sex to get further apart?
- What effect do you think this problem has on your partner?
- How do you get along in other aspects of your relationship?
- How do you negotiate closeness and distance?

*To the non-HSD partner*
- How do you feel when you want sex and your partner does not?
- What do you gain from having sex?
- How are love, sex, and intimacy related?
- How is sex and affection related?
- What do you do to deal with your sexual frustrations?
- How do you manage to not blame your partner for your frustrations?
- What do you think your partner doesn't say about this problem?
- What do you think this problem may be a symptom of?

*To the HSD partner*
- How do you feel when you want sex and your partner doesn't?
- What do you gain from having sex?
- What did you get out of having sex in the past when you felt desire?
- How are love, sex, and intimacy related?
- How are sex and affection related?
- What do you do to try to get yourself in the mood?
- What does your partner do to get you in the mood?
- What does your partner do to turn you off?
- What do you do to turn yourself off?
- How do you pressure yourself to be interested?
- What do you think your partner doesn't say to you about this problem?
- What do you think this problem may be a symptom of?

## Attending to the Affective, Cognitive, and Behavioral Aspects of HSD

Every psychological problem has at least three facets, the affective, cognitive, and behavioral. Many approaches to psychotherapy tend to deal almost exclusively with one aspect over the other. Sex therapy has tended to focus on the behavioral and methodologically operates within some loose framework of systematic desensitization. Treating HSD involves some behavioral assignments such as sensate focus exercises, nondemand intercourse, and expanding the "sexual" repertoire. All of these behavioral techniques are described elsewhere in this volume. However, the affective and cognitive facets of treatment have been underemphasized in the literature (Kaplan, 1979; Leiblum & Rosen, 1988).

HSD is basically about *absent* motivation and affect. The client does not feel sexy, in the mood, or turned on, for example. They are *not motivated* to do anything of a sensual and/or sexual nature. Additionally, the response anxiety they experience is a part of the turn-off cycle. The client's feelings need to be adequately discussed in the therapy, between the partners, and at home. In the sex therapy literature, the couple is rarely told they need to share how they feel as a couple about having this problem and how they feel as individuals about the absence of these feelings. Only by having this feeling-oriented discussion can the partners support and understand each other. Moreover, the therapist can educate the couple and help to normalize the feelings they are experiencing. Emotional validation is an integral part of any therapeutic process and has been strikingly absent in the sex therapy literature.

Most couples presenting with HSD are emotionally shut down. They have learned to avoid talking about this topic, because it leads to resentment, anger, hurt feelings, and sometimes arguments. The therapist will need to ask a number of probing questions and facilitate this discussion in the session. Once the couple has had the discussion in therapy, they can be coached on how to have the discussion at home. For example, the therapist might say, "What could you say to your partner when you want to do one of the exercises and your partner does not? What feelings would you want to express and how could you express those feelings in a nonblaming and nonhurtful way?"

The cognitive (see Dattilio et al., 1990) part of HSD has been virtually ignored in the literature with the exceptions mentioned in the first few chapters such as script theory. As we mentioned earlier, the client with HSD is *thinking* a number of *negative sexual thoughts*. They may not be fully aware of these thoughts, but they are present and do exert a powerful influence. A significant amount of time needs to be spent early in treatment assessing the negative sexual cognitions and working toward developing positive sexual cognitions. As the therapy proceeds, the therapist will need to continually check in regarding the reappearance of the negative thoughts and make an effort to keep the positive thoughts going.

The point of this discussion is to keep the focus of therapy flexible and balanced. All three facets of the problem require some attention, and, by focusing on all three areas, the therapist ensures that the pertinent issues are addressed.

## THE TREATMENT PLAN

We believe there are several goals that need to be addressed when treating HSD. The clinician can become overfocused on just treating the lack of desire and can overlook the larger picture. In our theoretical approach, we examine the problem in context. One way of accomplishing this task is to summarize the couple's major dynamic in a single or simple statement such as the reframing mentioned above. For example, the statement could be that one partner experiences HSD as a way to maintain a sense of control over the self. Another possible remark could be that the HSD in one partner aids the other partner in avoiding an underlying fear of rejection. The treatment plan identifies each problem to be changed and the strategies or techniques that will be used to effect the changes.

Treatment should also be a collaborative process in which the therapist shares his or her ideas with the clients and seeks their approval before proceeding. When given the opportunity clients like to participate in deciding what they want and will rarely turn down the opportunity to grow beyond the problem for which they sought therapy. The treatment plan may then include goals that extend beyond the presenting problem.

### Elements of the Treatment Plan

FOCUS ON THE LACK OF DESIRE

One of the goals of treatment should clearly be the lack of sexual desire. This was the problem that brought them to therapy and should be respected. However, it is the therapist's responsibility to put the HSD into perspective and suggest the best way to go about treating it. Part of the treatment plan should consist of talking about this issue and the plan to begin increasing the level of sexual desire.

IMPROVE THE OVERALL LEVEL OF SEXUAL FUNCTIONING

To put it succinctly, the second goal of sex therapy is to enhance the overall functioning of the couple sexually. What value is sexual desire if there is an erectile problem or some other sexual difficulty that will diminish the rewards in overcoming the lack of desire? Sometimes, it is also difficult to tell which is the cause and which is the effect of the HSD. Sexual communication is lacking in most couples in our experience. This problem is fairly easy to improve. It can be accomplished as part of treating the HSD case.

IMPROVE THE OVERALL QUALITY OF THE COUPLE'S RELATIONSHIP

In the traditional sexual therapy literature referred to earlier, *the couple* was not the focus of treatment. The sexual problem was treated as if it could be separated from the relationship. Many couples entering sex therapy do show improved marital functioning, although it was not an intended part of the therapy or part of the treatment plan. We believe these couples were able to generalize from their positive sex therapy experience to their relationship. Our experience over the past two decades has informed us that in general, couples therapists have not treated sexual problems and sex therapists have not treated couples problems. We prefer to think of ourselves as couples therapists treating couples as a whole, including their sexual relationship.

## Setting Treatment Priorities

Once a treatment plan has been formulated, we have a sense of which problems are to be treated and how they are to be treated. We have indicated that HSD cases usually involve a multitude of sexual and relational difficulties. Obviously, not everything can be treated at once. The clinician needs a flow chart of how to go about prioritizing treatment. We use the following guidelines in deciding on the implementation of the treatment plan, keeping in mind that some problems can be treated in an overlapping or concurrent way. As usual, we always recommend starting with the presenting problem, the HSD, except when relationship problems make the sex therapy impossible.

- Treat the HSD first and then begin treating other sexual difficulties such as an erectile dysfunction or inhibited female orgasm. Treatment may involve both individual and couples work depending upon the risk factors present. If another sexual problem is suppressing sexual desire, treat that problem first and/or concurrently with the HSD.
- Delay treating sexual problems in the non-HSD partner, until progress has been made with the HSD. The HSD partner will not be interested in any sexual interaction, including treatment of another sexual problem in themselves or their partner until they begin to feel they can derive more from sex.

- If attempts to treat the HSD fail because of the relationship, postpone treating the HSD and work on the relationship until the couple has reached a point where they are ready to resume the treatment of the HSD.
- Continue to mix the treatment of the couple with the treatment of the HSD.
- If the partners cannot work together, try splitting up the couple for some individual work on a short-term basis (see Weeks & Treat, 2001).
- Use the law of parsimony, starting with the simplest problems first and then moving to the more difficult. In general, we work from the surface to "in depth" and from the current to the historical. If you choose to do otherwise, be able to justify the reason. For example, if a family-of-origin issue is presented as a major factor, then this issue should receive priority.
- When the couple believe they have made sufficient progress on their relationship and the HSD, other sexual difficulties can be treated.
- When the couple believe they have essentially eliminated their relational and sexual problems, an offer can be made to help them optimize or enhance their sexual and couple relationship. For example, enhancement of intimacy and sexual passion via greater expression of feelings and learning new sexual techniques may be the final therapeutic agenda.

The key to keeping the couple in treatment is to have a focused, flexible, systematic treatment plan that is explained to the couple and is continually reshaped in collaboration with them. The couple can believe that the therapist knows what he or she is doing and why they are doing it. Having the couple participate in the development of their treatment program helps them feel they are part of the process, gives them a sense of control and responsibility, and fosters compliance with the treatment plan.

## Homework and Incremental Change

One of the hallmarks of sex therapy is *prescribed* change or "homework assignments." Homework is a way of extending the treatment beyond the confines of the weekly therapy hour. One hour per week provides limited opportunity for learning and is basically a verbal process. Homework, on the other hand, tends to be behavioral or action-oriented; clients learn by doing. In sex therapy, the homework increases the chances of success, lowers anxiety, and creates a safe environment in which to try new behaviors. Generally speaking, the couple is instructed to stop everything they have been doing to solve the problem. Also, sex is proscribed. They are told they will begin a process of doing homework assignments that are designed to help them relearn how to better function sexually. The incremental steps will lead to success rather than failure. In order to achieve success, the couple will need to proceed slowly and systematically. An underlying assumption is that the homework exercises help to control and slowly eliminate anxiety.

Homework has been a part of the behaviorally oriented approach to sex therapy, which stresses systematic desensitization, or the methodical reduction of anxiety (Heiman & Meston, 1997). For most sexual dysfunctions, the treatment protocols and the homework exercises have been formalized (Kaplan, 1979; Masters & Johnson, 1970). This is not the case for the treatment of HSD although Kaplan (1979) did suggest a few exercises. In all the literature on sex therapy, only McCarthy (1985) addresses the applicability and abuse of homework exercises. He pointed out that homework could be useful in changing attitudes, promoting behavioral change, and facilitating a change in feelings. He also mentioned several common errors made in giving homework, including not being specific enough, using a cookbook approach, reinforcing avoidance by not giving further homework when resistance is encountered, and setting up assignments which have criteria or goals, thereby increasing performance or response anxiety.

This section will describe how to use and give homework assignments rather than the content of the assignments. The content will emerge from the therapy sessions and from the literature referenced in these treatment chapters. It is important to think of homework as an extension of the therapy hour. *Clients must be ready and prepared to do the homework assignments.* Near the end of the therapy hour, the therapist begins to think about the homework for the next week. Sometimes the assignment is clear and at other times, it is not clear what might be helpful at that point. The therapist can describe the idea in mind and get the couples' reactions to the homework. Just as in creating a treatment plan, the therapist will find greater compliance with the assignments when the couple participates in its creation. Once the homework assignment is stated, the therapist may ask the following questions:

- How do you feel about this assignment?
- Do you think this will help you? Why?
- What do you expect will happen?
- What do you expect you will feel when you are doing it?
- Who will take the initiative?
- Can you think of any reason that you might not do it?
- Can you think of any reason that you might forget it or mess it up?

The therapist should ask the clients to do the homework assignment at least three times a week in most cases. Explain that in terms of effectiveness, one experience may be average, one above average, and one below average. If they hit the below average exercise the first time, they are likely to do better on another day. It is also useful to tell clients that sometimes exercises just do not work. There are two reasons they do not work. The first is that sometimes one or both partners are resistant. This can be reframed as an opportunity to examine the obstacles to moving ahead. If the clients resist doing the exercise, explain that this will be examined in close detail at the beginning of the next session. The second reason is that the therapist may have designed an exercise that was too advanced or complex. In the beginning of therapy, it is sometimes difficult to know just where to start. In both cases, the couple provides feedback, which is highly diagnostic. Thus, the couple should be told that no matter what happens in the exercises, useful information is always generated. If they are successful, they move to the next step, and if they are unsuccessful, the information is used for diagnostic purposes to help them understand the reasons why, and the therapist then develops another homework assignment. The therapist's responsibility is to always follow up promptly on the homework. If the therapist does not take it seriously, the clients will not take it seriously. Once the initial greetings are done, homework is the first order of business in sex therapy. Knowing what happened at home sets the stage for the therapy session and the next homework assignment.

Rarely does therapy follow a linear progression. This too should be explained to the couple. They may move ahead, get stuck, regress, and suddenly move forward. Their responses to the homework may reflect this process. When the couple has to back up a couple of steps, at least from their point of view, it is useful to reframe this process as a normal course of therapy. The therapist may also mix different kinds of assignments in treating HSD. It might involve a combination of behavioral, cognitive, couple, or family-of-origin assignments.

STRUCTURAL ELEMENTS OF HOMEWORK

The homework assignments include five structural elements: initiation, scheduling, duration, frequency, and place. A more thorough discussion of the homework assignments will follow in a later chapter on sex therapy with the couple detailing the sensate focus exercises.

*Initiation.* One of the greatest responsibilities of initiating is that of reminding the partner about the exercise and how this can be accomplished in a positive way. Before ending a session, an agreement should be made regarding *who* will initiate the homework assignments and *how* this will be done. In HSD cases, we often begin with the HSD partner taking responsibility for initiating all of the assignments. This involves choosing the time and place, but more importantly, working on getting themselves *mentally prepared* for the exercise. Since HSD clients are often resistant initially to doing any homework, initiating provides an opportunity to understand their resistance to doing the homework. Once it is clear that the HSD partner is able to initiate the exercises without hesitation, we suggest that the partners take turns initiating the assignments, unless there is a good reason not to proceed in this fashion. We explain our rationale for the initiation process and get feedback from the couple regarding what each would like to do.

*Scheduling.* We require that the assignments be scheduled. This part of the discussion can usually be held at home by comparing calendars and setting aside at least three times each week to do the homework. The couple should avoid trying to squeeze them all into the last few days before the next appointment. If the partners fail to plan appointments at home, the therapist provides an opportunity to uncover and comprehend the hidden obstacles. Sometimes couples object to the idea of planning time to do homework because they believe that intimacy should be spontaneous. They relate the exercise to the ultimate goal of having sex. Two points can be made to counter these feelings. First, unless they schedule times, nothing is likely to happen. It is much easier to deviate from a set time and reschedule than it is to try to fit it in at the end of the day. They should also set times that are mutually agreeable, free from distractions, and when they have enough energy to enjoy the experience. Second, they are not scheduling the activity itself, but an opportunity to do the activity. What this means is that the partners cannot force themselves to do the homework if they do not want to do it. By setting the time aside, they have created an opportunity to spend time together doing something meaningful. They may choose to do the homework or to use the time in any way they choose. Failing to do the exercises represents resistance and must be processed.

*Duration.* We recommend beginning with a short timeframe for first few assignments. If the couple can tolerate the amount of time, then extend it to some comfortable range. For the sensual touch exercises and sexual exercises, we usually begin with 5 to 10 minutes and progress to 10 to 20 minutes depending upon the couple's comfort level. Eventually as the experiences become more involved, 20 to 30 minutes will be needed. Typically, therapists ask couples to do assignments for too long a period of time. This error occurs because the therapist overestimates the amount of intimacy the couple can tolerate at a given point in treatment.

*Frequency.* Most sex therapy protocols require about three homework assignments per week. The therapist should remember that many couples presenting with HSD have not had any physical contact in many months.

The therapist could start the couple with one assignment a week, but the effect of starting that way would be to place a great deal of pressure on just one assignment. Desensitization only works through *repeated experiences*. Doing any less than three per week is not going to be productive. Prior to commencing the homework, it is important to have the couple talk about what it will be like to have so much physical contact so often. We will elaborate on this point extensively when we discuss the technique of sensate focus.

*Location.* For most couples, the bedroom is the natural place for making love. However, the bedroom may have many negative associations regarding sex. The HSD partner may think that if they are in the bedroom, they must have sex even though the therapist has proscribed it. Some couples will find that selecting another room in the home that gives them privacy works better. Many of our couples have started off in the living room or another bedroom for the simple over-the-clothing touching or hand massages. Once they begin to feel more comfortable outside the bedroom, they may move back to that room. This element means the therapist should ask the nonobvious question of where in the home they would like to do the homework.

PROMOTING COMPLIANCE TO HOMEWORK

An apparent assumption made in sex therapy is that clients will automatically comply with the assignments. Masters and Johnson (1970) ignored this topic and Kaplan (1979) briefly touched on the issue of resistance. In fact, it is surprising how little literature exists on the issue of homework in the field of psychotherapy and how to promote compliance to homework. Tiefer and Melman (1987) pointed out how poor compliance occurred in both medicine and psychotherapy. Clients often ignore, forget, deny, or distort their homework assignments in sex therapy and psychotherapy. Medical patients do not follow through with physician's recommendations and fail to take their medications as prescribed. In the next few paragraphs, we will present some ideas that can help to promote compliance to the needed homework assignments. These ideas are based the work of Strong and Claiborn (1982).

The first principle is that of choice. In general, people do not like to be told what to do. It tends to create a state of psychological *reactance*. The therapist can provide a basic outline of the assignment and then ask the couple to fill in the gaps. In those cases where the assignment is not clear, the therapist could discuss practicing those things discussed in the office and ask the couple to think of what they might do at home to practice what they learned in the session. The most important thing to remember is to develop a collaborative relationship with the couple around homework.

They simply need to feel part of the process. The more ownership they have of the process, the better. The therapist may also ask questions about the structural elements and let the couple make those decisions.

Another interesting aspect of homework is what to call it. For some clients, homework has a negative connotation because of how they did in school or felt about school. The therapist should think about the couple's background and use a term that will have some appeal for them. College professors, teachers, and other professionals like the term homework. They understand that people learn by doing homework and people have been successful in doing homework. The homework could be called an assignment, task, chore, exercise, or experiment. Experiment is an interesting choice and one that scientifically oriented clients like because it suggests there is no predetermined outcome. The therapist might even ask the couple what they want to call these assignments. Once again, the couple is given a choice.

The second principle is called *depersonalization*. In the paragraph above, we used the term psychological reactance to refer to the fact that people do not like to be told what to do, ordered, or commanded. Some clients are much more sensitive to this type of behavior on the part of the therapist than others. It is safer to discuss the fact that all sex therapy programs require homework and that the couples' homework assignments are best viewed as part of their uniquely designed program of treatment. The therapist should avoid saying, "I want you to . . . " When giving the assignment, the therapist can talk about what is "standard," "typical," or "needed," at that particular time in their treatment. By carefully positioning the homework so that it is a demand of the treatment program, the client(s) is unable to engage in a direct power struggle with the therapist.

For those partners who are oppositional or reactive in their behavior toward each other and the therapist, the third principle is most useful and involves giving implicit versus explicit directions. The first two principles assist in the implementation of the third. The therapist can use phrases such as, "You might try . . . ," thereby implicitly suggesting the kinds of thoughts, feelings, and reactions that may occur. The goal for the client with HSD is for he or she to feel something positive about physical, sensual, and sexual interactions. The therapist can phrase or suggest indirectly that some of these reactions may occur. The therapist might say:

• Notice any positive *thoughts* before and during the exercise or physical interaction.

• Notice any positive *feelings* before and during the exercise or physical interaction.

• Just let yourself feel whatever you feel.

- Enjoy whatever sensations you have from being touched.
- Enjoy whatever sensations you have from the sensual/sexual exercise.
- Let your senses tell you what they are feeling.
- See whether you can enhance the positive thoughts you are having.
- Notice what you do when you are in a positive sexual mood.
- Do not try to force any of your feelings—just let them happen.
- Whatever happens during the exercise is fine—this is not a test.
- You are free to try whatever you like.

Some of these indirect suggestions grow from the work of Milton Erickson and have been described by Weeks and L'Abate (1982).

## TREATING OTHER SEXUAL DYSFUNCTIONS

From a statistical and experiential perspective, sexual dysfunctions rarely occur in isolation. We usually find several problems within the couple's relationship. The couple may have entered therapy to work on the male's erectile dysfunction and then "discovered" the HSD. The number of possible combinations of sexual problems and difficulties is quite extensive. From the clinician's perspective, the question is which problem to treat first. Of the major sexual dysfunctions, we are referring to erectile dysfunction, premature ejaculation, inhibited orgasm, inhibited female orgasm, and vaginismus. In general, the HSD is the first problem to treat whether it was the presenting problem or not. Without some sexual desire, the client is not going to be motivated to work on the other problems that might make sex more feasible or pleasurable. Why would a woman want to help her partner overcome premature ejaculation if she is not interested in having sex anyway? Why would a man want to help his wife overcome inhibited female orgasm if he is not interested in having sex?

The problem is that the HSD may in part be a function of another sexual difficulty such as a lack of sexual communication or incompatibility, erectile dysfunction, or vaginismus. For example, assume the woman is experiencing vaginismus or painful intercourse. Over time, the pain associated with intercourse will probably diminish her desire for sex. Helping the couple make this link is important because it will suggest to them that both problems need concurrent work. The vaginismus is a risk factor for the HSD. Even though the woman may have little to no desire, she can understand that she did have desire when she was pain free or might have desire if she could ever have pain-free intercourse. In this sense, treating other sexual dysfunctions is no different than treating other risk factors. The client(s) needs to understand the possible connections between problems and then commit to working on removing the risk factors.

## PROMOTING SEXUAL INTIMACY

We have suggested that when HSD has a psychological foundation, the contributing factors are largely based on the inability to be intimate. The goal of treatment is not about any particular type of sexual performance, but rather on developing feelings of sexual desire based on the desire to be intimate through sexual expression. The clinician is informed and guided by this principle. Aside from Weeks and Hof (1987) and Schnarch (1991, 1997), very little has been written about this issue. Lobitz and Lobitz (1996) elaborated on the sexual intimacy paradox that was first suggested by Weeks and Hof (1987) and further elaborated by Weeks (1995). The paradox or contradiction is that the closer, more intimate some couples become, the less one or the other desires a sexual relationship. Lobitz and Lobitz's contribution was to offer a developmental model based on Erikson's developmental theory consisting of five elements: conflagration, merger, fusion, differentiation, and integration. This paper is highly theoretical and blends Erickson's theory with traditional family systems theory.

McCarthy (1987) published an interesting paper on how men are socialized to develop nonintimate sexual relationships. He suggested it is part of the male double standard to be mechanically sexual and strong but to be perceived as weak if one has any needs. Sexually, it means a real man needs nothing from a woman in order to function sexually—certainly nothing of an intimate nature. The double standard learned early in life has far-reaching consequences. While the focus is on men, McCarthy does discuss how to work with couples around the problem of HSD. He suggested three areas that require attention in order to promote intimacy. These are comfort, self-disclosure, and increasing the range of emotional and sexual expression. Comfort refers to being comfortable with one's body, sexual language, communication, and most importantly, asking for what one needs. Young men, in particular, are afraid to ask for what they want and to express discomfort with any aspect of the sexual experience. The second focus is on self-disclosure. Men have more difficulty self-disclosing than do women. One way of being intimate is to share one's thoughts and feelings with another. Some men are able to share some of their positive feelings, but none of their negative feelings. The third focus of therapy is to improve the level of intimacy by increasing the range of emotional and sexual expression. In this regard, men need to be helped to identify and express their feelings (see Weeks and Treat, 2001) and expand the notion that sex equals intercourse.

Our approach to promoting sexual intimacy involves four parts.

1. Help the couple conceptualize the relationship between sex and intimacy. This involves changing attitudes, beliefs, or cognitions about the relationship between the two. Some partners have fragmented or split these concepts. They fail to see any connection or link between them. One man in his early 30s commented that he had never thought of sex as having anything to do with intimacy. He saw it as a separate part of a relationship. He was also attracted to other women and acted out through public masturbation. This was another symptom of the extent to which he had separated these concepts.

2. Help the couple redefine sexuality as being more than intercourse or some particular sexual performance. It involves an opening up to a richer and deeper form of sexuality, based on thoughts and feelings— shared and unshared.

3. The couple needs to share some idea of what it means to be intimate. In the case just mentioned, the husband quickly learned that sex could be more than just intercourse. He started to enjoy the touching and caressing without having to engage in intercourse. Even though he professed a radical change in his thinking, his wife kept returning to the issue to make sure that he actually meant what he was saying. She questioned whether he was being honest. She too was conditioned to the idea that men only derive sexual satisfaction if it involves intercourse. Many couples do not have the same notion of what sex means to them. They are out of sync or have discrepant views regarding intimacy.

4. The partners must develop a greater awareness of their underlying fears of intimacy and how those fears are barriers to sexual desire and to being closer. These final two points were discussed in Chapter 4.

## RELAPSE PREVENTION

Very little attention in the clinical literature has been given to the topic of relapse prevention in sex therapy and in particular, in treating HSD. McCarthy (1993, 1999a) addressed this persistent problem and suggested the following strategies in treating HSD:

- Sexual avoidance is damaging to desire, and desire is maintained through active sexual and pleasurable contact. Circumvention of the homework exercises is one of the earliest signs that a couple is relapsing.

- Help the couple broaden and increase their touching repertoire to include *sensual* caressing. In too many cases, touching is sexually focused.

- Help the couple solve nonsexual conflicts and anger.
- Facilitate an understanding between sex and intimacy.
- Help the couple agree on what is mutually desirable from the initiation stage to the completion of sexual activity.
- Help the couple achieve a good balance of intimacy.
- Establish a regular sexual rhythm in terms of time spent together and having sexual dates.

McCarthy (1999a) also suggests follow-up sessions to ensure continued treatment maintenance. Our approach is similar. We begin to phase out treatment by spacing the last few sessions over a 2- to 3-week period and then monthly. We also suggest that at the first sign of trouble, the couple talk about what might be happening, and if they are unable to resolve the problem, they must return for some therapy work. Couples will sometimes think that returning after treatment has terminated is a failure. The therapist predicts that couples sometimes return for maintenance and that failing to do so can lead to a relapse. These ideas can be discussed before the final session, giving the couple permission to have these thoughts, yet also encouraging them to return if necessary.

We also use a paradoxical strategy to help prevent relapses (Weeks & L'Abate, 1982). We ask a couple to think of all the ways they might undo treatment or what they have learned in treatment. We might challenge them to think of ways they will "screw up" their sexual relationship. This conversation should be held in the context of reminding them that desire is variable and sometimes we have sex even when the mood is absent. Additionally, couples may go through "dry spells" when not much is happening sexually. If the dry spell continues, then it is time to seek help again. They are also told that desire is fragile, new factors may come along that interfere with desire, and old conditions may reappear. Paradoxically, predicting the problems that might occur increases the likelihood of nonoccurrence. Should the puzzle come up again, the couple will remember the therapist's prediction and return to the therapy.

## IMPLEMENTATION AND PROCESS

### Implementation

The execution of the principles and strategies of treating HSD requires experience, training, comfort, and skill. During the past 20 years of practice, we have each treated many sex therapy cases and HSD cases that had been handled without success by other therapists, some of whom were not knowledgeable about sex therapy and especially the treatment of HSD. A qualified sex therapist is someone with the appropriate credentials, experience, supervised training, and, in our opinion, a strong foundation in couples and family therapy. In other, less frequent cases, the clients were treated by sex therapists, but they may not have had the broad range of training required to treat HSD which involves so much emphasis on couples' work.

Another problem contributing to sex therapy failure is the lack of proper implementation of techniques in the existing texts. With the exception of Wincze and Carey (1991), one formula is typically recommended for every couple. We have personally seen many cases where the correct technique or set of techniques were used, but were not properly executed because they were not tailored to the specific relational needs of the couple. When a client has had ineffective treatment with another therapist, we never suggest that therapist was incompetent. We proceed directly to collect a thorough history of the treatment, asking detailed questions about the techniques, how the techniques were implemented, and how the homework was reviewed in therapy.

Experience is also a major factor in implementation. The more a therapist uses a strategy or technique, the more he or she should learn about what works and what does not. We certainly see these phenomena in the field of surgery. Most surgeons are trained in the same procedure, but the surgeon who does the most liver transplants, for example, will have the best success rate. Treating a large number of cases or being supervised by a therapist who has treated a large number of cases is one of the best ways to overcome this therapeutic difficulty. When the client has failed with another therapist, why should they start over and do some of the same techniques that failed the last time. The best way for the therapist to explain this situation is to say that the other therapist was on the right track, but did not have enough experience or did not attend to issues of implementation sufficiently. Each time a technique is implemented, the client should know:

- why the technique is being used
- the expected outcome
- possible problems in implementing the technique
- ways to overcome those problems
- how the technique fits into the overall treatment program

Questions should be solicited from the couple and answered to their satisfaction. It is not as simple as telling the client to do something and having the client blindly comply.

## Process

Process is a key concept in the field of psychotherapy. It refers to "how" therapy is done rather than what (the technique) is done. Process has much more to do with the relationship issues of therapy. The therapist and the client continually assess how they are doing as a team and how the team is doing in terms of implementing a treatment program. Process is directly related to the idea of developing a collaborative relationship with the couple so that they own their therapy. Today's clients are more educated and sophisticated than in the past. Many have read self-help books about their problem and have had prior therapy. Many sex therapy clients are very sophisticated consumers such as doctors, lawyers, and other professionals. They expect to be treated with respect and want a rationale for why they are being asked to do what the therapist thinks is useful. Every couple is also different; therefore, each treatment program is slightly different and needs to be uniquely designed for that particular couple. One size does not fit all as some texts suggest.

One of the first process issues to cover in treating HSD is the couple's expectation. Most expect a quick fix, especially those who have read that sex therapy is a brief approach to treatment. They need to understand that change will be gradual or incremental, with occasional plateaus. Staying on track and working through one problem at a time rather than suddenly finding a state of sexual passion is, in fact, the best measure of success. The therapist needs to ask the partners how they feel about being in therapy for a sexual problem. The majority of couples are embarrassed or ashamed; they feel the problem is uniquely theirs. With HSD cases, they assume that almost everyone else has a higher level of sexual desire and make other erroneous assumptions about what it means to lack desire. The therapist explains that many questions will be asked about their sexual and couple relationship. The sexual questions will be explicit and may be difficult to talk about. One of our favorite sayings about sex therapy to the couple is, "The hardest part is getting started." The therapist's attitude must be nonjudgmental and openly accepting of great sexual variation. Clients will be wondering if what they tell the therapist will be viewed judgmentally, and, if this is suspected, it is useful to ask the client to talk about what they think the therapist thinks of their behavior. The therapist could make some opening statement such as, "I have been a sex therapist for years. Over that time, I have heard just about everything. I spend hours a day talking about sex with people, so I have become so used to it I sometimes do not stop to remember that this is all new to you. I want you to let me know how you feel about my questions and how you feel about this process. I will check in with you from time to time, but you can let me know at any time when a question is difficult for you to answer or whether you would rather not have your partner hear your answer. I think there must be some boundaries between you. You do not need to know everything about each other. Some things are just old garbage left over from our past or irrational ideas that really have nothing to do with the partner."

The therapist must also keep checking in with the couple about the pace of therapy. Some couples are ready to jump right in, full-speed ahead. Others need to go at a much slower pace. The therapist and the couple decide which problems are to be treated, the sequence in which they are to be treated, and, as the process unfolds, the pace at which they are to be treated. From time to time, the therapist can ask whether the pace feels right. The therapist will need to change pace from time to time depending upon the issue at hand. Couples will aggressively tackle some issues and approach others with trepidation.

## CONCLUSION

This chapter has reviewed some of our guiding principles used in treating HSD. These concepts provide the foundation for treatment and are generic to the treatment of many other sexual as well as nonsexual difficulties. Unless we remain cognizant of these beliefs, the techniques are much less likely to work, the clients are less likely to adhere to treatment, and the dropout rate is likely to escalate. Understanding the principles helps us understand what we are doing and why. It also allows us to individualize the therapy, making it not only the best fit for the couple, but cost-effective as well. A tailored plan need not contain all the techniques of every treatment program for HSD, but only those relevant for the couple being treated.

As we have mentioned, in Chapter 4, there are several common relational issues that can contribute to a lack of sexual desire such as struggles over power, control, and intimacy. These will be discussed in greater detail in the next chapter.

# 9

# Treating Risk Factors
# in the Couple

IN CHAPTERS 3, 4, AND 5, WE IDENTIFIED a number of factors in the couple's relationship that would place one or possibly both partners at risk for developing HSD. There are numerous possible risk factors that can be conceptually divided into individual, interactional, and intergenerational categories. However, our experience has shown that the vast majority of cases are *secondary* HSD, with at least one of the major risk factors being the couple's relationship. The purpose of this chapter is to describe the treatment of some of those aspects of the couple's relationship that would predispose them to HSD.

## INTIMACY-BASED APPROACH TO TREATMENT

In Chapter 4, an intimacy-based approach was presented for the assessment of the couple's risk factors. This chapter will describe an intimacy-based approach to treating these couples. Schaefer and Olson (1981) were the first to illustrate seven areas of intimacy in a relationship. They included sexual intimacy in their inventory. A theoretically and empirically based model of love in adult relationships helped to improve our understanding of how these different types of intimacy may affect each other (Sternberg, 1986). Sternberg postulated that love in adults (marital love) consists of three components in about equal proportions: commitment, intimacy, and passion. What has been missing in the sex therapy literature is a clinically based model of treatment that includes the many areas of intimacy and love described above. Our contention is that difficulties in one area of intimacy may affect or create problems in other areas of intimacy, thereby affecting sexual enjoyment. Sternberg was the first to propose this concept, and our clinical experience categorically supports it.

## Commitment

Commitment is the cognitive component of the intimacy-based model for the treatment of HSD. It refers to the intellectual decision to commit to another person and live in an exclusive relationship. Further, commitment can be expressed through fidelity, engagement, marriage, living together, and so on.

## Intimacy

The second component of this triangular theory of love is intimacy, the emotional part of the triangle. In fact, Prager (1997) devoted an entire volume to this topic by identifying 13 different concepts of intimacy and 45 measures of intimacy and related concepts. For our purposes, Sternberg's (1986) concept of intimacy is most useful. It includes, but is not limited to, the following characteristics:

- a sense of closeness
- being connected or bonded
- having a sense of welfare for the other
- wanting happiness for the other
- regarding the other highly
- being able to count on the other in time of need
- sharing oneself
- talking intimately
- giving emotional support
- being honest and empathic

## Passion

The third component of the triangle is passion, which is described as romance, sex, physical attraction, and longing to be with the other person.

Sternberg (1986) states that passion is the motivational part of the triangle serving to bring partners together physically.

This volume deals with the absence of sexual passion. Our argument is that the therapist cannot evaluate and treat sexual passion as an isolated phenomenon. Cognitive/behavioral approaches to sex therapy tend to focus on the individual rather than the couple. Moreover, treatment involves keeping a focus on the sexual problem(s) and using traditional techniques of sex therapy. We believe that passion exists within the context of commitment and intimacy in the relationship. This view of the problem is systemic and contextual. The problem of HSD cannot be separated and isolated from the couple's relationship nor can it be decontextualized. Thus, problems in one area of the triangle can have significant impact on another area. Occasionally, we have treated couples that claim to have terrible relationships, but great sex. Somehow, these partners are able to compartmentalize sex from the rest of their relationship. In our clinical experience, most couples report a causal association between their relationship as a whole and their sexual desire.

In Chapter 3, we reviewed the data on the relationship between marital satisfaction and sexual desire. Being in a happy marriage is a strong predictor of sexual desire and satisfaction. What then does it mean to be in a happy or satisfied marriage? This question can be approached from a variety of perspectives. One perspective is simply to argue that working marriages are relatively free of problems or difficulties. In other words, the couple is not pathological or dysfunctional, and the partners have found a way to work out their difficulties. The perspective that we will present is that couples in happy relationships:

1. have the skills to effectively work through problems,
2. have been able to reach consensus on issues of intimacy, and
3. do not allow underlying fears of intimacy to sabotage their relationship.

## STAGES OF TREATMENT

### Defining the Relationship

For every relationship we form, all parties involved seek a definition. The alliance can function only if the individuals reach some consensus about what constitutes the relationship or how it is to be defined. Using Sternberg's (1986) theory as a guide or a model, we can help the couple define or redefine their relationship. The first step of this process is to educate the couple about Sternberg's theory of love. A brief description of the three components and the fact that the components are interlocking is usually sufficient to set the stage. (Of course, before continuing this line of treatment, the couple must be at a point where they comprehend the connection between the lack of sexual desire and the difficulties in their relationship.) At this stage of treatment, the therapist should assess and possibly help the couple work through six issues.

1. *Do both partners desire all three components as described in the triangle?* We set the stage for this discussion by asking the partners to think about and discuss how they would characterize love and intimacy. Their definitions inform us about how they want to characterize their relationship. This simple process is extremely productive in that basic differences in partners and areas of agreement are uncovered. Some couples can identify several areas of intimacy; others focus on just one area. One older couple had only been married a couple of years. They were both professors in the same academic area. When asked to define intimacy, they focused on working well together as colleagues but could not conceive of any other type of intimacy. Interestingly, sex was not defined as a type of intimacy but as a necessary part of a marriage. When asked about whether they had thought about emotional intimacy, they both replied that was something neither one was comfortable expressing.

   Next, we move on to ask about the partners need to have all three components in their relationship. These are basically yes/no questions. Are you committed to each other? Do you want to have an intimate relationship? Do you want to have passion in this relationship? If the answer is no or if there is a discrepancy in answers, there is probably a significant problem. For example, in one case a couple had only been married for about a year. They had just started to experience major disagreements. Prior to this time, the partners had never had a fight and said that they were perfectly matched because they saw everything the same way. The arguing meant to them that their marriage was irrevocably flawed and a mistake. They requested help with divorcing at the outset of treatment. A recent secondary problem for them was lack of desire. Because they believed they were in the process of dissolving their commitment, they felt that being sexual would send the wrong message, thereby violating each partner's view that the marriage had been a mistake.

   In other cases, we have seen lack of desire when couples are having trouble committing to each other, when one has commitment to the relationship and the other does not, or when one or both partners are ambivalent about being committed. For instance, one partner may only want a relationship based on companionship or may seek a parallel relationship (Sager & Hunt, 1979). Conversely, there are individuals who want relationships lacking in intimacy who successfully find partners that want the same type of relationship. Similarly, there are partners who form celibate relationships because both lack sexual desire. These relationships can work because they are not discrepant. However, if one wants passion and the other does not or thinks the other partner will change, then there is a fundamental disparity in the definition of the relationship and the partners are at risk for HSD.

Also, the therapist should assess for the presence of underlying fears regarding intimacy in one or both partners. The term "commitment phobic" has become a common term in everyday language. Couples will sometimes present this concept as the presenting problem. Our stance is that commitment is a process that occurs after some degree of attraction is experienced and intimacy has been established. Discussions of commitment disguise the fact that problems exist in the area of *intimacy*. The partners have not been able to identify these problems due to the fact that they are often beyond conscious recognition. These problems are the underlying fears of intimacy to be covered later.

2. *Does each partner want the same level of intensity for each of the three components?* Assume both partners answer yes to the three questions above. They both want commitment, intimacy, and passion. How much of each of these do they want? This issue is one of degree. The reason they are in therapy is because they have different degrees of passion or desire. Commonly, this reflects the fact that one partner wants more closeness than the other. The partner who desires less intimacy will find ways to distance from the relationship. One method is to be asexual. Conversely, the partner who is pursuing may become resentful, angry, or frustrated and eventually turn off desire because they can never get what they want.

Underlying this conflict over how much closeness and distance is wanted, most couples are actually well matched. Although partners may complain about the lack of intimacy, when they get what they say they want, they often find ways to undo it. It is easy for the therapist to be seduced by the idea that just one partner has a problem with intimacy when the other protests so loudly and angrily. When this pattern is revealed, it is clear that the other partner also had a problem they could hide by externalizing the issue onto their distancing partner.

3. *How much togetherness and individuation does each partner want in his or her relationship?* At the beginning of a relationship, couples are generally striving to find ways to get closer. They make dates, spend as much time together as possible, have long discussions, and are sexual with each other. Once the relationship has been established, the next

issue is how to balance togetherness and individuation. Couples are much better at negotiating for togetherness than they are for distance. Partners are often afraid to say they need some time for themselves or some "space." Rather than verbalize this need, it gets acted out in a way that sends the wrong message. One partner, for example, might spend hours on the computer in order to legitimize time for self. Another partner could claim he or she is working on getting some needed recreation. Couples can be encouraged to discuss their evening and weekend time so they achieve a mix of time together and time apart. Discussing the need for individuation will be described later in this chapter under fear of loss of control of self.

4. *What prevents the partners from being able to identify and/or express these three components openly and freely?* Often, the concepts of intimacy, commitment, and passion are grasped intellectually, but expressing them emotionally is difficult. We hear many definitions, such as, "my wife brings me tea," to "I give my partner backrubs." The partners may be unable to identify or express these features of a relationship for many reasons. One reason is that they have never experienced it. They may have been reared in a family that was cold or detached. The use of a focused genogram will help to disclose the partner's experiences in their family-of-origin. Specifically, the attachment genogram described by DeMaria and colleagues (1999) will provide the clinician with a picture of how love was expressed in the family-of-origin. The partners may feel embarrassed or incompetent about expressing some of these features because of messages they internalized about what was acceptable role behavior.

   Men typically have more difficulty expressing feelings than women because they are socialized in different ways. Men are often socialized to be strong and self-sufficient. They learn not to complain or express feelings that would make them appear vulnerable and they can feel embarrassed or incompetent if they demonstrate vulnerability. Successful professional men who run large companies or perform surgery have said they do not know how to express a feeling. An attempt to do so threatens their sense of self-worth and competence. Also, we have seen a number of women who were socialized to be sexually passive or to not show passion. Showing sexual desire is antithetical to their upbringing.

5. *Does each partner have a realistic perception of what love involves?* As the discussion unfolds about love and intimacy, the therapist will begin to gain a picture of how realistic each partner is about what constitutes a loving relationship. Some partners have unrealistic perceptions of love that can never be met thus, they will inevitably experience a sense of

disappointment and loss. There are many myths about love in our culture. Even though we may intellectually know that some ideas are fic-
tion, it can be hard to escape their impact. The idea that in a good
marriage couples never disagree or fight is a common myth. Another
prevalent idea is that the partner should automatically know what the
other is thinking or wanting and immediately supply it. Believing that
the partner should be able to read the other's mind is a pervasive belief
leading to the feelings mentioned above. When the expected behaviors
from the partner are not forthcoming, it is often believed that one is
consciously trying to hurt the other or to withhold what is wanted or
needed. This pattern becomes a simple formula for lack of desire. The
HSD partner is unconsciously thinking, "If you are going to withhold
from me, then I am not going to be turned on to you and give you sex."

6. *Does each partner have a realistic perception of what he or she can
   actually offer?* People come to therapy to change, and many do change.
   However, there are limitations to how much and whether some people
   can change. Part of therapy is also helping couples adapt or adjust to
   that which is not changeable or probably will not change. Sally and
   Mark were a classic example. They did not seek therapy until they were
   in their early 60s and all their children were living on their own. With
   the long overdue departure of the last child from the nest, they were
   confronted with the reality of their marriage. This couple had been married well over 30 years. Sally was ready to leave the marriage if Mark
   could not make some major changes. Her complaint was that he was
   cold, unfeeling, unemotional, and distant. He had spent his career as a
   professional engineer—a business that does not value emotion. Sally had
   reared four girls and was accustomed to getting her emotional needs met
   through them. Once all of her daughters were adults and had moved
   some distance from the couple, Sally was forced to see the marriage as
   it had always been. She had not felt sexual desire for years but still
   fulfilled her conjugal duty. She wanted the therapist to remake her husband into an emotionally expressive man and help her find sexual desire
   for her "new" partner. After some exploration of Mark's history and
   his motivation for change, it was clear he was not going to meet her
   expectations. The therapy shifted to coming to terms with what the marriage had been and what it would continue to be. The positives and
   negatives of their situation were explored. Mark did make some minor
   changes, and Sally decided that he was an honest and good man who
   was "emotionally limited." Sally did not want to examine her part of
   staying in a marriage that for over 30 years was lacking in intimacy. It
   was enough for her to know that she had issues as well and would

probably not be able to tolerate too much closeness should she move on to another relationship. They were able to find some equilibrium and stability in their relationship in spite of accepting much lower goals than Sally had set for the relationship.

Ultimately we must be prepared to help partners accept limited change and/or changeability. Some partners have no desire for desire and will not change. The other partner must decide what this fact means to them and move forward in the way that makes the most sense to them. Other partners will want to feel more passion, but, in spite of the best treatment we can provide, will not move ahead. Fortunately, these cases do not take too long to assess. Those partners who are going to stay stuck are stuck from the beginning. When the expected course of treatment is stalled after a reasonable period of time, strategies must shift from what they want to change to what can realistically be changed. While this idea may represent an acceptance of failure, we believe that accepting a lack of motivation or ability in some people is a more realistic view.

## Creating Greater Intimacy

Once the couple has defined intimacy and has agreed upon some common idea about what intimacy should be in their relationship, the discussion is taken to the next level. Now that the partners have come to a consensus about what they want, they must see if they are able to achieve it through their actions. First, each partner is asked to make a list of what they can actually do in order to demonstrate intimacy in the areas they have identified. The items on the list should be actions rather than obtuse constructs. As they make this inventory, they should keep in mind what they feel positively about giving and whether the partner will value what they offer. If one partner gives something that the receiver does not value or see as part of intimacy, it will not help to bring the couple closer. Partners are instructed to read their list daily and at the end of the day to do a self-assessment of whether they did what they intended and, if not, what stopped them. Couples usually start slowly, then build some momentum. With practice, giving behaviors that are viewed as intimate become more automatic and hopefully reinforced through a reciprocal process.

We also suggest the use of an exercise that we call the three A's. The A's refer to *affection, appreciation,* and *affirmation.* Affection is letting the other person know how much you value and like them through verbal and nonverbal statements. Physical gestures of affection without any sexual connotation are important. Responding favorably to what the other person does and appreciating them is another way of showing affection. Appreciation means taking nothing for granted and acknowledging gratefulness. Affirmation refers to declaring the relationship with statements such as, "I am glad I found you," or "I love you." These statements cannot be professed often without losing their meaning, but should be stated occasionally. We have seen marriages of long duration where a statement of love had never been made.

Waring (1981) stressed the importance of emotional and cognitive sharing as a part of intimacy. Sharing cannot take place without effective communication, and this work with couples can take many forms. For instance, the therapist models affective communication by asking questions that focus on the emotional processes occurring between the partners. Hopefully, the couple will begin to generalize from what they have learned in the sessions and use some of the same concepts at home. Since most couples are more comfortable talking at a level of *content* rather than *process*, they can be taught these distinctions and coached on *process-oriented* conversation. It is a difficult skill to acquire, as many therapists know, with practice during the session being ongoing. The key is to help the couple communicate about their relationship.

Therapists often tell couples they need to deepen their conversation without explaining how. Another tool for the clinician is the schema developed by Bernal and Barker (1979) which helps couples gauge and code their level of communication on a continuum of cognitive through affective. One level of communication is not considered better than another as they are all necessary, but if the couple never moves beyond the first level, the best they can hope to achieve is intellectual intimacy. Couples are asked to practice adding depth to their conversational interactions. The levels are described below:

1. *Objects.* This level of communication involves talking about things outside of oneself in an impersonal or detached way. It is similar to giving a newspaper account of something that has happened. It is a factual recounting of some event.

2. *Individual.* This term almost seems to be a misnomer. Each partner talks about his or her behavior in terms of how it was "caused" by someone else. Self-responsibility is not present at this level.

3. *Transactional.* At this level, process or affective discussion is present. Partners are able to comment on their behavior and that of their partner. They can step back and observe themselves engaging in a transaction. Moreover, the interlocking and reciprocal nature of the relationship is comprehended, for example, "you were withdrawn, I became resentful, and the more resentful I became, the more you withdrew, and somewhere along the way I stopped feeling desire for you."

4. *Relational.* Couples who can talk at this level have a deeper understanding of their underlying assumptions and the emotional contract or set of operating principles in their relationship. They can talk about patterns in their alliance and have explanations for why things work the way they do, for example "I was reared to think that sex was bad and it was the man's responsibility."

5. *Contextual.* This level of communication adds the historical context to the former level. The partners can connect their current behavior to past behavioral experiences in their family-of-origin, other early relationships, and the context of the current relationship. For example, "Early on in this marriage, you made it clear you did not ever want to be bothered by sex; that is the reason I never initiate."

The partners are asked to set aside some time each week for talking about family business matters and their relationship, and for light, playful, affectional, and bonding interchanges. Communication must be made a priority and the only way to demonstrate that it is a priority is to practice effective communication. It also helps if couples adopt three assumptions about their communication:

1. It must be viewed as a commitment.
2. They should assume good will or good intent.
3. Understanding is a goal.

By the time many couples enter therapy, they are ascribing malicious intentions to almost everything the partner says. To reverse this negative spiral, they start with the default assumption that the intent was good even though the effect may have been less than good. Most couples have also lost their sense of efficacy. They feel they can no longer communicate and that if they communicate, they will end up nowhere. Their unconscious motto has become "Why start if you cannot finish or have a good finish." Communication is a struggle; it takes time to achieve understanding. Couples will frequently give up before they begin. Once they realize that they must start and stay committed to the process of eventually working through a problem or coming to an agreement, they can stay engaged in the struggle.

Couples may need to be taught other communication skills such as making *I statements*, using *reflective listening, validating each other*, learning to *edit* what they say. They can also be instructed about some of the common obstacles to communication such as mind reading, personalization, using polarizing language and distracting, for example (Weeks & Treat, 2001). The empirically based work of John Gottman (1994) on couples and communication is helpful in building intimacy. He has demonstrated that in working marriages there is at least a 5 to 1 ratio of positive to negative exchanges. Thus, it is important for couples to work on creating the positive behavioral exchanges described above. He also found that four types of communication were highly predictive of divorce and marital dissatisfaction: stonewalling, criticism, contempt, and defensiveness. The therapist can assess the couple for these patterns in the session, teach the couple about these destructive communication styles, and help them master the communication skills necessary to solve problems and share intellectually and emotionally.

## Working with Underlying Fears of Intimacy

The fear of being intimate is common, as every couple must confront the dilemma of how much closeness and distance they can comfortably tolerate in their relationship. When the intimacy fears are strong, the effects often create marital or couple dysfunction such as HSD. In humans, the response to fear is biologically programmed. We either fight or we flee in an effort to regulate a comfort level in the relationship. Sometimes, this self-regulation takes the form of fighting with each other, avoiding each other, or alternating between these two behaviors. What can sometimes be confusing is that the same behavior can be used in diametrically novel ways to produce different outcomes. Thus, sometimes the purpose of fighting is to connect or get closer and at other times, it may be a way to create emotional distance.

Although many of the intimacy fears are unconscious or outside of the person's awareness, they have the same behavioral consequences as do other fears. The first step is to help the client become aware of what the fears might be and then to help resolve them. The therapist will need to support the assumption of unconscious fears of intimacy through behavioral examples such as a pattern of undermining every relationship just as it begins to solidify. Ask the client to think about his or her history (doing a genogram) and to focus attention on what might underlie the client's patterns of behavior.

COMMON INTIMACY FEARS

A few fears are so universal that it is possible to list them and suggest that the couple will want to consider these fears first. These include the fears of loss of control; anger or conflict; dependency; rejection/abandonment; feelings; and exposure. In our experience, the first two fears account for the majority of risk factors in HSD from the couple's perspective; therefore, treatment should focus on them. We will return to the first two fears after discussing the following general concepts that apply to the treatment of all of these fears.

GENERAL GUIDELINES FOR THE TREATMENT OF INTIMACY FEARS

1. Identify the fear.
2. Analyze historical data using a genogram to trace its origin and development. This analysis promotes self-understanding, helps to remove self-blame, and allows the individual to see how they internalized various messages and experiences.
3. Rework the cognitions associated with the fear. Cognitive therapy helps to neutralize the negative or fearful thoughts. Then, adaptive cognitions are substituted to help the partner approach rather than avoid fear-provoking situations.
4. Develop a behavioral plan that interrupts the avoidance pattern. Practice the behavior that is needed.
5. Discuss the partner's fearful emotions for the purposes of validation. Be careful not to agree with the client's fears because he or she believes that there must be a good reason to be fearful and to avoid the behavior (an irrational belief described by cognitive therapists as emotional reasoning). Suggest that the fear serves no purpose and moreover threatens the survival of the current intimate relationship.
6. Examine the ways in which the partners may have interlocking fears that keep them stuck in the same patterns. When one partner is identified as having intimacy fears and the other also has unrecognized fears, the partner who has escaped identification will undermine the therapy or progress made by the client who is working. Couple therapy is defined by keeping a systemic focus. The agenda is always what each person contributes to maintain the problem.

As stated earlier, the two most common fears we have targeted in couples with HSD are the fear of loss of control and the fear of anger and conflict. We will discuss these at some length.

FEAR OF LOSING CONTROL

Every relationship must deal with the issues of control, power, and self. Healthy relationships are based on mutual control and shared power, and allow for the autonomous development of self. Unhealthy relationships do not share these features. A partner who feels or thinks they will lose control, be controlled, or lose themselves will undoubtedly manifest some behavioral symptoms that serve to defend the self against a perceived threat to autonomy. The understanding of this problem can be at two different levels.

The first way this problem is manifested in relationships is by an imbalance of power and control in which one partner takes a dominant position and the other a submissive position. In the literature, this pattern has been referred to as the parent-child relationship (Sager & Hunt, 1979). It appears that one of the partners has the power to control another, but in fact, each contributes by assuming prescribed roles. Thus, the one who is being controlled must allow it to happen. Each partner gains something from this type of arrangement. Unfortunately, as the roles become more polarized over time, the parent figure begins to feel more burdened and the child figure begins to feel more helpless and ineffective.

Sex in a relationship defined in this way would be incestuous. The "powerless" partner usually exhibits the lack of sexual desire. Given the culture in which we live, this partner is frequently the woman. The powerless partner has a dilemma. How does she continue to obtain secondary gains from playing the child role, yet find some way of holding on to power and control? The fact that marriage is supposed to be based on mutual sharing of power and control increases the conflict. The symptom of HSD is one possible solution. Sexual desire is an internal state that cannot be forced, although the partner may "force" the HSD partner to have sex by using guilt or coercion, for example. Trying to tell someone how to feel is a futile endeavor. The HSD partner unconsciously chooses to feel turned off. It is a way to maintain control in one area of her life.

The treatment for this problem would follow the general guidelines outlined above. It is clear they have formed an interlocking pattern of behavior that appears one way on the surface, but is supported by a complex set of dynamics and secondary gains underneath. What is interesting about such a relationship is that *both partners* are powerless to change and confront themselves. The power is in the game that they have created (L'Abate, Weeks, & Weeks, 1977). Behavioral contracting can be used to help break some of the well-established patterns of conduct and to encourage new behaviors that would help to stabilize the power and control in the relationship (see Weeks & Treat, 2001). The partner who has given up control in certain areas could be given unqualified or unconditional decision-making power over certain aspects of the couple or family. The partner who has been taking all the control could be given control in areas that are more limited, and the partners could be taught how to negotiate solutions in other areas. Of course, they would each need to examine the secondary gains they are receiving from their patterns of behavior and what they have avoided by being so outwardly focused.

FEAR OF LOSS OF SELF

An extension of the intimacy fear is the relationship in which the loss of control goes beyond being defined in behavioral terms but is perceived as a loss of self. These clients feel that their partners want to control them—what they do, how they think, what they feel. It is a much deeper and insidious pattern of feeling engulfed, smothered, or fused to the other person. The "controlling" partner continues to define who they are—not just what they do. The HSD partner believes that eventually they will have *no* self. The one place that can be protected is the control over sexual feelings. A dynamically oriented therapist might think of this individual as having weak ego-strength. A family-oriented therapist would think in terms of lack of differentiation (L'Abate, 1976). The undifferentiated individual defines self as being the same as or opposite from others or in more extreme cases as being symbiotic with others or completely cut off from others. Differentiated individuals can think of themselves as being both similar to and different from others. The primary task in treating this couple is to help each partner become more differentiated.

Bowen (1976), a family theorist, and Fogarty, (1976), a couples theorist, wrote about the treatment of undifferentiated couples. Their theories blended dynamic and systems therapies, especially family-of-origin work, over an extended course of treatment and suggest that these couples are driven by powerful emotional forces outside their control and are not able to modulate these feelings. The therapist is seen as instrumental in modeling differentiation and in helping the couple defuse emotion and cognition. These more traditional family therapy theories can be integrated with more contemporary approaches such as cognitive therapy (Dattilio & Padesky, 1990) and new research in genograms (DeMaria et al., 1999) in helping the couple become more differentiated.

In the chapter on psychological risk factors, we mentioned a couple in which the husband was still highly enmeshed with his parents and his wife was experiencing a lack of desire because she felt she had no control or self-definition. This particular case ran a course of about 2 years and involved the integration of many of the techniques mentioned in this volume. The partners worked on differentiating from their respective families. Initially, the husband did not understand this concept and fought against it just as she fought against reconnecting with her family. The wife learned to be more assertive and take greater control as the opposite happened for the husband. We reframed the situation for the husband by suggesting that sometimes the best way to take control is to give it away. He was thinking and acting for everyone in his life. She also needed to work specifically on what she wanted for herself. She did exercises that consisted of thinking about her wants and needs, how she would undermine herself, and how she was to approach her husband. Simultaneously, he was to help her achieve what she needed by staying out of her way and listening to what she wanted rather than what he thought she should want. Most of the therapy centered on the couple issues, with the sexual issue being postponed until the couple issues were resolved. Then the sensate focus exercises produced the desired response, especially since she was already beginning to find she was feeling more desire for her husband. In fact, she once commented that because the bed was no longer so "crowded," she felt better able to express herself.

FEAR OF ANGER AND CONFLICT

The second common risk factor in the couple is the inability to deal with anger and conflict. As we pointed out in Chapter 4, the problem could be that the HSD partner is chronically overtly angry, living in fear of anger from the higher desire partner, or is experiencing "chronically suppressed anger." In the pages to follow, we will summarize a model the primary author has developed (see Weeks & Treat, 2001) for treating anger and conflict that is more comprehensive than most of the existing behaviorally oriented models available (Kassinove, 1995; L'Abate & McHenry, 1983). The paradigm is comprehensive enough to deal with alleviating both of the patterns mentioned above (fear of losing control and fear of anger) in the HSD partner and helping the couple deal with anger more effectively.

Couples that handle anger poorly tend to have one of two different attitudes. Often, both partners believe that being angry and expressing this feeling without any consideration for the other person is appropriate. Their expression of angry feelings is raw and unmodulated. The more common attitude, however, occurs when partners view anger in only negative terms. They think anger is bad, to be avoided, has only destructive consequences, and perhaps means that the relationship is flawed or defective. This attitude leads partners to suppress, repress, or to attempt to hold anger inside until they explode. An explosion of anger for some individuals is barely noticeable; it might just be a short and simple statement such as, "I really appreciate the way you take care of me," said sarcastically. For others, it might look like an uncontrolled explosion.

The first step in helping couples deal with anger is to first explore their attitudes toward it. Clients will not follow the behavioral program if they have the belief that the expression of anger will create more difficulties and hurt feelings. We believe that the couple could and should be taught behavioral techniques from the outset of treatment. In order to assess the partners' attitudes toward anger the therapist can ask a series of questions listening carefully to what they say, how they say it, and asking probing follow-up questions. These questions include:

- What is anger to you?
- What other feelings are associated with or underlie your anger?
- What does it mean when you are angry?
- What does it mean when you are angry with your partner?
- What does it mean when your partner is angry?
- What does it mean when your partner is angry with you?
- How do you respond to your partner's anger?
- How do you respond to your own anger?
- How do you let your partner know you are angry?
- How long does your anger usually last?
- How would you rate your anger on a scale from one to ten?

The first two questions in this list require considerable discussion. The first question elicits information about how the person defines anger, but the real intent of this question is to begin assessing their attitude about anger. A follow-up question could actually be about the extent to which they believe anger is a positive or a negative force in their lives. In all probability, a negative attitude will be discovered, and the therapist can then begin to work on changing this. The next question involving the feelings that underlie anger requires not only considerable discussion but also continued exploration by the clients in their day-to-day living. We ask clients to draw an "anger iceberg," with a line differentiating the above-water part from the hidden component which is under water. We then explain that when we feel anger we are almost always feeling a host of other feelings that are under the surface. Anger is just the feeling of which we are most aware.

Anger is often used as a defense against other feelings because they are more difficult for us to recognize or acceptable for us to experience. Both partners are given the assignment of noticing when they feel angry and what feelings underlie their angry feelings. Our experience has taught us that two feelings are almost always present. Those feelings are *fear* (fear of intimacy) and *hurt*. Thus, we always ask that the clients pay particular attention to whether they are also experiencing those feelings. Other feelings that may be covered over with anger are guilt, shame, depression, sadness, grief, insecurity, and low self-worth. It is important for the client to recognize that anger may simply be the mechanism to express some of these unrecognized feelings. Once the client has an awareness of the underlying feelings, he or she is encouraged to articulate those feelings to his or her partner.

In the HSD cases, individuals are not aware of the resentment or anger that underlies their words and actions. Sometimes the hostility is noticeable but usually it is latent and difficult to pinpoint. The frustrated partner usually observes that something is wrong yet feels helpless in his or her efforts to correct the problem. Moreover, the role of the lack of desire in expressing anger is rarely understood. The HSD clients can be helped to recognize what they are feeling by having their partners point out what they perceive in a nonblaming way. First, both partners must learn that anger can be expressed indirectly or covertly. The therapist can use a variety of psychoeducational strategies to achieve this objective. The following self-monitoring strategies are useful.

## Self-monitor for Passive-aggressive Behavior

The most common forms of passive-aggression are forgetting, procrastinating, or constantly claiming to misunderstand some request. Instruct about how these ways of expressing anger can be veiled, powerful, and destructive.

### SELF-MONITOR FOR SELF-RIGHTEOUSNESS

One partner often claims to know the truth or to have the high moral ground. By implication, the other partner has a weaker position or is "one down." Another variation is the need to see the other as "wrong" in order to view oneself as "right."

### SELF-MONITOR FOR SELF-VICTIMIZATION

The lower-desire partner acts as a helpless victim, sending a message such as "you are responsible for my problems and for taking care of me." Typical tasks in life are burdensome, and often there are complaints of somatic problems. HSD clients do not feel they can "fight back" because they will always lose. They will talk about the partner being smarter, more verbal, more aggressive, and so on, to prove that they are helpless in defending themselves.

SELF-MONITOR FOR AN OVERRELIANCE ON REASON AND RATIONALITY

When intellectualization replaces the expression of emotions, this may be the best disguise for anger. Emotional expression is viewed as undesirable and the person needs to have reason and rationality on their side. Sometimes it is even difficult for the therapist to see how the client uses this defense.

## Use of the Anger Genogram

The other major tool that can be used is the anger genogram developed by DeMaria, Weeks, and Hof (1999). Collecting this information from both partners will increase the awareness of how anger is experienced and expressed. Also, it provides the historical context and a view of how each partner internalizes messages about anger.

The anger genogram is a narrative consisting of nine questions:

1. How did your parents deal with anger/conflict?
2. Did you see your parents work through anger/conflict?
3. When members of your family (name each one) got angry, how did others respond?
4. What did you learn about anger from each of your parents?
5. When your parents became angry with you, how did you feel and what did you do?
6. How did members of your family respond when you got angry? For example, who listened or failed to listen to you?
7. Who was allowed/not allowed to be angry in your family?
8. What is your best/worst memory about anger in your family?
9. Was anyone ever hurt as a result of someone's anger? Who?

The first therapeutic strategy is to normalize anger and help the couple understand that it can be a positive force in their relationship by explaining that it is impossible to be in a close relationship and not feel anger from time to time. The couple could be asked to think about how anger can be a positive force, how it can bring them closer together, and how it can be used to reaffirm one's boundaries and expectations in an appropriate way. The therapist may wish to incorporate some cognitive therapy techniques by having the partners catalog their negative thoughts about anger and then, with the therapist's assistance, list counter thoughts. When clients have only had negative experiences with anger, it is difficult to convince them that it can be positive. Mainly, the therapist is trying to create a positive mindset that will at least allow them to get started. Getting started means expressing anger using the behavioral techniques we will describe later.

## Bibliotherapy

Bibliotherapy can be a useful adjunct at the beginning of therapy. The texts we usually recommend are *The Dance of Anger* (1989) by Harriet Lerner-Goldhor and *Your Perfect Right* (1995) by Alberti and Emmons. Both books place a positive connotation on expressing anger appropriately. The first book focuses more on anger and the family-of-origin and is written expressly for women, but men can find much value in it. The second book covers communication, assertiveness, and anger from a behavioral perspective. Partners can benefit from all these topics.

## Guidelines for Arguing Constructively

Arguments or fights usually take place when the partners' needs or perceptions are in conflict. The therapist can provide the couple with a set of guidelines to follow during a fight or disagreement to help them preserve the integrity of their relationship in spite of these differences. The following general guidelines are given to the couple:

1. Explore the feelings and underlying emotions first.
2. Make a clear complaint without blaming.
3. Take responsibility for your feelings.
4. Take time-outs as needed.
5. Maintain an attitude of negotiation and compromise.

When an argument occurs, the first task of the couple is to talk about their feelings or emotions. One of the most common mistakes is skipping or skimming over this task. This is a twofold task. Ask that the partners describe *the problem* and also the *feelings about the problem*. Women are much more inclined than men to want to discuss their feelings about the issue, while men are much more inclined than women to want to immediately fix or solve it. As a result of this difference, women often feel their partners are being insensitive, and men lament that women want to complain without fixing the problem. The HSD client has a tendency to avoid anger and conflict. When the feelings have not received enough attention, the couple will find that the problem-solving phase is interrupted by angry or tearful outbursts and the argument will continue in circles. The feelings need to be discussed for *as long as it takes* in order for both parties to feel

heard and validated. The couple may need to revisit the issue several times
just to deal with the emotions before moving to the next phase.

The next guideline is to offer the complaint without blaming the other
person. Blame tends to beget counterblame and so on. The partner who is
angry must first sort out what he or she is angry about, how he or she
feels, and then be calm enough to offer the complaint in a way that it can
be heard. Screaming a complaint or expressing it indirectly is likely to elicit
a nonproductive response from the partner. The accusation may be re-
hearsed before anything is said. It must be expressed in terms of an "I"
statement and *not* a "You" or "It" statement.

Taking responsibility for one's feeling is the third guideline. Using an
"I" statement permits the person who feels anger to take responsibility for
how he or she feels without placing the blame or "cause" for the feelings
onto the partner. A question that frequently emerges at this point is how
to deal with overreactions and underreactions. In either case, the emotional
response does not appear proportional to the situation. When the therapist
suspects an overreaction, the anger may be about some other behavior,
some other person, a culmination of feelings, or some unresolved historical
behavior. Furthermore, some HSD clients are chronically angry. They do
not know their anger is based on one or more of the reasons just mentioned. Helping them sort out their feelings brings the situation and feelings
into perspective. Other HSD clients are unconsciously resentful with their
partners and this is expressed through chronic avoidance. One of our male
clients with HSD was angry with his wife for not living up to his unex-
pressed expectations. He wanted his wife to be like his first love (who
rejected him) and he mentally compared the two. Whenever they fought,
he would underreact and then feel even more resentment. Clients with this
propensity must be helped to see that they are underreacting and to stop
to think about how much they feel. The therapist can also discuss how he
or she might feel in various situations brought up by this client and press
the client to amplify on his or her muted feelings of anger.

The fourth principle is to take time-outs when the emotions are so intense that being heard or understood is unlikely. Time-outs should be used
sparingly since they are a safety net allowing the partner(s) to regroup and
calm down. Effective time-outs require several rules. The first is that the
time-out be at least 20 minutes. Gottman's (1994) research showed that
most spouses need at least 20 minutes to calm down or for their physiology
to return to baseline. The person who calls the time-out is responsible for
reengagement or setting a time to resume the discussion. When we pre-
scribe a time-out, we state it in the following way: "If you think the emotions are taking over the conversation either partner may call a time-out.

You may call it if you think you or your partner is getting too upset. Simply say you want a time-out for x number of minutes and invite the partner to resume the conversation at that time. When the timeout is called, the conversation should cease immediately without another comment from either partner. We will discuss the reason and necessity for the time-out in the next session and how well you did at resuming the argument."

The therapist will need to follow up on time-outs to make sure they are being used appropriately. Make sure the couple understands the instructions and they are both willing to stop when the conversation becomes too emotionally laden. They may need to discuss what it will be like to stop midstream when they both may be feeling so emotional.

The fifth guideline is to think in terms of negotiation and compromise rather than winning or loosing an argument. If one person must win, then the other is compelled to lose; hence, both lose. A more useful attitude is that giving in somewhat on one's position will have the most positive benefit for the individual and the relationship. The idea is that in order to win, as a couple, both must be willing to give up or sacrifice something. A number of behavioral concepts related to negotiation can now be implemented.

Fighting fairly or learning to use conflict constructively requires time and practice. The couple will need time and practice to master the skills now required of them. Setting aside time to discuss issues is a foreign concept for most couple; however, it is essential to begin the process. The couple is instructed to put relatively short periods of time aside (30 to 60 minutes) to discuss matters. Some altercations have to be segmented or talked about over several sessions. (Most couples expect and want to be able to solve all problems in 5 minutes.) Creating a reasonable timeframe can be very useful. Initially, the couple will practice working on the less emotional and difficult issues in the session and at home. The therapist can ask them to divide their problems or conflicts into three areas—those that are cold, warm, and hot. Over the course of several weeks, the couple begins to tackle the issues in each of these categories. The therapist's function is to educate, provide feedback, sort out underlying issues, and help the couple master the behavioral skills.

For the new productive behaviors to be integrated, the old patterns need to be identified and kept in check. The therapist can ask about these "bad habits" requesting that each describe what the other has done to shut down the process of effective conflict resolution in the past. Each partner is asked to be self-responsible for eliminating these bad habits by offering what they will use as a positive substitute. In addition to the bad habits they are able to identify in the session, we also give them a list of *behaviors to avoid when arguing*:

- Avoid complaining; instead ask for a *reasonable change* that will resolve or reduce the complaint.
- Avoid bringing up counterdemands until the original requests have been thoroughly discussed.
- Do not assume you know what your partner thinks, feels, wants, or means. If you have any doubt about what something means, ask. If you have any doubts about your partner understanding you, ask.
- Avoid making sweeping, labeling judgments about your partner.
- Do not use contempt, stonewalling, criticism, or defensiveness.

## Steps in Conflict Resolution

The final task is to help the couple to implement the following behavioral steps for productive conflict resolution:

- The partner with the dilemma is responsible for initiating a discussion immediately. If the situation does not permit this, schedule a time that would be better.
- Describe the problem and the feelings associated with it. For example, "I am feeling angry and hurt over the way you acted last night. I tried to initiate an exercise with you and felt that you were ignoring me."
- Ask the partner to reflect back both the initial complaint and the associated feeling. This process is for clarification of the problem statement. Both partners should respect and understand the problem as the other person perceives it.
- Both partners should discuss the feelings first.
- Next, each should agree on the behaviors that accompanied the feelings.
- Then, the partner who had the issue may propose a solution or a request. The other partner may make a counterproposal, and that idea is discussed.
- Consider as many options as possible without prejudging their merits.
- Select the idea that appears most workable.
- Once you have agreed on an idea, talk about how you will implement it thoroughly.
- Return to the proposed solution periodically to see how it is working. If both parties are not satisfied, then change it.
- Working through a conflict can stir up a lot of negative emotion. Discuss how you feel at the end of each discussion and focus on what was positive. Congratulate each other and celebrate your small successes.

Paul and Nancy responded well to this treatment approach. They were in their late 20s and were married for 4 years. Paul experienced a lack of sexual desire for Nancy. She complained that they were never able to have a disagreement. She thought this was an unhealthy situation because they had little opportunity to voice their differences and resolve problems together. In an effort to avoid arguing, he would try to disregard his feelings and get busy doing something else. Ignoring these feelings caused his resentment to increase. He did not connect his lack of sexual desire with repressed anger toward Nancy.

Paul recounted that he had never seen his parents argue. He assumed that fighting must be something terrible and destructive if his parents never disagreed. Additionally, when unfair things would happen to Paul at work, he would sometimes tell Nancy and she would become angry for him. He then felt uncomfortable that she was incensed with his work colleagues. Any form of animosity would cause him to feel uncomfortable. In therapy, Paul learned to work on his attitudes and beliefs about anger and to acquire the fighting skills.

We would also like to briefly mention the treatment of two other risk factors that have been underemphasized in the sex therapy literature. The first is when one partner has been sexually traumatized and the second is the presence of clinical depression in a partner.

## Sexual Trauma

As we discussed in Chapter 5, sexual trauma can have significant effects on both desire and performance. Sexual trauma could include anything from physical abuse to the more covert intergenerational boundary violations involved in latent incest. The prevailing model for conceptualizing and treating sexual trauma involves long-term treatment combined with group support (Courtois, 1988). Much of this work involves recounting the early trauma, dealing with self-blame and guilt, dealing with deeper psychodynamic issues, and healing the wounded "inner child." Moreover, in some cases this view constrains the abused person to identify him or herself as a "victim," conveying to the partner that the capacity for sexual intimacy is conditional at best. A partner accepting this definition reinforces the belief that limitations must be accepted until the person has completed a long-term course of recovery.

In 1986, McCarthy challenged the traditional notion of treating sexual trauma by suggesting a broad-spectrum cognitive-behavioral treatment modality that is short-term and involves blending the recovery from the trauma with sex therapy. He made two important contributions. The first was that the survivors rework their cognitions in order to view sexuality in a more positive manner. This involves reworking the negative cognitions carried over from the abuse and viewing sexuality as an integral part of their personality and as a behavior that is freely chosen to enhance their life. The second element was that the therapy be conducted with *the couple*, not with the survivor alone, reformatting the couple's view of sex to become more hopeful or optimistic. To the extent that the nonabused spouse accepts the idea of the inherent "victim" limitations, he or she may be sexually avoidant, continue the pattern of secrecy and confusion, or be sexually coercive and insensitive. Additionally, McCarthy emphasizes the condition that the survivor must feel in control of the exercises and have the behavioral methods to deal with the flashbacks, fears, and anxieties.

McCarthy (1986, 1997) published two additional papers advocating a cognitive-behavioral approach to treatment. In the most recent paper cited, he described the use of the CERTS model which includes the following concepts: C = consent, E = equality, R = respect, T = trust, and S = safety (Maltz & Holman, 1987). All the prescribed and nonprescribed sexual interactions should occur with these five ideas in mind.

We have successfully treated cases involving a partner with a history of sexual trauma using the CERTS model without the need to refer the survivor for individual treatment. In these instances, we utilized as flexible a format of individual and conjoint sessions as necessary. We have also treated cases where longer-term work appeared necessary because the severe and phobic limitations of the survivor precluded the use of the conjoint format exclusively. We think that therapists should be aware of both treatment options and try to work as efficiently as possible.

## Depression

Depression is one of the psychiatric risk factors for HSD mentioned in Chapter 3. In our experience, therapists treating depressed clients tend to think of two treatment modalities, either cognitive-behavioral therapy or medication. As clinicians, most of us were trained to think of depression in individual psychological terms. Also, an impressive array of literature supports both of the two therapeutic modalities mentioned above.

Only during the past few years has depression been linked to marital discord, conflict, and dissolution (see Howard & Weeks, 1995). About 50 percent of maritally discordant couples seeking treatment have at least one depressed spouse. Researchers have not yet answered the question of how marital discord and depression are causally liked.

When marital discord and depression are present in a couple with HSD, the therapist should maintain a systemic perspective unless there is reason to do otherwise. This assumption is basic to doing systemic work. Therefore, we begin with the supposition that we need to rule out a relationship between the marital discord and depression before assuming the depression will only respond to medication or to an individually oriented approach (Jones & Asen, 2000). To clarify further, we are not suggesting that medication should not be used to help the client feel better and make the situation more workable. We utilize the interactional conceptual framework and couple-oriented treatment models developed by Howard and Weeks (1995). In many cases, the depression in one partner *masks* the depression in the other. The task of the therapist is to show that both partners are depressed even though only one partner shows symptoms. In other cases, the nondepressed partner maintains and exacerbates the depression by trying to force the depressed partner to *not be depressed*. A variety of combinations are possible as far as etiology is concerned. Once the causative connections have been dissected, work may proceed with the couple. Resolving the depression in this manner has a double-benefit for the HSD partner. They are no longer depressed and marital satisfaction is greatly enhanced.

## CONCLUSION

Treating HSD requires an integration of sex and couple therapies. Some risk factors deal primarily with the sexual relationship. Traditionally oriented sex therapy techniques may be of value in dealing with this aspect of HSD. However, many other risk factors are found in the relationship and the family-of-origin. These are best treated in the couple context. Moreover, our philosophy is that sex is an expression of intimacy within and inseparable from the couple relationship. Unless there is good reason for splitting off part of the therapeutic work, the couple is best served by solving the problems together.

# 10

## Sex Therapy with Couples: Basic Techniques

THIS CHAPTER PROVIDES A DESCRIPTION of the most common techniques we have developed in the treatment of HSD. These treatment strategies have emerged as a result of working with hundreds of individuals and couples who have struggled with sexual dysfunctions. Our approach involves designing specific strategies tailored to the needs of *the couple*. This is a departure from the formulaic therapy recommended by Masters and Johnson (1970) in their volume on sex therapy. In prior chapters, we cautioned the reader against such a simplistic or cookbook approach that is likely to produce only limited results for a finite period of time. With HSD, the etiology is usually multicausal, thus, treatment should be based on a theoretical rationale that is specific to the etiology presented by the couple.

### PSYCHOEDUCATIONAL INFORMATION AND BIBLIOTHERAPY

During the past several years, information about the topic of sexual desire and the lack of desire has become commonplace in the media. Many radio programs, a few primetime shows, daytime television talk shows, magazine articles, and books discuss the topic of HSD. Numerous remedies for sluggish or nonexistent sexual desire have been proposed for the individual.

These have included activities designed to "prime the pump" sexually speaking, such as thinking about, reading, and focusing one's interest on sexual material. A healthy diet, exercise, and even hormone replacement therapy have been suggested as "cures" for many women who lack desire. A number of magazine articles contain simple advice for the couple about how to "spice up" one's sex life. We consider these remedies to be palliative at best, because they do not offer any understanding about the nature of HSD. Many of our clients know about these strategies while others come to therapy after having read one or more textbooks on the subject including Kaplan's (1979) original text about HSD, which includes many of the reasons for lack of desire. Unfortunately, it also suggests that the treatment outcome is very poor. Some couples enter therapy with a sense of pessimism based on having read Kaplan's early book.

One of the first techniques in treating HSD is to *find out what the client(s) have learned and believe about the disorder*. Ask specifically about information that might have originated from the popular media such as television programs, magazine articles, and books. They may have acquired a good deal of information on prevailing beliefs about HSD, and it is always important to know what the clients know. In fact, having them share this kind of information is a useful way to begin to work together. Acknowledge their information without judgment and proceed to understand their beliefs about the causes of their sexual problems. We find that couples often selectively attend to certain facts and ignore others. Typically, there is a mixture of accurate information and misinformation about this problem and about sex in general.

*It is imperative that the couple is asked about their expectations of therapy and the therapist with regard to information about HSD.* Couples may enter therapy believing the therapist knows of a medication or new medical treatment that will help them due to all the publicity given these treatments lately. The medicalization of erectile dysfunction has contributed to this belief. If a man can be helped to achieve an erection with a pill, then why can't women be helped with sexual desire with a pill? This kind of presentation often reflects an unrealistic expectation that therapy will provide a simple, rapid, and magical cure for HSD. Many clients also believe that sildenafil (Viagra), the erectile dysfunction medication, will also serve as a psychological sexual stimulant. We have even heard reports from our clients that the woman was encouraged by her partner to take Viagra without a prescription. One couple reported that the wife took Viagra at the insistence of her husband and suffered from an unpleasant and frightening generalized reaction of flushing with a severe headache.

Others have read that sex therapy is a brief approach to sexual problems. *Determine what the couple expects in terms of a timeframe.* Often they think the treatment will be unrealistically shortterm. Also, ask about how they expect treatment to proceed based on their information and beliefs about sex therapy. For instance, they may have read magazine articles giving simple advice and incorrectly assumed that a single uncomplicated method is used to treat all sexual problems. Typically, couples have attempted some degree of self-treatment which has failed, exacerbating their sense of frustration and helplessness. The couple may have tried the advice offered by the popular media, yet they think that it was just the wrong advice when it fails. They might expect then that the therapist will be able to give them different, simple advice that is effective. In some cases, the client may have tried a technique that could be useful when properly implemented in the context of an overall treatment program, yet these techniques did not help the problem. Clients should be assured that the therapist understands their self-help efforts and that these strategies failed for particular reasons. Explain how the current treatment program is more likely to work.

The information acquired from popular sources usually complements the person's belief system about sexual functioning. *Inquire about what each individual believes to be true about sexual functioning in general.* Next, *ask the couple about how they view themselves sexually speaking.* Look for areas of agreement and dissention. Some of the sexual myths relevant to HSD we have encountered include:

- Women lose their sexual desire after marriage or after a few years of marriage.
- Men who lose their desire must be getting sex elsewhere.
- Men with low desire are really gay.
- Everyone is more turned on than me (us).
- I should be more interested than I am.
- I should be able to get turned on quicker.
- When I get turned on, I need to have sex immediately.
- Sexual desire diminishes with age.
- Men and women are on different wavelengths about sex.
- Desire is just something that happens.
- Sex should be a natural and spontaneous act.
- Scheduling sex is a bad idea and will kill desire.
- Sexual fantasy about someone other than my partner is wrong.
- Masturbation is wrong and can diminish desire for my partner.

- There is no place for erotic literature, films, or devices in lovemaking with my partner.
- My partner should know what I want and need.
- Talking about sexual needs will ensure that I will not get what is wanted.
- Because I am (too heavy, thin, large, small, hairy, old, etc.) I am not attractive to my partner.
- Because I am an incest survivor, I am "damaged goods."
- If my desire declines, I must not be in love with my partner.

The therapist wants to correct as much misinformation as possible about sexual desire, the lack of desire, or about sexuality in general at the beginning of therapy. *Listen carefully to what clients say about their problem.* Once they have described their particular variation of the presenting problem, attend to the clients' beliefs and ideas about the nature of their problem, what caused it, and how it affects their sexual intimacy. Then the therapist can spend a few minutes educating the clients about the fact that HSD is usually caused by multiple determinants and that the treatment requires addressing all of the risk factors.

The couple will talk about the sexual problem in ways that give the therapist many opportunities to correct misinformation and provide accurate data. The therapist should let the clients know that this education will be a part of the therapy and that correcting them is not intended as criticism. Normalizing the lack of accurate information is helpful. Most men and women have had no formal education in human sexuality, therefore, we do not expect that they understand the complexities of sexual anatomy and physiology. In fact, men have often learned about sex from pornographic material and other men. Women usually learn about sex from their female peers and from the popular media. If the couple knows they are not alone in believing many sexual myths, they will be less likely to feel they are being criticized or corrected. The power of this intervention cannot be underestimated. Some clients have been carrying sexual ideas that have engendered tremendous anxiety or guilt over the years. They feel unburdened by being able to express these notions and by being told these are typical ideas even if they have no basis in fact.

The revision of some misconceptions may take time and repeated discussions, whereas others seem to evaporate the moment the conversation is over. Some beliefs will not be revealed until they are uncovered by an experience reported in the therapy or through a discussion with the therapist. The processes of dispelling inaccurate information and correcting cognitive distortions continue throughout the duration of therapy. Recommending books such as *The New Male Sexuality* by Zilbergeld (1992) reinforces the therapeutic task of providing accurate information in an interesting and nonthreatening format.

Thus, bibliotherapy is often important at the beginning of therapy. During the past 20 years, many excellent texts have been written for the layperson on sexual problems, sexuality, and relationships. We cannot mention all the superb books that are now available, but we list a few of the better texts below. These cover some of the basic areas about which couples are ill informed and need the most help in understanding. Some of these manuals were written primarily for women, others for men. We suggest that each partner read the book in order to gain a better understanding of the other gender. Moreover, we instruct each partner to underscore significant passages and share these with the other. Some partners use a different color highlighter to distinguish one from the other. Always recommend a finite amount of material to be covered between sessions and be sure to review what the clients will be discussing.

In 1990, Knopf and Seiler wrote a lay text called *I.S.D: Inhibited Sexual Desire*. This was a well-written, factual book about the lack of sexual desire. We used this book for a number of years, and clients had a positive reaction to it. A few years ago, the book went out of print and it has not been reprinted. We still suggest that clients try to find a copy in their local or university library. We found that with the I.S.D. book, clients were able to see themselves, particularly in the chapters on the causes of lack of desire. This insight helped them move through the diagnostic phase of treatment faster. The same should prove to be true with the chapter on etiology in this volume.

Couples can also benefit from obtaining general information about sexuality. We suggest three books at this point. The first book to obtain is a copy of any undergraduate level textbook on human sexuality. A few of these are available in some of the better bookstores and through the Internet. The therapist may have a favorite or be familiar with what is available at the local university bookstore and use that title. These texts tend to be long and comprehensive. We have several copies in our libraries and often lend them to clients. We ask the couple to read the chapters out of sequence starting with sexual behavior, anatomy and physiology, sex and aging, and sexual development. Other chapters may also be selected. One of the most readable human sexuality texts is by Crooks and Baur entitled *Our Sexuality* (1999).

Two other books are simpler to read and a bit less difficult. The first half of Heiman and LoPiccolo's *Becoming Orgasmic* (1988) is about female sexuality in general. We tell the couple to postpone reading the second half until they are ready. We mentioned earlier Bernie Zilbergeld's (1992) very popular book on male sexuality. The first half deals with commonly held sexual myths and suggestions about how to understand and communicate with women. The second half of the book describes a number of sexual problems and the process of aging. There is much in this book for both genders.

We often recommend other books dealing with broader areas of sexual intimacy. Of course, the timing of the recommendation is critical. It is also prudent to pace the bibliotherapy in order to ensure that the material is discussed by the couple and then understood. The following are a few of our favorites:

- Barbach, L. (1982). *For each other: Sharing sexual intimacy*. New York: Doubleday. We often recommend this book to couples that wish to enrich their sexual intimacy. It is extremely sensitive and accurate.
- Comfort, A. (1994). *The new joy of sex*. New York: Crown. This is a technique-oriented text, which can be helpful in providing new ideas about lovemaking and eroticism.
- Friday, N. (1998d). *My secret garden: Women's sexual fantasies*. New York: Pocket Books.
- Friday, N. (1998c). *Men in love*. New York: Dell. The two books by Nancy Friday deal with the topic of sexual fantasy in women and men. They are phenomenological treatments of the variety, range, and normalization of sexual fantasies.

The therapist will need to assess the couple's potential for being able to read any material. Some couples or partners just do not like to read or refuse to read anything that is of the self-help variety. In those cases, we use the technique described above in order to educate throughout the therapy and do not press the couple to comply with the recommended readings. For those couples that will read, we give small assignments suggesting that they spend at least 30 minutes during the week discussing what they have read. This assignment helps them to start discussing sexual matters. When the couple comes to the session, the therapist begins by asking what they have read and which ideas were most pertinent or interesting to them. In general, clients are trying to relate themselves to what they read and are likely to tell you about ideas that are similar to or discrepant from theirs. The reading and discussions take a lot of extra time between therapy sessions. Praise the couples for this effort and be sure to point out how much they are learning from the process. Couples may not connect what they are reading to their problem nor are they likely to praise each other for their commitment to the therapeutic process. Suggest to the couple that you will be asking them to talk about their own sexuality and needs in a few sessions. The reading and discussions are one way to ease them into being ready to talk about more personal issues and to help reduce the anxiety they feel when talking about sex.

## Using Sexual Fantasies

One of the identifying characteristics of HSD is the absence of sexual fantasies. We discussed in Chapter 2 that this clinical observation has been noted in the research literature. For example, an investigation by Nutter and Condron (1983) confirmed that clients with HSD have fewer fantasies than individuals without HSD. Loren and Weeks (1986) found that most college students had sexual fantasies, the fantasies were highly varied, and the most common reason for having a sexual fantasy was to get "turned on" or to get more turned on. Partners use fantasies prior to sex in order to become aroused and during sex to become more aroused. Weeks (1987) suggested using sexual fantasies to increase desire, rehearse a particular behavior, and create a more positive sexual self-image.

It may be safe to argue that those men and women who have no or little fantasies can benefit from developing and expanding the use of fantasy to increase sexual desire. However, the overuse of fantasies and/or the use of fantasy material to depersonalize sex may be detrimental to linking sex, love, and intimacy. Nutter and Condron (1983) found that some males used fantasies in a way that would depersonalize sex with the partner. As an example, we recall one of our cases involving a man who primarily aroused to women who were tall with blond hair. Initially, we had him masturbate and look at pictures of women who fit his ideal body type. Gradually we had him move to other pictures with women of different body types. Finally, the process was repeated using sexual fantasies alone while masturbating and then during sex with his wife.

There are several different techniques that can be used to help clients develop and use fantasies. Developing sexual fantasies is actually easier than getting clients to use them. Some clients have never had sexual fantasies and think that to have a fantasy involving anyone other than their partner would be a form of sexual betrayal, or a sin. Time will need to be spent discussing fantasies and why they are normal. Sexual fantasies tend to fall into two broad categories, planned and spontaneous. There are those that are like little movies in one's head in the sense that they are conjured up, have some theme, and go on for a few seconds to minutes. Conversely, there are fantasies that are fleeting and just seem to appear. Masters and Johnson (1979) made this distinction. Our goal is to help clients develop the longer-term fantasies. The therapist will need to discern how the client feels about having sexual fantasies. If the attitude about fantasies is nega-tive, then some work will need to be done to help bring about an attitudinal change. Permission giving is a powerful tool in helping clients have or use fantasies, particularly when the fantasy material is inconsistent with the person's religious belief system. The client who attributes power, control, and authority to the therapist simply needs to hear that having fantasies is normal and useful to building desire. Each of the client's concerns should be dealt with respectfully as far as altering their belief system.

In order to understand what clients believe about sexual fantasies, have them discuss their definition of the term, fantasy. Often, there are onerous connotations associated with the notion. Once all parties agree about what constitutes a sexual fantasy, proceed with psychoeducation. The following points should be covered at the start.

## Psychoeducation

### SEXUAL FANTASIES ARE NORMAL

It is normal to have or not have sexual fantasies. However, people who have fantasies are more likely to feel desire and to be able to use fantasies to create desire. The most common function of sexual fantasies is to build or enhance desire.

People report a wide range of sexual fantasies ranging from the mundane to the most exotic that one could imagine, including bondage and rape fanta-sies. It is common to have a fantasy that a person would *never* want to act out or act on. The fact that the fantasy will never happen can make it even more pleasurable. Sometimes fantasies can be personally distressing. Typi-cally, this is because of the individual's *judgments* about the content rather than the actual scene or image. They deem themselves to be perverted, sick, or gay if the fantasy contradicts their value system. Interestingly, Masters and Johnson (1979) found that homosexual images were common among heterosexuals and did not usually mean they were homosexual. The converse was also true. Homosexual individuals sometimes had heterosexual imagery, but that did not mean they were heterosexual.

### SEXUAL FANTASIES ARE HIGHLY VARIED

Younger, less sexually experienced individuals have a wide range of fanta-sies and may fantasize about their newly established partner (Loren & Weeks, 1986). As individuals become more sexually experienced, they are much less likely to think about their permanent partner. Masters and John-son (1979) found that the most common sexual fantasy of both men and women was to fantasize about a "replacement" partner.

A FANTASY IS JUST A FANTASY

Sometimes people worry that if they begin to fantasize about something it must mean they want to act on it. When the sexual fantasy is something the person would not want to act out, it is highly unlikely they would act it out. One female client reported that she consciously stopped her sexual fantasies that pertained to a former lover because she felt they were wrong. Stopping the fantasies also halted her arousal and she sometimes found herself disinterested in continuing sex with her husband because she had turned herself off. She recognized in therapy that one can fantasize or think about almost anything without being compelled to act on it. Fantasy and behavior are not synonymous.

A SEXUAL FANTASY DURING SEX IS NOT AN ACT OF BETRAYAL

Many subjects in our study (Loren & Weeks, 1986) and our clients have reported having a sexual fantasy while having sex with their partner. The occurrence of a fantasy does not represent dissatisfaction with the partner or betrayal. It is a way to enhance arousal because it introduces novelty into the situation. Couples who fall into the pattern of having sex the same way every time suffer from sexual boredom and can use fantasy as a way to compensate for the lack of variety. Often we hear that partners feel they are being disloyal if they have fleeting fantasies about another person during sex. We try to explore the genesis of this belief and reinforce that sexual desire is a stimulating experience, that sometimes the mind is so aroused that many ideas enter the awareness at once, and that this is a good thing. Interrupting the spontaneous flow of sexual fantasies can diminish desire and arousal.

Our experience has been that talking to couples about sexual fantasies is one of the most personal experiences one can have in therapy. It is actually much easier for partners to talk about all kinds of sexual behaviors than it is to talk about their sexual fantasies. Discussion of sexual fantasies often triggers guilt, shame, embarrassment, and anxiety over what the partner will think of them.

We ease into the whole discussion of fantasies using several questions:

- Do you have sexual fantasies? When? How often?
- How do you feel about having these fantasies?
- Do you think all your fantasies are normal?
- Do some of your fantasies make you feel uneasy or distressed?
- Do you use fantasies to build your desire?
- Do you ever share your fantasies with your partner?
- Are there fantasies you would not want to share?

Note that we never ask about the specific content of the fantasies at this point. At a later time, we might ask whether it is acceptable to discuss specific fantasies, but in general, the therapist does not need to hear the content unless it is distressing to the client.

When the therapist begins to educate and discuss the use of fantasy in the session, one of the natural questions flowing from this discussion is whether the partners should share their fantasies. We think this is a matter for the couple to decide. We remain neutral about this issue, but structure a conversation so the couple can decide. We ask them to think about the advantages and disadvantages of sharing their fantasies and whether they would want to selectively share their fantasies. We might suggest that fantasy is one form of *mental preparation* we use to try to decide what we might like to actually try. If a person keeps coming back to the same fantasy, they might want to share it with their partner as something that they would like to partially or fully enact. Some couples will choose to share everything, some to share selectively, and some will keep the fantasy life to themselves. It is extremely important to reemphasize the harmlessness of the replacement of established partner fantasy and how the partner would feel if they were to hear this fantasy. In general, the more ego-strength each partner has and the more secure the couple is in their relationship, the easier it is for them to risk sharing fantasy life.

There are three techniques we commonly use to help couples develop their sexual fantasy life: permission giving, mental priming, and guided fantasy.

1. *Permission Giving*. The first is the simplest and involves just giving the partners permission to be creative in developing whatever fantasy works best for them. They are asked to put some time aside just to work on developing a fantasy that is a turn-on. They can think about it or try writing it down. We want them to develop two or three favorite fantasies that they can use to increase their level of arousal. These fantasies do not necessarily need to be shared. We want the partners to become used to the idea that they can create their own enjoyable fantasies and that fantasies do not always happen spontaneously.

2. *Mental Priming*. The second technique is used with those individuals who say they do not know where to begin. They may have never had a sexual fantasy and cannot imagine having one. They require some mental priming by reading the fantasies of others. Fortunately, Nancy Friday has published a series of books on sexual fantasies reported by men and women. They help to normalize the fact that people have varied and "outrageous" fantasies and provide some content for developing a sexual fantasy. We suggest that the client skim the book to find the fantasies they like and forget about the rest. We do not want clients to spend time thinking about fantasies that are a turn-off. Her books are compilations of sex-

ual fantasies and include *Forbidden Flowers* (1998a), *Women on Top* (1998b), *Men in Love* (1998c), and *My Secret Garden* (1998d). The first two books are the tamest, the third book is about men's fantasies, and the last book contains some of the more unusual and aggressive female fantasies. Men often report to us that they find the women's books more of a turn-on than the book about men's fantasies. The purpose of the books is to provide ideas for the individual who is unable to provide his or her own, but we also suggest reading a few pages a day of the stimulating fantasies in order to help build some desire. Over a course of two to three weeks, we hope the client will be able to create a fantasy they find arousing. If an individual is unable to follow this process, this must be processed in therapy in order to find out what is blocking them.

3. *Guided Fantasy.* The third technique is a bit more elaborate and time consuming in session. It involves developing a guided fantasy. In other words, the therapist asks the client to listen to a verbal outline during the session, to mentally fill in the answers to the questions, and to put all the material together in one fantasy (Weeks & Gambescia, 2000). The following questions are verbalized and then a long pause follows. The client may signal when they are ready for the next question. The process continues in an uninterrupted way until the end of the questions unless the client gets stuck on some particular question. The questions and statements are:

- Think about the fact that you are feeling somewhat aroused. What does it feel like? What are you thinking?
- You want to develop a fantasy of an ideal encounter with your partner.
- Think about how you want to get this encounter started. What do you each do to create a close, sensual, erotic setting?
- What happens at the very beginning of this encounter?
- Think about who is in charge or initiates, what you want, what you give.
- Imagine the interaction building from a sense of closeness and affection to it being sensual and erotic.
- Where do you like to be touched? What are the sensations like?
- Let the experience unfold in your mind. Let one thing flow into another, each experience being more sexual.
- Imagine what you would say to your partner or how you would let him or her know what you like and how you would find out what your partner likes.
- Focus on the sexual part of the interaction, choreograph it in your mind down to every detail. Imagine that everything is flowing perfectly.

- Now imagine that things get a little off track. How would you get things back on track?
- How do you want this encounter to end and slowly wind down?
- Replay this experience in your mind again and again, changing whatever you like in order to have a satisfying experience.

The therapist can go through this exercise with the couple in the session, which usually takes 15 to 20 minutes. Each partner is asked to describe what he or she fantasized about. They then try to combine their ideal encounters into a single experience, which they try to enact. As the therapist listens to their wishes, he or she may discover that the partners do not understand basic physiology and he or she may be able to suggest things that would work better. Men, for example, will sometimes want to have their orgasm first and then expect to be able to have intercourse. Many men think that vaginal stimulation is what turns women on rather than clitoral stimulation, when the focus is to try to produce an orgasm. Many women do not know how to touch the penis to produce an erection, causing the men to feel teased and frustrated. Depending on where the couple is in the therapeutic process, part or all of the guided fantasy may be implemented. Early on in treatment, they may just try the first part of the fantasy, saving the sexual part for later. Implementing the fantasy gives them a real-life opportunity to discover what actually does and does not work for them.

## Creating a Sexual Environment

Many factors contribute to creating a sexual environment, and a number of techniques may be used to help promote these conditions. In this section, we will focus on two sets of environmental techniques that are used in the treatment of HSD. The first pertains to the individual factors and the second to relational factors.

## Individual Factors

### REALISTIC EXPECTATIONS

From time to time, it is useful to check in with the partners to determine what expectations they have of the therapist, themselves, and the relationship. They need to realistically anticipate what can be gained from therapy during any given period of time. They also require practical guidelines about what can be accomplished with their desire and with their sexual relationship. For example, partners may think they are going to suddenly feel the level of desire they felt when they first met or that they should magically feel what they think others feel. Having unrealistic expectations can sabotage the therapy. Furthermore, the sense of skepticism and pessimism discussed earlier can predispose the couple to give up prematurely if they are disappointed in their progress. The therapist must be mindful that clients' goals can be impractical, and when it appears that this is happening, these goals can be discussed and modified.

SYNTONIC SEXUALITY

Some HSD clients do not accept themselves as sexual beings. They often feel alienated from their sexual selves or they may believe they do not have a sexual self at all. It is impossible for them to accept the idea that one is entitled to feel sexual pleasure. For them, sexual desire is ego-dystonic or foreign. The issues causing individuals to become alienated from one's sexuality are often deep and beyond the awareness of the conscious mind, often having historical roots in strict, antisexual religious or family beliefs, or a family norm that stressed life's difficulties and lack of enjoyment. In other scenarios, there may have been a history of physical, emotional, or sexual abuse. Nonetheless, these individuals are left with strong feelings of guilt, embarrassment, and humiliation regarding sex and the presence of sexuality within the self. Less frequently, we have noticed that a personality disorder, such as the obsessive-compulsive personality, alienates the person from the feeling part of the self. Sexual feelings would therefore be excluded from the affective repertoire. Hypoactive sexual desire clients need to feel they own their own sexuality, are deserving of pleasurable feelings, and that sexual feelings are syntonic with their experience of themselves.

The therapist has two tasks. The first is to determine the reasons for not owning and enjoying one's sexuality and the second is to effectively treat the problem. Because there is not just one cause for this problem, the therapist may need to use several techniques, including cognitive, behavioral, and insight oriented. We have used writing exercises as a starting point. Some of the following questions may be used:

- What is sexuality?
- What does sexuality mean for you?
- In what ways are you a sexual being?
- In what ways do others think you are a sexual being?
- What do you like most about being a sexual being?

- What do you dislike most about being a sexual being?
- What would it mean to experience sexual pleasure?
- What would be good about experiencing sexual pleasure?
- What are some of the negative consequences of experiencing sexual pleasure?
- How do you feel about letting yourself feel any kind of pleasure or enjoyment?
- Which senses allow you to feel pleasure?
- Which senses do you cut off from feeling pleasure?
- What are the negative consequences of feeling pleasure/sexual pleasure?
- Was it hard for members of your family to enjoy themselves?
- Would someone in your family be upset if they knew how much pleasure you got out of life?

The therapist can develop as many questions as are needed in order to pinpoint the hypothesized difficulties in feeling sexual. The questions will generate material that will be addressed through a variety of treatment strategies. The therapist treating HSD will need to be patient and flexible.

Another technique that we employ is called the "sexual bill of rights." We introduce the idea that everyone is entitled to and has the right to have sexual feelings. This concept is foreign to some HSD clients, thus, the therapist will need to promote and support the acceptance of a sexual bill of rights. Initially, we briefly describe this assignment. Then the client is asked what they heard and how they feel about constructing their own sexual bill of rights. We expect that our HSD clients will begin with a vague sense about this task and may struggle with the concept because it is so foreign to them. We state that they will need to spend time developing it at home and during the session. This sometimes takes several weeks. We feel this assignment helps create acceptance and ownership of one's sexual feelings, an important component in the treatment of HSD.

One of our clients was reared in a family that stressed religious duty and devotion over any enjoyment of life. Developing a sexual bill of rights forced her to reexamine her religious belief system because she believed it would be disloyal to her religion to feel sexual in any way. Her first attempt to write the sexual bill of rights was ineffective. She had to work and re-work her beliefs in order to have a statement representing her own thoughts and feelings. The locus of power needed to shift from outside to inside regulation of her own beliefs and feelings. In some cases like this one, it is useful to have a clergy member provide some pastoral counseling in an effort to assist the client to accept a broader definition of religion that allows a place for sexual feelings. Obviously, the clergy person would need to be known and trusted by both the therapist and client.

## Being Responsible for Sexual Desire

The vast majority of HSD clients and their spouses think that sexual desire is just something that *happens to them*. They feel powerless with respect to owning and controlling their sexual feelings. Although this concept might be difficult for our clients to grasp initially, teaching them that they have some authority over their desire is empowering. Responsibility for sexual desire can be promoted through many of the procedures mentioned earlier in this section. We prefer to use the psychoeducational and cognitive techniques which encourage the use of sexual fantasy to "prime the psyche" into a sexual state. Each partner must take responsibility by deliberately thinking and fantasizing from time to time, especially on those days when sexual interaction is possible.

## Expressing Desire in Solo Sex

In Chapter 2, we discussed that sexual desire is manifested in both solo and dyadic sex. In cases of global HSD, there is little or no sexual appetite whether alone or with partners, thus the individual is not motivated to masturbate. Since the capacity for sexual pleasure is learned initially through masturbation, the prescription for solo sexual stimulation is often used to "prime the pump" for sexual desire. Desire and sexual pleasure are inextricably linked. If there is sexual gratification or enjoyment, there is likely to be more sexual desire. We believe that our clients should be able to give themselves sexual pleasure effectively and efficiently via masturbation. Therefore, we recommend the use of cognitive strategies in conjunction with solo masturbatory exercises in order to create a positive mindset for sexual desire. This is not always acceptable to our HSD clients as in the case of a 29-year-old woman in a 4-year committed relationship. She stated in the first session, "Don't think about recommending masturbation or vibrators. There is no way I will even consider touching myself!" Since sexual pleasure begets sexual pleasure, the sexual experiences leading to orgasm should promote the desire for more sexual activity (Arafat & Cotton, 1974; Hoon, 1983).

## CONCLUSION

The procedures described in this chapter are general and basic to the treatment of the *couple* experiencing HSD in one or both partners. Even though some of our approaches may be primarily directed toward the partner with the HSD, we try to keep a balanced perspective that involves looking for how the higher desire partner may have helped to cause or maintain the current problem. The role of psychoeducation, fantasy, and the couple's responsibility for creating an intimate environment were discussed. These techniques form the groundwork for the focused, specific, behavioral strategies to be covered in Chapter 11. The couple is now ready to address the sexual aspects of their relationship through progressive sex therapy techniques.

# 11

## Sex Therapy with Couples: Advanced Techniques

THE STRATEGIES WE WILL DESCRIBE in this chapter stress the importance of working with the couple *as a couple*, addressing the sexual part of the relationship. The techniques used for the couple often parallel those that we use with the individual partners. The underlying principles include the acceptance of sexual feelings and promoting conditions that allow for sexual intimacy between partners. We recommend creating opportunities for three kinds of intimacy: affectional, sensual, and sexual.

### CREATING AFFECTIONAL INTIMACY

Displays of affection that were so important in the earlier phases of the relationship often diminish over time. Additionally, due to the pattern of avoidance that often accompanies sexual problems, affectional ties can often be broken. Each partner can take responsibility to show more affection in all situations. This will promote good will and reinforce the positive quality of the relationship. We therefore suggest showing affection at least three times a day in some physical or verbal way. It is important, however, not to confuse displays of affection with being sexual. In some cases affection leads to sex, but always linking the two can exacerbate the problem of avoidance and HSD.

196

Many of the couples we treat operate with the myth of naturalism. Sex should be a natural act that just happens. Our lives are too busy and filled with activities for this idea to work. Instead, we recommend that partners *create* opportunities to be sensual with each other. An opportunity requires that they set time aside to be together in a sensual way. If either person is not in the mood, they could suggest doing something else that is enjoyable and will help them feel connected. Being sensual takes time and planning. It could involve many forms such as a brief backrub or holding and caressing in bed just prior to falling asleep. Creating an opportunity helps to promote positive anticipation about that time they will share in a pleasing way. Sensuality and sexuality are not synonymous, but they often overlap and one can lead to the other.

Anyone who has ever dated has thought at some point about how they were going to seduce their partner. After marriage, the idea of seduction seems foreign and forgotten. An insession exercise for the couple is to talk about how, when, and where they would like to be seduced. We encourage them to include as many details as possible and to describe the setting as they would depict a scene in a movie. Many of our female clients complain that their partners usually select a time or setting based on their own needs rather than considering what is known to be relaxing for their partner. We invite discussion about gender differences or partner differences regarding readiness for sexual intimacy. Also, we encourage an understanding of the difference between *seducing* and *making demands* of each other. The partners can then discuss what they would like and the therapist can help them agree on what we call a "seduction ritual" with some variations, and other key elements.

McGuirl and Wiederman (2000) conducted a study of the characteristics of an ideal sexual partner. They found that ten factors were important:

1. openness to discussing sex
2. being uninhibited
3. physical attractiveness
4. being knowledgeable
5. receiving compliments during sex
6. clear communication of desires
7. being easily aroused
8. the ability to experience orgasm
9. the ability to enjoy erotic videos, books, and magazines
10. being able to take a dominant role during sex

All of these factors can be part of the discussion of what it means to help create a state of desire because they reduce negative viewpoints about the partner and increase positive perceptions. The McGuirl and Wiederman research data are consistent with our clinical observations about factors necessary to build and maintain sexual desire over the duration of a long relationship. There were some gender differences in the study. Men placed more value on physical attractiveness, being able to experience an orgasm easily, and liking erotic media. Women placed more value on being able to discuss sex, receiving compliments during sex, and having the man take the dominant role.

## Sensate Focus Exercises

In treating HSD, the therapist begins with psychoeducation, bibliotherapy, and cognitive therapy and then incorporates other approaches such as physical assignments and couples therapy. The physical assignments consist of a series of sensual massage exercises performed by the couple in the privacy of their home. The general principle underlying the physical tasks is to create an environment that is *safe, nondemanding*, and *free from anxiety*. It is safe in the sense that the couple is asked to do *only* what the therapist says. The exercises are incremental in nature. Couples take small steps in order to experience success rather than failure. Each small step *desensitizes* the couple to sexual anxiety. The graduated increments must be so tiny that each exercise is experienced as a success, not a failure. The exercises do not demand any particular performance. For men and women with HSD, the emphasis is on feeling pleasurable sensations rather than sexual desire. If there is no demand for sexual desire, then there can be no anxiety over not experiencing it. If desire happens, that is permissible. It is also acceptable if the exercises yield no desire. This *nondemand* approach helps to eliminate the *response anxiety* accompanying HSD.

The physical homework is called *sensate focus*, a term first coined by Masters and Johnson (1970) and later used by Kaplan (1979) who called the homework *pleasuring* exercises. Sensate focus exercises have two primary purposes in treating HSD. They enable the couple to connect physically with the hope of producing 1) pleasant sensations, and 2) positive cognitions. Moreover, the cycle of avoidance, which often accompanies sexual dysfunctions, is interrupted. Additionally, the act of being physically close and doing something sensual gives the partners and therapist many opportunities to identify the hidden negative cognitions about physical intimacy that may arise and to correct them.

The following few pages will review how we conceptualize and implement these exercises.

## Purposes of Sensate Focus Exercises

Most descriptions of sensate focus exercises have overlooked the complexity and multiple purposes of exercises that appear to be so simple. The therapist who understands these purposes can help the couple understand what they are doing and why. This improves compliance, combats pessimism, and creates a positive expectancy. The couple expects to see many changes in their relationship as a result of carrying out the assignment. Without this set of expectations, they may focus on just one aspect of the assignment, failing to link this assignment with the risk factors they have thus far uncovered. The sensate focus exercises can serve nine different purposes.

1. *To help the partners become more aware of their own sensations.* Men and women with HSD become so highly focused on their lack of sexual desire or response anxiety that they are removed from their partners. They worry so much about their relationship that they begin to lose touch with the pleasurable sensations of physical intimacy. In fact, as the HSD progresses, most couples become more and more cut off from the sensations that partners normally crave. Physical sensations become suppressed to the point of not having them at all. The partners are simply told to focus on what they feel in the moment and not worry about anything else. One male partner commented about how pleasurable it was for him to feel his wife's skin on his fingertips while giving a back massage. He focused on the tactile sensations that accompanied the giving role.

2. *To help the partners become more in touch with their own needs for pleasure and worry less about the other partner's.* The individual with the HSD usually feels they are letting the partner down, disappointing them, and not living up to their conjugal duties. They worry about how the other feels and whether he or she will become angry, resentful, and possibly leave them. They therefore become so other-focused that the ability to feel and express their *own* physical needs is lost. In most cases we have treated, the goal of much of their sexual activity was to please the partner, not the self. Moreover, the HSD partner often fears that if they ask to be held, they must in turn give sex, thus they avoid asking to be held. The HSD partner must realize that they still have the need to feel pleasure and the need to be touched. They then learn how to ask for that need without feeling guilty or feeling that they will not be able to reciprocate in the way the partner would like.

3. *To communicate sensual and sexual needs, wishes, and desires.* Once there is some awareness of the sensual and sexual needs, wishes, and

desires, the next step is to verbalize them. Most couples we have treated are too inhibited in their sexual communication to ask for what they would like. As simple as an exercise appears to be, couples have great difficulty expressing or verbalizing what they actually want. This difficulty means the exercises must start at a level where each partner can verbalize what they want. Two basic instructions are given to the couple. They are told to *notice* what they are feeling on a moment-to-moment basis and to *verbalize* what they need in order to keep the feelings pleasurable. Couples will need a significant amount of encouragement, praise, and patience in getting started.

4. *To facilitate an awareness of each other's sensual and sexual needs.* The third purpose is an extension of the first two points described above. Often, individuals with HSD do not know what they desire and therefore cannot express their sexual needs. Also, they are afraid to ask for too much, fearing that they will be viewed as selfish or self-centered. Their partners never know what the other wants and feel burdened because they are trying to read the other person's mind all the time. In addition, the partners often feel a sense of rejection or alienation in the sexual setting. Over time they can become so angry, resentful, or feel so rejected that they do not want to fulfill the needs expressed.

   Gaining more awareness and learning to appreciate the sensual and sexual aspects of being together is one component of sensate focus. Partners are given permission to think about and ask for what they want and to explore what the other person would like. Each is asked to verbalize their sensual and sexual needs to the other. This interactional process heightens sensitivity to self and to the other's needs.

5. *To expand the repertoire of intimate, sensual, and sexual behaviors.* Couples with HSD either have no sex by the time they enter treatment or have sex infrequently. When they do have sex, they both know it is out of obligation and the goal is to get it over with as quickly as possible. They fall into a pattern of having perfunctory sex that allows the act to be done quickly. In addition to the HSD, both partners are usually suffering from sexual boredom. Sexual boredom is also an inhibitor of sexual desire. During the sensate focus exercises, the couple is encouraged to be experimental, creative, and to try new things. The therapist might say, "Try as many things as you can think of to give yourself and your partner pleasure. Be creative. Think about what you would like, tell your partner, and listen carefully to what your partner tells you." In the next session, encourage the couple to discuss the new behaviors they have attempted.

6. *To learn to appreciate foreplay, or nongoal-oriented sex, more fully.* This purpose is similar to the last. For the partner with HSD, the goal of any sensual or sexual activity is to *feel* sexual desire more easily and intensely than in the past. Prior to therapy, these couples often develop a routine that eliminates foreplay for the HSD partner. After all, if one partner lacks desire and the goal of sex is to get the act over as quickly as possible, then there is no purpose for foreplay. Unfortunately, the HSD partner learns to focus on the partner's orgasm in order to *act* interested in the sexual experience. Some of the HSD partners we have treated have admitted that they "go through all the motions" *as if* they were enjoying sex for the sake of their partner.

   We recommend that the couples discuss and plan what they would like to include in foreplay. Since intercourse is proscribed, the couple can appreciate foreplay as an *end* in itself rather than as a means to an end. This directive creates a nondemand condition that promotes an unhurried, relaxed, sensual experience. One couple described how they enjoyed varying the kinds of touch they included in the homework assignments. They especially enjoyed touching each other's face, hands, and feet—activities they had avoided for years prior to therapy.

7. *To create positive relational experiences.* The sensate focus exercises are intended to create positive physical and sensual experience. In order for this to happen, the couple must work together, make their relationship a priority, want to solve this problem together, and reinforce each other for being self-responsible. The partners are also told to discuss what was good about each experience. Whenever possible, they should compliment each other on any aspect of the exercise. The therapist wants the couple to generate as many positive interactions out of this assignment as possible. Gottman (1994) has empirically shown that couples that have happy, stable relationships are those who experience the most positive interactions. These positive interactions give the couple the sense that they are moving in the right direction, competence about what they have done, and a good feeling about the relationship in general. One couple described how they took the day to investigate massage oils in a quaint shopping village, a 1-hour drive from their home. They had a delightful day of browsing, dining, and discovering how much they enjoyed each other's company.

8. *To decrease physical avoidance and enhance sexual desire.* Couples with HSD begin to avoid any physical or sexual contact over time. The exercises allow them to slowly reconnect in ways that are mutual and mutually satisfying. The combination of techniques being used should begin

to increase the desire. Desire is difficult to measure as an abstraction. We look at two indices; the couple's reaction to previous exercises and their motivation to repeat the experience with future exercises. When the HSD partner feels they want to initiate some of the exercises and they talk about feeling turned on during the exercises, they know the therapy is helping them solve the desire problem.

9. *To enhance the sense of cohesion, love, caring, commitment, coopera-
tion, and intimacy between partners.* The sensate focus exercises will either create successes for the couple or generate useful diagnostic information. In order for the exercises to occur and to continue, the couple must be committed to working together at a variety of levels. While they may have entered therapy thinking that just one person had a problem, they begin to appreciate how the problem has impacted their relationship and how their relationship may have contributed to the problem. The therapeutic process opens up to the couple far more exploration than they had anticipated. A problem once defined as an individual one has been redefined as one in the couple. Working together as a couple, with each partner taking responsibility for their part, is a powerful message for them regarding the strength of their relationship. As the therapy unfolds, issues of intimacy are often examined showing the couple how the HSD partner was manifesting a symptom of dysfunction in their ability to be intimate with one another. Working through the intimacy problems further strengthens the relationship.

The nine purposes of the sensate focus exercises reveal just how complex and powerful they may be when implemented properly. The therapist should keep these points in mind and remind the couple often about what they are gaining from these exercises. Such reminders combat pessimism and allow for positive interactions between the therapist and the couple. Thus, the therapist is modeling being positive, and the couple feels more optimistic. Moreover, the couple experiences a sense of mastery over their symptoms because they can understand some of the underlying causes, rather than feel the HSD is just happening to them.

## Structure and Implementation of Sensate Focus Exercises

In order to carry out this part of the treatment plan, the couple must be ready to do incremental homework exercises involving physical contact with each other. The degree and type of physical contact is under the control of the therapist although the couple may help in designing the exercises. Also, they must be willing to suspend attempts at intercourse until asked to do so later under prescribed conditions. The rationale for not attempting intercourse is usually self-evident to most couples. Some will ask why, and others need to be told that proscribing intercourse helps to create a nondemand environment that promotes relaxation. Most couples will greet the sensate focus exercises with relief, primarily because they will no longer have to avoid each other. Typically, the HSD partner is relieved not to have to feel desire and have intercourse. The other partner is glad that treatment has started and that they can begin to do something to get their physical needs met.

The prohibition against intercourse and going beyond the bounds of the exercise should be very clear and agreed upon by both partners. They can be asked to discuss how they feel about these prohibitions. Often we hear complaints that the couple is not where they would like to be in their treatment. Most clients would like to be finished before they start. They begin with a compelling impatience, driving them to try to force things to happen *before they are ready*. The therapist must set the pace and cannot give in to their impatience.

We begin the process by discussing the need for physical contact and the benefits as described earlier. Briefly discuss the purposes of the sensate focus exercises explaining that they are designed to reduce sexual anxiety and as such constitute a form of systematic desensitization (Wolpe, 1991). The couple needs to comprehend that gradually they will be reintroduced to physical intimacy in small, safe, graduated increments. Sensate focus exercises are sensual in the beginning and eventually become sexual, but *only* when the couple is ready. Many couples, particularly those with HSD, are not ready for the level of physical contact demanded by the first sensate focus exercise described by Kaplan (1979) and Masters and Johnson (1970). The therapist must structure the exercises to fit the couple rather than try to fit the couple to the exercises. This approach is quite different from the therapist arbitrarily assigning homework for the couple to do. The therapist provides the general structure and facilitates feedback loops, letting the couple take charge of what they choose to do behaviorally. We approach the exercises from a more systematic and contextual perspective. The context is the couple's *readiness* to begin a physical touching exercise. The feedback from each exercise helps us design the next exercise.

For instance, we begin by asking the couple to describe some touching exercise they can do at home that will be mutually enjoyable. To help them get started, suggestions can be made about hand massages, foot massages, scalp and facial massages, and over the clothing touching such as a back-rub, pointing out that these are to be sensual and loving and *not* therapeutic massages that one would seek from a professional. Alice and Marty, for example, had been sexually avoidant for years. They had learned to show each other little physical affection. They were asked where they thought they could begin the process. Alice, the client with the HSD, stated she thought a hand massage in the living room using lotion would be nice and a safe place for her to begin. Marty agreed that it would be a safe place to start. He was afraid that any place they started might scare her away from therapy. He had wanted to get help for years, but she had refused. Now that they were ready, she needed some time to discuss her fears and he needed some time to talk about his frustration, resentment, and the loss of the sexual relationship. They were encouraged to talk about how they would feel about this exercise and what they anticipated next. Some couples can predict what they would like to try the next two or three weeks. Their predictions help them begin to formulate a part of their treatment plan.

Tell the couple that any distractions such as telephones, beepers, cell phones, and televisions are to be eliminated during the homework exercises. Have the couple agree on a specific time that is sufficient and unhurried, yet not too long. Have the couple recognize that time together in a relaxed manner is the priority. Discuss a setting that is private and relaxing. We usually recommend a location outside of the bedroom, if possible. The couple is instructed to create an environment that appeals to the senses. We suggest pleasant music, massage oil, scented candles, warm temperature, and the use of comforters, for example. We often discuss those objects and settings that are desirable and tasteful to each partner. The use of recreational drugs is prohibited. Sometimes couples ask if it is acceptable to drink wine, and, while we do not recommend it, a small amount can promote relaxation, if desired. Then we explain that there is a giver and a receiver for each exercise. Sometimes we flip a coin to determine who is to be the first giver, in an effort to remove anxiety about initiation. We have found it useful to have the giver also set the environment such as choosing the location and music. The couple alternates responsibility for "taking charge" of the environment. Also, the giver becomes the first receiver during the next exercise.

In the following session, the therapist asks about the homework exercises that the couple completed. We often use specific questions when inquiring about homework and these are listed below under sensate focus-I. In general, we are interested in what the couple enjoyed best and least, if the exercises went smoothly, and if there were any problems for either partner. In contemplating the next assignment, the therapist considers the hierarchy and the importance of small steps in order to ensure success. The couple is asked what they would like to do next in the way of touching. Determine if they have chosen an incremental progression that could promote closeness and reduce anxiety. At some point, the couple will be ready to do the more traditional Sensate focus exercises, which we have divided into two categories for the purpose of this discussion. Sensate focus-I consists of a series of graduated *sensual* touch exercises, which do *not* progress to genital touching. In sensate focus-II, the sensual touch exercises gradually incorporate the breasts and genitals and eventually become *sexual*.

## SENSATE FOCUS-I

The intention of the nongenital touching exercises is for the couple to experience physical and emotional intimacy through sensual touch. The sensate focus-I exercises are progressive, nonsexual, and nondemanding of sexual performance of any kind. At first, the giver chooses the type of touch, but the receiver quickly becomes an active participant directing the giver. These are generally less threatening and anxiety provoking than the sensate focus-II exercises, although both groups of exercises serve the nine purposes mentioned above. The following statement is typical of how we set up this activity:

> During the next week, your first task will be to do a touching exercise. It is not a sexual exercise, but a sensual exercise. You will need to set aside about 20 minutes (shorter for earlier exercises) for the main part of this experience. During that 20 minutes, take turns massaging each other. This is not to be a therapeutic massage, but a sensual massage. Are you both clear about how a sensual massage is different from a sexual or therapeutic massage? Each of you will have about 10 minutes. Rather than massaging each other at the same time, please take turns. By taking turns, you will be able to focus either on what you are feeling or what your partner would like to receive from you. The goal of this exercise is not to get sexually excited or feel aroused, nor is it to get turned-on sexually. If that should happen, just take note of it.

At this point, ask the partners how they would feel if one were to get turned-on or if the male gets an erection. They need permission to do nothing about these feelings or behaviors except let them be. A humorous comment, such as, "No one ever died from an erection or from feeling turned-on," might help to ease some of the tensions.

> When you are on the receiving end, allow yourself to experience as much pleasurable sensation as possible. Concentrate on what is feeling good. Think about how the experience feels good. Let your partner know what you would like to keep the feelings pleasurable.

Communicating with your partner is essential. This will give you practice in learning how to ask first for sensual things and later for sexual things. Be creative and experimental. Ask your partner to try different techniques in order to give you different sensations. Do not worry about your partner when you are on the receiving end; just focus on yourself. This sounds like an easy exercise to do, but we have found that couples need a lot of practice before everything begins to flow, especially the communication. Explain that it would be better if you did not make this into a cold and clinical exercise.

Try to get in the mood for it by thinking positive thoughts, remembering past pleasant experiences together, and saying things to each other during the day to create a positive mood.

(To the partner with the HSD) Take note of any negative thoughts or feelings that occur during the exercise. Write them down later so we can discuss them in the next session. You may have a tendency to monitor how much desire you are feeling. Just feel whatever you feel. On the other hand, you can work on changing your thoughts and the interaction. You can think about the positive thoughts we have talked about, you can push the negative thoughts aside with the counter-thoughts, and if something is not working for you, tell your partner and ask that he or she do something else. If you really get caught up in negative feelings and cannot get out of them, take a short break. Just tell your partner you are having some negative thinking and you need a couple of minutes of quiet to try to work through it. Hopefully, you will be able to complete the exercise. If you still cannot get out of the negative thoughts and feelings, tell your partner that you need to stop. Write down what you were thinking and feeling so we can talk about it here. Try the exercise three times even if the first or second time did not work. The more you try, the more feedback you can give me.

At the beginning of the session following the first assignment, the therapist asks the couple how the exercise unfolded, gaining as thorough a picture as possible in order to optimally design the next exercise and to identify continuing or new negative cognitions. The following questions are typical of what we ask in the follow-ups.

*To the couple*
- How did the exercise go? (Start with an open-ended question to see what they thought was most significant.)

- Tell me about the setting. What did you/your partner like best?
- How many times did you do the assignment? (If not three, then why not?)
- What times worked best for you?
- Was it difficult to find time?
- Who initiated the exercises?
- Did your partner have to remind you?
- What was the experience like?
- What did you like most about it?
- What did you like least about it?
- What was it like being on the giving/receiving end?
- Did you let your partner know what felt good?
- Do you think your partner let you know what felt good?
- Do you think there was enough communication?

*To the partner with HSD*
- Were you able to stay focused on just the sensual experience and not think about getting aroused?
- Were you able to stop monitoring yourself regarding your level of desire?
- What kinds of unpleasant feelings and negative thoughts did you experience?
- How did you deal with these feelings and thoughts?
- What was effective for you in dealing with these thoughts and feelings?
- How can you use these ideas the next time you have unpleasant feelings and thoughts?
- What was it like not to worry about having to feel desire when you were interacting?

The couple continues the sensate focus I activity until both are comfortably able to give each other a full-body nongenital massage. This process can take from one to several weeks, depending on the steps set up in the hierarchy and the severity of the HSD. The therapist should never push the couple or accelerate the pace because the couple is getting impatient. Go at a pace likely to produce pleasurable experiences and success. Sometimes the therapist will start the process in the wrong place or with an exercise that is too advanced. The feedback from the couple will quickly disclose this mistake. Back up a few steps then work forward. When couples move ahead of what they have been prescribed to do, perhaps they can go on to another step. They should be warned that if they move too quickly, they might have to stay where they are or take a step back. For now, the therapist can press forward because the couple will not diminish their progress unless they experience a failure. Failure may present itself in many versions such as the HSD partner feeling pressed, not wanting to do the exercise, feeling turned off about doing the exercise, and feeling anxious that they have not moved forward quickly enough. In other words, the homework fails if it has had the effect of exacerbating the symptoms of their HSD.

<h2 align="center">Sensate Focus-II</h2>

The next step in the traditional models of Masters and Johnson (1970) and Kaplan (1979) is the sensate focus-II exercises, which are similar in structure to sensate focus-I exercises. They go beyond the parameters of sensate focus-I exercises in that they involve genital stimulation. The prohibition against intercourse is still in effect. The intent of the sensate focus-II exercises is to help the client(s) reconnect with genital sensations in *an anxiety-free environment*. There should be no pressure to feel desire in the presence of genital stimulation. Hopefully, the genital stimulation will produce some physical sexual arousal accompanied by feelings of desire. *This goal is never stated*. This exercise is more difficult for the HSD client because it raises the expectation that desire should be experienced if something of a sexual nature is happening. Like the sensate focus-I exercises, this level is intended to interrupt the cycle of negative thinking associated with feeling desire. For instance, the HSD client anticipates feeling no desire, or anxiety instead of pleasure. It is the self-monitoring and negative thinking rather than performance anxiety per se that inhibits sexual functioning (Wincze & Carey, 1991).

The instructions for the sensate focus-II exercises are basically a modified version of the directions that are presented for the sensate focus-I exercises. Nevertheless, we repeat the complete instructions as given above. We usually divide the sensate focus-II exercises into three sub-steps. First, the couple is instructed to start with nonsexual touching and toward the end of the session to *gradually* move to breast and genital stimulation. This part of the experience is exploratory. The goal is to find out which body areas are most sensitive to sexual stimulation and to experiment with trying different ways of being touched.

Second, the couple is instructed to start with nonsexual touching and move *more quickly* to breast and genital stimulation. This exercise is more focused on experiencing pleasurable genital sensations. In spite of trying to maximize the pleasurable genital sensations, the HSD client is told that he or she is *not to try to force* feeling desire or sexual pleasure. Third, the couple begins nonsexually and then moves to genital stimulation. This time they are told to *let the genital sensations build* to whatever level they like. At this stage, some partners with HSD will experience an orgasm, but only if they choose to do so. We are careful to tell them that it is not necessary to feel desire to have an orgasm. They are two separate phenomena. Desire will facilitate having an orgasm, but is not necessary. An orgasm is a pleasurable activity and when it can be easily achieved may have a positive effect on lowering anxiety, thereby increasing desire.

Each of these steps is moved through in succession depending upon the success of the last step. We ask the same types of questions on follow-up as in the section on the sensate focus-I exercises. It is normal to witness erratic "performance" at the beginning of this phase. If desire is beginning to return more consistently, it may be more or less present during each exercise.

Sandie and Rick were typical of many couples given the sensate focus-II exercise. They had done the sensate focus-I without any difficulty. When they reported back after being given the assignment, they said they had not done the exercise. Sandie, the HSD client, said the week was just too hectic to get to it. Rick had suggested it several times, but she always said it was a bad time. The fact was the week was no different than any other week in their lives, hectic yet manageable. Sandie was confronted on her difficulty in finding time to do the exercise and her cancellations of the few times that were set. As soon as she was asked what happened, she replied that she did not want another fight. When asked to explain, she said she knew Rick would get turned-on and want to have sex even if he did not say anything. Sandie was assuming responsibility for *his* sexual response and assuming that if he got an erection he would later become sullen and take out his feelings on her. Thus, she anticipated a fight would occur after the exercise that would purportedly have nothing to do with the exercise. She had to learn to stop making assumptions for him and to let him be responsible for his own sexuality.

## Transitioning to Intercourse

Kaplan (1979) discussed the importance of creating a context of nondemand intercourse for clients with HSD. She used this same procedure to treat other sexual dysfunctions such as erectile dysfunction. Nondemand intercourse by definition does not require any particular types of performance, including orgasm, erection, or desire. It is actually an extension of

Masters and Johnson's (1970) idea of prohibiting intercourse and never prescribing the problem in question.

In 1988, Apfelbaum published a thought-provoking chapter on "An ego-analytic perspective on desire disorders" (Leiblum & Rosen, 1988). We have already mentioned that his primary contribution to the literature on HSD has been the concept of response anxiety. Apfelbaum readily credits Masters and Johnson (1970) with the idea that performance anxiety was a cause of much sexual difficulty and that couples must avoid goal-directed sexual activity. Apfelbaum presents an interesting review of ideas regarding sexual desire and performance. He pointed out that from the seventeenth century onward, sex was viewed as an animalistic drive that had to be tightly controlled. People were warned about having too much sex, the detrimental effects of ejaculating too much, and the need to keep desire under control. In short, individuals in that era were told they should feel anxiety over feeling too much desire and/or sexual pleasure.

In the 1920s, the sexual world of this earlier era was turned upside down. Van de Velde (1930) wrote a bestselling book on sexuality entitled *Ideal marriage: Its physiology and technique*. This book and the ones to follow emphasized sexual performance and technique. He made the claim that foreplay should be short because everyone should be aroused within 15 minutes, orgasm and ejaculation were the goals of sex, and simultaneous orgasm was a goal for which every couple should strive. During this era, married couples were supposed to be highly sexual and experts in giving and receiving sexual pleasure. The first era we described would have contributed to a *fear of feeling sexual pleasure*; the second era would have contributed to a *fear of not feeling pleasure*. The effects of this second period are still embedded in the culture. Today, sexual technique continues to be emphasized in books (Comfort, 1994), popular educational tapes such as the Better Sex series, erotica, and pornography. The underlying message of pornography is that everyone is very turned on and will act on it if given the opportunity. Interestingly, Masters and Johnson (1970) designed and described their exercises in a way that would not suggest any intensification of erotic feelings. There exercises were presented in such a way as to suggest they be done in a cold and clinical manner.

The transition to intercourse is difficult for two reasons. First, most couples view intercourse as the ultimate goal or expression of their sexuality. The implication is that if having intercourse does not turn you on, or, by the time you get to intercourse during a physical interaction, you are not turned on, then something must be wrong. This belief would only reinforce the response anxiety. The act of having intercourse must also be nondemanding in and of itself. If a person does not want to have intercourse, they should be free of the demand. Hopefully, the prior experiences of the sensate focus-I and II exercises, have taught the couple to expand their sexual repertoire allowing them to experience sex in a variety of ways. *Intercourse is just one way of having sex; it is not the ultimate goal of sex.* The second reason is that intercourse inherently carries the expectation of sexual arousal and desire. In order for a male to have intercourse, he must be physically aroused (unless he uses a drug to produce the erection). A woman does not need to be aroused to have intercourse nor does she need to feel desire. Feeling desire is a desirable and pleasurable state that facilitates the experience, but is not a necessity. However, in our experience, women tend to equate having intercourse with having the desire to have intercourse. Thus, men and women believe they should derive sexual pleasure from intercourse and should feel a consistent desire for intercourse. As Weeks and Treat (2001) pointed out, marriage not only *allows* couples to have socially sanctioned sex, but it *requires* them to want to have sex and to enjoy it.

Apfelbaum (1988) states that treating HSD must therefore involve eliminating the fear of having pleasure and the fear of not having pleasure. Also, the fear of feeling desire and the fear of not feeling desire needs to be eliminated. He claims that HSD cases are easy to treat using this method and his success rates are extremely high for those who stay in treatment (he reported about a 15% dropout rate). His theory focuses on the immediate cause (and effect) of HSD. He does not think the therapist needs to look beyond the immediate cause in order to treat the problem effectively. We believe and most other theorists believe (Leiblum & Rosen, 1988) that HSD is multicausal. His approach may work with a select group of couples, but would not be sufficient to be effective with the vast number of couples we have treated.

The transition to intercourse does not occur until the HSD client begins to feel some sexual desire. When the couple is ready to move to intercourse, the following instructions may be given:

> You have now successfully done the sensate focus-I and II exercises. Your desire for sex is beginning to return. Now it's time to see how you feel about having intercourse. Once again, create three opportunities to do something sexual. Try to see if you can use your thoughts and the other ideas we have talked about to create a desire for intercourse. If you do not feel like having intercourse, it is fine; do something else that you would feel good about doing. If you decide to have intercourse, focus on the sensations, positive thoughts, fantasies, and other techniques that have helped you rekindle your sexual desire. Do not let the response anxiety get the best of you and watch the self-monitoring. Use the techniques you have learned to avoid

getting into these turn-off patterns. The feelings of pleasure and desire before and during intercourse are highly variable; sometimes you will feel more desire, sometimes less. Do not worry about what you feel except to feel that you are doing something that brings you closer to your partner and pleases both you and your partner.

## CONCLUSION

Treating HSD involves a number of contradictions. Most clients present a lack of desire but *want to* feel desire. (As we said, some have no desire to feel desire). In order to feel desire, they must turn on their turn-on mechanism and turn off their turn-off mechanism. They cannot do this by trying to force their feelings, a strategy that most use. They cannot be forced to feel desire or force themselves to feel desire. The harder they try to feel desire, the less they are likely to feel desire. The therapist can only manipulate a number of cognitive, behavioral, and relational conditions to eliminate the immediate and underlying risk factors. As far as the feeling of sexual desire goes, the therapist takes the paradoxical stance (Weeks & L'Abate, 1982) of accepting whatever feeling position (the concept is called positioning) or state the client has as being normal and appropriate for that moment. The acceptance and normalization of these feelings is intended to reduce the fears discussed by Apfelbaum (1988). Once these fears are quelled, some desire may return in some cases and in others, it removes the most immediate surface layer of a problem that may have many contributing risk factors. This exercise is very difficult for most HSD couples. When Randy and Rhoda first attempted this exercise, Rhoda, the HSD client, found that the progress she had made earlier seemed to be lost. She had been able to keep her response anxiety in check during the sensate focus I- and II exercises. When they switched to intercourse, she found that she was overanticipating when they would have intercourse, wondering whether she could feel desire, and how much desire she would feel. She wanted to prove that she could feel desire and that she was better. The more she obsessed about her progress as measured by desire, the less she felt desire. Rhoda was a woman who constantly set high standards for herself. She did not like to fail, did not want to think that she had any psychological problems, and always needed to prove that she could do any job well. Discussing how her personality factored into her view of the exercise helped her relax and accept whatever happened without judgment. It took several attempts before she could break this habit and she knew it would be something that she would have to watch indefinitely.

# References

Adams, K. (1991). *Silently seduced: When parents make their children partners: Understanding covert incest.* Deerfield Beach, FL: Health Communications.

Alberti, R. E., & Emmons, M. L. (1995). *Your perfect right* (25th ed.). San Luis Obispo, CA: Impact.

American Psychiatric Association. (1980). *Diagnostic and statistical manual of mental disorders* (3rd ed.). Washington, DC: Author.

American Psychiatric Association. (1987). *Diagnostic and statistical manual of mental disorders* (3rd ed., revised). Washington, DC: Author.

American Psychiatric Association. (1994). *Diagnostic and statistical manual of mental disorders* (4th ed.). Washington, DC: Author.

American Psychiatric Association. (2000). *Diagnostic and statistical manual of mental disorders* (4th ed., text revision). Washington, DC: Author.

American Psychological Association. (1995). Training in and dissemination of empirically validated psychological treatments: Report and recommendations. *The Clinical Psychologist, 48,* 3–24.

Apfelbaum, B. (1988). An ego-analytic perspective on desire disorders. In S. Lieblum & R. Rosen (Eds.), *Sexual desire disorders* (pp. 75–104). New York: Guilford.

Arafat, I., & Cotton, W. (1974). Masturbation practices of males and females. *Journal of Sex Research, 10,* 293–307.

Ashton, A., Hamer, R., & Rosen, R. (1997). Serotonin reuptake inhibitor-induced sexual dysfunction and its treatment: A large-scale retrospective study of 596 psychiatric outpatients. *Journal of Sex & Marital Therapy, 23,* 165–175.

213

Ashton, A., & Rosen, R. (1998). Accommodation to serotonin reuptake inhibitor-induced sexual dysfunction. *Journal of Sex & Marital Therapy, 24,* 191–192.

Atwood, J., & Gagnon, J. (1987). Masturbatory behavior in college youth. *Journal of Sex Education and Therapy, 13,* 35–42.

Avery-Clark, C. (1986). Sexual dysfunction and disorder patterns of working wives. *Journal of Sex & Marital Therapy, 12,* 93–107.

Baggish, M., and Miklos, J. (1995) Vulvar pain syndrome: A review. *Obstetrical and Gynecological Survey, 50*(8), 618–627.

Bahr, J., & Weeks, G. (1989). Sexual functioning in a nonclinical sample of male couples. *The American Journal of Family Therapy, 17,* 110–127.

Ballard, S., & Morris, M. (1998). Sources of sexuality information for university students. *Journal of Sex Education and Therapy, 23,* 278–287.

Ballon, R. (1999). Sildenafil and sexual dysfunction associated with antidepressants. *Journal of Sex & Marital Therapy, 25*(4), 259–264.

Bancroft, J., Sanders, D., Davidson, D. W., & Warner, P. (1983). Mood, sexuality, hormones and the menstrual cycle. Sexuality and the role of androgens. *Psychosomatic Medicine, 45,* 509–516.

Barbach, L. (1982). *For each other: Sharing sexual intimacy.* New York: Doubleday.

Barlow, D. (1986). Causes of sexual dysfunction: the role of anxiety and cognitive interference. *Journal of Consulting and Clinical Psychology, 54,* 140–148.

Bartlik, B. D., & Kaplan, P. (1999). Testosterone treatment for women. *The Harvard Mental Health Letter, 16,* 4–6.

Basson, R. (1999). Androgen replacement for women. *Canadian Family Physician, 45,* 2100–2107.

Basson, R. (2000). The female sexual response: A different model. *Journal of Sex & Marital Therapy, 26,* 51–65.

Basson, R., Berman, J., Burnett, A., Derogatis, L., Ferguson, D., et al. (2001). Report of the International Consensus Development Conference on Female Sexual Dysfunction: Definitions and classifications. *Journal of Sex & Marital Therapy, 27,* 83–94.

Beck, A. T. (1976). *Cognitive therapy and the emotional disorders.* New York: International Universities Press.

Beck, J., & Bozman, A. (1995). Gender differences in sexual desire: the effects of anger and anxiety. *Archives of Sexual Behavior, 24,* 595–612.

Beck, J., Bozman, A., & Qualtrough, T. (1991). The experience of sexual desire: Psychological correlates in a college sample. *The Journal of Sex Research, 28,* 443–456.

Bennun, I., Rust, J., & Golombok, S. (1985). The effects of marital therapy on sexual satisfaction. *Scandinavian Journal of Behavior Therapy, 14,* 65–72.

Bergen, R. K. (1996). *Wife rape: Understanding the response of survivors and service providers.* Thousand Oaks, CA: Sage.

Berman, L., & Hof, L. (1987). The sexual genogram: Assessing family-of-origin factors in the treatment of sexual dysfunction. In G. R. Weeks & L. Hof (Eds.), *Integrating sex and marital therapy: A clinical guide* (pp. 37–56). New York: Brunner/Mazel.

Bernal, G., & Barker, J. (1979). Toward a metacommunication framework of couples intervention. *Family Process, 18,* 293–302.

Blumstein, P., & Schwartz, P. (1983). *American couples: Money, work, sex.* New York: William Morrow.

Bowen, M. (1976). Theory in the practice of psychotherapy. In P. J. Guerin (Ed.), *Family therapy: Theory and practice* (pp. 42–90). New York: Gardner.

Brodsky, I. G., Balagopal, P., & Nair, K. S. (1996). Effects of testosterone replacement on muscle mass and muscle protein synthesis in hypogonadal men: A clinical research center study. *Journal of Clinical Endocrinology and Metabolism, 81*(10), 3469–3475.

Buckler H. M., Robertson, W. R., & Wu, F. C. (1998). Which androgen replacement therapy for women? *Journal of Clinical Endocrinology and Metabolism, 83*(11), 3920–3924.

Burris, A. S., Banks, S. M., Carter, C. S., Davidson, J. M., & Sherins, R. J. (1992). A long-term prospective study of the physiological and behavioral effects of hormone replacement in untreated hypogonadal men. *Journal of Andrology, 13*(4), 297–304.

Byers, E., & Heinlein, L. (1989). Predicting initiations and refusals of sexual activities in married and cohabiting heterosexual couples. *Journal of Sex Research, 26*, 210–231.

Campbell, J. C., & Alford, P. (1989). The dark consequences of marital rape. *American Journal of Nursing, 89*, 946–949.

Carnes, P. (1990). Diagnostic criteria for sexual addiction . *American Journal of Preventive Psychiatry and Neurology, 2*(3).

Carnes, P. (1991). *Don't call it love.* New York: Bantam Books.

Carnes, P. (1997). *Sexual anorexia.* Center City, MN: Hazelden.

Casper, R., Remond, D. Jr., Katz, M., Schaffer, C., Davis, J., & Koslow, S. (1985). Somatic symptoms in primary affective disorder. *Archives of Genetic Psychiatry, 42*, 1098–1104.

Casson, P., Straughn, A., Umstot, E., Abraham, G., Carson, S., & Buster, J. (1996). Delivery of dehydroepiandrosterone to premenopausal women: Effects of micronization and nonoral administration. *American Journal of Obstetrics and Gynecology, 174*, 649–653.

Cohen, A. J., & Bartlik, B. (1998). Ginkgo biloba for antidepressant-induced sexual dysfunction. *Journal of Sex & Marital Therapy, 24*, 139–143.

Comfort, A. (1994). *The new joy of sex: A gourmet guide to lovemaking in the nineties.* New York: Crown Publishing.

Confrancesco, J., & Dobbs, A. S. (1996). Transdermal testosterone delivery systems. *The Endocrinologist, 6*, 207.

Cooper, A., Delmonico, D., & Burg, R. (2000). Cybersex users, abusers, and compulsives: New findings and clinical applications. *Sexual Addiction and Compulsivity, 7*(1–2), 5–30.

Courtois, C. (1988). *Healing the incest wound.* New York: Norton.

Crenshaw, T. (1985). The sexual aversion syndrome. *Journal of Sex & Marital Therapy, 11*, 285–292.

Crenshaw, T., & Goldberg, G. (1996). *Sexual pharmacology.* New York: W. W. Norton.

Crooks, R., & Baur, K. (1999). *Our sexuality* (7th Ed.). Pacific Grove, CA: Brooks/Cole.

Crowe, M., Gillan, P., & Golombok, S. (1981). Form and content in the conjoint treatment of sexual dysfunction: A controlled study. *Behaviour Research and Therapy, 19*, 47–54.

Dattillio, F., & Padeskey, C. (1990). *Cognitive therapy with couples.* Florida: Professional Resource Exchange.

Davis, G. D., & Hutchinson, C. V. (1999). Clinical management of vulvodynia. *Clinical Obstetrics and Gynecology, 42*(2), 221–233.

Davis, S. R. (1998a). The clonical use of androgens in female sexual disorders. *Journal of Sex & Marital Therapy, 24,* 153–163.

Davis, S. R. (1998b). The role of androgens and the menopause in the female sexual response. *International Journal of Impotence Research, Supplement 2,* 82–83.

Davis, S. R. (1999a). The therapeutic use of androgens in women: A commentary. *Journal of Steroid Biochemistry & Molecular Biology, 69*(1–6), 177–184.

Davis, S. R. (1999b). Androgen replacement in women: a commentary. *Journal of Clinical Endocrinology and Metabolism, 84*(6), 1886–1891.

DeAmicus, L., Goldberg, D. C., LoPiccolo, J., Friedman, J., & Davies, L. (1985). Clinical follow-up of couples treated for sexual dysfunction. *Archives of Sexual Behavior, 14,* 467–489.

DeMaria, R., Weeks, G., & Hof, L. (1999). *Focused genograms: Intergenerational assessment of individuals, couples, and families.* Philadelphia: Brunner/ Mazel.

Donahey, K., & Carroll, R. (1993). Gender differences in factors associated with hypoactive sexual desire. *Journal of Sex & Marital Therapy, 19,* 190–205.

Dove, N., & Wiederman, M. (2000). Cognitive distraction and women's sexual functioning. *Journal of Sex & Marital Therapy, 26,* 67–78.

Dunn, K .M., Croft, P., & Hackett, G. (2000). Satisfaction in the sex life of a general population sample. *Journal of Sex & Marital Therapy, 26,* 141–151.

Everard, W., & Laan, E. (2000). Drug treatments for women's sexual disorders. *The Journal of Sex Research, 37,* 195–204.

Fava, M. (2000). Management of nonresponse and intolerance: Switching strategies. *Journal of Clinical Psychiatry, 61,* 10–20.

Fava, M., Rankin, M., Alpert, J., Nierenberg, A., & Worthington, J. (1998). An open trial of oral sidenafil in antidepressant-induced sexual dysfunction. *Psychotherapy and Psychosomatics, 67*(6), 328–331.

Ferguson, J. M., Shrivastava, R. K., Stahl.S. M., Hartford, J. T., Borian, F., Ieni, J., McQuade, R. D., & Jody, J. (2001). Reemergence of sexual dysfunction in patients with major depressive disorder: Double-blind comparison of nefazodone and sertraline. *Journal of Clinical Psychiatry, 62,* 24–29.

Finkelhor, D. (1994). The international epidemiology of child sexual abuse. *Child Abuse and Neglect, 18,* 409–417.

Firestone, R. W. (1990). Voices during sex: Application of voice therapy to sexuality. *Journal of Sex & Marital Therapy, 16*(4), 258–274.

Fogarty, T. F. (1976). Marital crisis. In P. J. Guerin (Ed.), *Family Therapy: Theory and Practice* (pp. 325–334). New York: Gardner.

Frank, E., Anderson, C., & Rubinstein, D. (1978). Frequency of sexual dysfunction in "normal" couples. *The New England Journal of Medicine, 299*(3), 111–115.

Frankl, V. (1952). The pleasure principle and sexual neurosis. *International Journal of Sexology, 5.*

Fredrickson, B., & Roberts, T. (1997). Objectification theory: Toward understanding women's lived experiences and mental health risks. *Psychology of Women's Quarterly, 21,* 173–206.

Freud, S. (1962). *Three essays on the theory of female sexuality.* New York: Avon.

Friday, N. (1998a). *Forbidden flowers: More women's sexual fantasies.* New York: Pocket.

Friday, N. (1998b). *Women on top: How real life has changed women's sexual fantasies.* New York: Pocket.

Friday, N. (1998c). *Men in love.* New York: Dell.

Friday, N. (1998d). *My secret garden: Women's sexual fantasies.* New York.

Gelfand, M. M. (1999). Role of androgens in surgical menopause. *American Journal of Obstetrics and Gynecology, 180,* 325–327.

Gelman, D., Doherty, S., Murr, A., Drew, L., & Gordon, J. (1987, Oct. 26). Not tonight, dear. *Newsweek,* 64–66.

Gold, S., & Chick, D. (1988). Sexual fantasy patterns as related to sexual attitude, experience, guilt, and sex. *Journal of Sex Education and Therapy, 14,* 18–23.

Goldstein, I., Lue, T., Padma-Nathan, H., Rosen, R., Steers, W., & Wicker, P. (1998). Oral sidenafil in the treatment of erectile dysfunction. Sidenafil study group. *The New England Journal of Medicine. 338 (20),* 1397–1404.

Goodman, A. (1992). Sexual addiction: Designation and treatment. *Journal of Sex & Marital Therapy, 18*(4), 303–314.

Goodman, A. (1993). Diagnosis and treatment of sex addiction. *Journal of Sex & Marital Therapy, 19*(3).

Gottman, J. (1994). *What predicts divorce: The relationship between marital processes and marital outcomes.* Hillsdale, NJ: Lawrence Erlbaum.

Grodstein F., Stampfer, M. J., Colditz, G. A., Joffe, M., Rosner, B., Fuchs, C., Hankinson, S., Hunter, D., Hennekens, C., & Speizer, F. (1997). Postmenopausal hormone therapy and mortality. *The New England Journal of Medicine, 336,* 1769–1775.

Hawton, K. (1995). Treatment of sexual dysfunctions by sex therapy and other approaches. *British Journal of Psychiatry, 167,* 307–314.

Hawton, K., & Catalan, J. (1986). Prognostic factors in sex therapy. *Behavior Research and Therapy, 24,* 377–385.

Heiman, J., & LoPiccolo, J. (1988). *Becoming orgasmic: A sexual and personal growth program for women.* New York: Simon & Schuster.

Heiman, J. R., & Meston, C. M. (1997). Empirically validated treatment for sexual dysfunction. *Annual Review of Sex Research, 8,* 148–194.

Hof, L., & Berman, E. (1986). The sexual genogram. *Journal of Marital and Family Therapy, 12,* 39–47.

Hoon, P. (1983). A path analysis model of psychosexuality in young women. *Journal of Research in Personality, 17,* 143–152.

Howard, B., & Weeks, G. (1995) A happy marriage: Pairing couples therapy and treatment of depression. In G. Weeks & L. Hof (Eds.), *Integrative solutions: Treating common problems in couples therapy,* (pp. 95–123). New York: Brunner/Mazel.

Hunt, M. (1974). *Sexual behavior in the 1970's.* Chicago: Playboy Press.

Hurlbert, D. F. (1993). A comparative study using orgasm consistency training in the treatment of women reporting hypoactive sexual desire. *Journal of Sex & Marital Therapy, 19*(1), 41–55.

Hurlbert, D., & Apt, C. (1994). Female sexual desire, response, and behavior. *Behavior Modification, 18,* 488–504.

Hurlbert, D., Apt, C., & Rabehl, S. (1993). Key variables to understanding female sexual satisfaction: an examination of women in nondistressed marriages. *Journal of Sex & Marital Therapy, 19,* 154–165.

Hurlbert, D. F., White, C. L., Powell, R. D., & Apt, C. (1993). Orgasm consistency training in the treatment of women reporting hypoactive sexual desire: An outcome comparison of women-only groups and couples-only groups. *Journal of Behavior Therapy & Experimental Psychiatry, 24*(1), 3–13.

Hurlbert, D., & Whittaker, K. (1991). The role of masturbation in marital and sexual satisfaction: a comparative study of female masturbators and nonmasturbators. *Journal of Sex Education and Therapy, 17*, 272–282.

Johnson, S. M., & Greenberg, L. S. (1985). Differential effects of experiential and problem-solving interventions in resolving marital conflict. *Journal of Consulting and Clinical Psychology, 53*, 175–184.

Jones, E., & Asen, E. (2000). *Systemic couple therapy and depression.* United Kingdom: Karnac Books.

Jordan, W. (1997). Allergy and topical irritation associated with transdermal testosterone administration: A comparison of scrotal and nonscrotal delivery systems. *American Journal of Contact Dermititis, 8*(2), 103.

Kaplan, H. (1979). *Disorders of sexual desire and other new concepts and techniques in sex therapy.* New York: Brunner/Mazel.

Kaplan, H. (1983). *The evaluation of sexual disorders: Psychological and medical aspects.* New York: Brunner/Mazel.

Kaplan, H. (1985). *Comprehensive evaluation of disorders of sexual desire.* Washington, DC: American Psychiatric Association.

Kaplan, H. (1995). *The sexual desire disorders: Dysfunctional regulation of sexual motivation.* New York: Brunner/Mazel.

Kaplan, H. (1996). Erotic obsession: relationship to hypoactive sexual desire disorder and paraphilia. *American Journal of Psychiatry, 153*, 30–41.

Kaplan, S., Reis, R., Kohn, I., Ikeguchi, E., Laor, E., Te, A., & Martins, A. (1999). Safety and efficacy of sidenafil in postmenopausal women with sexual dysfunction. *Urology, 53*(3), 481–486.

Kassinove, H. (1995). *Anger disorders: Definition, diagnosis, and treatment.* Philadelphia: Taylor & Francis.

Katz, R., & Jardine, D. (1999). The relationship between worry, sexual aversion, and low sexual desire. *Journal of Sex & Marital Therapy, 25*, 293–296.

Katznelson, L., Finkelstein, J. S., Schoenfield, D. A., Rosenthal, D. I., Anderson, E. J., & Klibanski, A. (1996). Increase in bone mass density and lean body mass during testosterone administration in men with acquired hypogonadism. *Journal of Clinical Endocrinology and Metabolism, 81*(12), 4358–4365.

Kilmann, P., Boland, J., Norton, S., Davidson, E., & Caid, C. (1986). Perspectives of sex therapy outcome: A survey of ASSECT providers. *Journal of Sex & Marital Therapy, 12*, 116–138.

Kinsey, A., Pomeroy, W., & Martin, C. (1948). *Sexual behavior in the human male.* Philadelphia: W. B. Saunders.

Kinsey, A., Pomeroy, W., Martin, C., & Gebhard, P. (1953). *Sexual behavior in the human female.* Philadelphia: W. B. Saunders.

Kinzl, J., Mangweth, B., Traweger, C., & Biebl, W. (1996). Sexual dysfunction in males: significance of adverse childhood experiences. *Child Abuse and Neglect, 20*, 759–766.

Kinzl, J., Traweger, C., & Biebl, W. (1995). Sexual dysfunctions: relationship to childhood sexual abuse and early family experiences in a nonclinical sample. *Child Abuse and Neglect, 19*, 785–792.

Knopf, J., & Seiler, M. (1990). *ISD: Inhibited sexual desire*. New York: Morrow.

Kolodny, R. C., Masters, W., & Johnson, V. (1979). *Textbook of sexual medicine*. Boston: Little Brown.

L'Abate, L. (1976). *Understanding and helping the individual in the family*. New York: Grune & Stratton.

L'Abate, L., & McHenry, S. (1983). *Handbook of marital interventions*. New York: Grune & Stratton.

L'Abate, L., Weeks, G., & Weeks, K. (1977). Protectiveness, persecution, and powerlessness. *International Journal of Family Counseling, 5*, 72–76.

Laan, E., & Everaerd, W. (1995). Determinants of female sexual arousal: Psychophysiological theory and data. *Archives of Sexual Behavior, 23*, 153–170.

Laan, E., Everaerd, W., van der Velde, J., & Geer, J. (1995). Determinants of subjective experience of sexual arousal in women: Feedback from genital arousal and erotic stimulus content. *Psychology, 32*(5), 444–451.

Laumann, E., Gagnon, J. H., Michael, R., & Michaels, S. (1994). *The social organization of sexuality*. Chicago: University of Chicago.

Laumann, E., Paik, A., & Rosen, R. (1999) Sexual dysfunction in the United States. *Journal of the American Medical Asociation, 281*(6), 537–544.

Lazarus, A. (1988). A multimodal perspective on problems of sexual desire. In S. Leiblum & R. Rosen (Eds.), *Sexual desire disorders* (pp. 145–167). New York: Guilford.

Leiblum, S., & Rosen, R. (1988). *Sexual desire disorders*. New York: Guilford.

Leitenberg, H., & Henning, K. (1995). Sexual fantasy. *Psychological Bulletin, 117*, 469–496.

LeMone, P. (1996). The physical effects of diabetes on sexuality in women. *The Diabetes Educator, 22*(4), 361–366.

Lerner-Goldhor, H. (1989). *The dance of anger*. New York: HarperCollins.

Levin, S. (1984). An essay on the nature of sexual desire. *Journal of Sex & Marital Therapy, 10*, 83–96.

Levin, S. (1988). Intrapsychic and individual aspects of sexual desire. In S. Leiblum & R. Rosen (Eds.), *Sexual desire disorders* (pp. 21–44). New York: Guilford.

Lief, H. (1977). What's new in sex research? Inhibited sexual desire. *Medical Aspects of Human Sexuality, 2*, 94–95.

Lief, H. (1985). The evaluation of inhibited sexual desire: Relationship aspects. In H. S. Kaplan (Ed.), *The comprehensive evaluation of disorders of sexual desire*. Washington: American Psychiatric Press.

Lobitz, W. C., & Lobitz, G. K. (1996). Resolving the sexual intimacy paradox: A developmental model for the treatment of sexual desire disorders. *Journal of Sex & Marital Therapy, 22*(2), 71–84.

LoPiccolo, L. (1980). Low sexual desire. In S. R. Leiblum & L. A. Pervin (Eds.), *Principles and practice of sex therapy*. New York: Guilford.

LoPiccolo, J., & Friedman, J. (1988). Broad-spectrum treatment of low sexual desire: Integration of cognitive, behavioral, and systemic therapy. In S. Leiblum and R. Rosen (Eds.), *Sexual desire disorders* (pp. 107–144), New York: Guilford.

Loren, R., & Weeks, G. (1986). Comparison of the sexual fantasies of undergraduates and their perception of the sexual fantasies of the opposite sex. *Journal of Sex Education and Therapy, 12*, 31–36.

Lund, B., Bever-Stille, K., & Perry, P. (1999). Testosterone and andropause: the feasibility of testosterone replacement therapy in elderly men. *Pharmacology, 19*(8), 951–956.

Mackey, M. A., Conway, A. J., & Handelsman, D. J. (1995). Tolerability of intramuscular injections of testosterone ester in oil vehicle. *Human Reproduction, 10*(4), 862–865.

Mahoney, P., & Williams, L. (1998). Sexual assault in marriage: Prevalence, consequences and treatment of wife rape. In J. Jasinski & L. Williams (Eds.), *Partner violence: A comprehensive review of 20 years of research*, Thousand Oaks, CA: Sage.

Maltz, W. (1988). Identifying and treating the sexual repercussions of incest: A couples therapy approach. *Journal of Sex & Marital Therapy, 14*(2), 142–170.

Maltz, W. (1995). *The sexual healing journey: A guide for survivors of sexual abuse.* New York: HarperCollins.

Maltz, W., & Holman, B. (1987). *Incest and sexuality.* Lexington, MA: Lexington.

Masters, W. H., & Johnson, V. (1966). *Human sexual response.* Boston: Little, Brown.

Masters, W. H., & Johnson, V. (1970). *Human sexual inadequacy.* Boston: Little, Brown.

Masters, W. H., & Johnson, V. (1979). *Homosexuality in perspective.* Boston: Little, Brown.

Matthew, R., Weinman, M., & Claghorn, J. (1980). Tricyclic side effects without tricyclics in depression. *Psychopharmacological Bulletin, 16*, 58–60.

Maurice, W. (1999). *Sexual medicine in primary care.* St. Louis: Mosby.

McCarthy, B. W. (1985). Use and misuse of behavioral homework exercises in sex therapy. *Journal of Sex & Marital Therapy, 11*, 185–191.

McCarthy, B. W. (1986). A cognitive-behavioral approach to understanding and treating sexual trauma. *Journal of Sex & Marital Therapy, 12*(4), 322–329.

McCarthy, B. W. (1987). Developing positive intimacy cognitions in males with a history of nonintimate sexual experiences. *Journal of Sex & Marital Therapy, 13*(4), 253–259.

McCarthy, B. W. (1992). Erectile dysfunction and inhibited sexual desire: cognitive-behavioral strategies. *Journal of Sex Education and Therapy, 18*, 22–34.

McCarthy, B. (1993). Relapse prevention strategies and techniques in sex therapy. *Journal of Sex & Marital Therapy, 19*, 142–146.

McCarthy, B. W. (1994). Sexually compulsive men and inhibited sexual desire. *Journal of Sex & Marital Therapy, 20*, 200–209.

McCarthy, B. (1997). Strategies and techniques for revitalizing a nonsexual marriage. *Journal of Sex & Marital Therapy, 23*, 231–240.

McCarthy, B. W. (1999a). Relapse prevention strategies and techniques for inhibited sexual desire. *Journal of Sex & Marital Therapy, 25*, 297–303.

McCarthy, B. (1999b). The nonsexual marriage: Assessing viability and treatment Options. *Journal of Sex & Marital Therapy, 25*, 227–236.

McGuirl, K. E., & Wiederman, M. W. (2000). Characteristics of the ideal sex partner: Gender differences and perceptions of the preferences of the other gender. *Journal of Sex & Marital Therapy, 26*, 153–159.

McKibben, L., De Vos, E., & Newberger, E. (1989). Victimization of mothers of abused children: A controlled study. *Pediatrics, 84*, 531–535.

MacPhee, D. C., Johnson, S.M., & Van der Veer, M.C. (1995). Low sexual desire in women: The effect of marital therapy. *Journal of Sex & Marital Therapy, 21*(3), 159–182.

Michael, R., Gagnon, J. H., Laumann, E., & Kolata, G. (1994). *Sex in America: A definitive survey.* Boston: Little, Brown.

Michelson, D., Bancroft, J., Targum, S., Kim, Y., & Tepner, R. (2000). Female sexual dysfunction associated with antidepressant administration: A randomized, placebo-controlled study of pharmacologic intervention. *American Journal of Psychiatry, 157,* 239–243.

Modell, J., May, R., & Katholi, C. (2000). Effect of bupropion-SR on orgasmic dysfunction in nondepressed subjects: A pilot study. *Journal of Sex & Marital Therapy, 26,* 231–240.

Montejo-González, A. L., Llorca, G., Izquierdo, J., Ledesma, A., Bousoño, M., Calcedo, A., Carrasco, J., Ciudad, J., Daniel, E., De la Gandara, J., Derecho, J., Franco, M., Gomez, M., Macias, J., Martin, T., Perez, V., Sanchez, J., Sanchez, S., & Vicens, E. (1997). SSRI-induced sexual dysfunction: fluoxetine, paroxetine, sertraline, and fluvoxamine in a prospective, multicenter, and descriptive clinical study of 344 patients. *Journal of Sex & Marital Therapy, 23*(3), 176–94.

Morales, A., Nolan, J., Nelson, J., & Yen, S. (1994). Effects of replacement dose of dehydroepiandrosterone in men and women of advancing age. *Journal of Clinical Endocrinology and Metabolism, 78,* 1360–1367.

Morokoff, P., & Gillilland, R. (1993). Stress, sexual functioning, and marital satisfaction. *The Journal of Sex Research, 30,* 43–53.

Moser, C. (1992). Lust, lack of desire, and paraphilias: some thoughts and possible connections. *Journal of Sex & Marital Therapy, 18,* 65–69.

Mosher, D. (1979). Sex guilt and sex myth in college men and women. *Journal of Sex Research, 15*(3), 224–234.

Nathan, S. (1986). The epidemiology of the DSM-III psychosexual dysfunctions. *Journal of Sex & Marital Therapy, 12,* 267–281.

Nurnberg, H., Hensley, P., Lauriello, J., Parker, L., & Keith, S. (1999) Sildenafil for women patients with antidepressant-induced sexual dysfunction. *Psychiatric Services, 312,* 1076–1078.

Nutter, D. E., & Condron, M. K. (1983). Sexual fantasy and activity patterns of females with inhibited sexual desire versus normal controls. *Journal of Sex & Marital Therapy, 9*(4), 276–282.

Nutter, D., & Condron, M. (1985). Sexual fantasy and activity patterns of males with inhibited sexual desire and males with erectile dysfunction versus normal controls. *Journal of Sex & Marital Therapy, 11,* 91–98.

O'Carroll, R. (1991). Sexual desire disorders: A review of controlled treatment studies. *The Journal of Sex Research, 28*(4), 607–624.

Orzack, M. H., & Ross, C. J. (2000). Should virtual sex be treated like other sex addictions? *Sexual Addiction & Compulsivity, 7*(1–2), 113–126.

O'Sullivan, L., & Allgeier, E. (1998). Feigning sexual desire: consenting to unwanted sexual activity in heterosexual dating relationships. *The Journal of Sex Research, 35,* 234–243.

Parker, S., & Armitage, M. (1999) Experience with transdermal testosterone replacement therapy for hypogonadal men. *Clinical Endocrinology, 50*(1), 57–62.

Persky, H., Lief, H., Strauss, D., Miller, W., & O'Brien, C. (1978). Plasma testosterone levels and sexual behavior of couples. *Archives of Sexual Behavior, 7,* 157–173.

Piletz, J., Segraves, K., Feng, Y., Maguire, E., & Halaris, A. (1998). Plasma MHPG response to yohimbine treatment in women with hypoactive sexual desire. *Journal of Sex & Marital Therapy, 24,* 43–54.

Poppen, P. J., & Segal, N. J. (1988). The influence of sex and sex role orientation on sexual coercion. *Sex Roles, 19,* 689–701.

Prager, K. (1997). *The psychology of intimacy.* New York: Guilford.

Radin, M. (1989). Preoedipal factors in relation to psychogenic inhibited sexual desire. *Journal of Sex & Marital Therapy, 15,* 255–268.

Rako, S. (1996). *The hormone of desire: The truth about sexuality, menopause and testosterone.* New York: Haworth.

Regan, P., & Berscheid, E. (1996). Beliefs about the state, goals, and objects of sexual desire. *Journal of Sex & Marital Therapy, 22,* 110–120.

Randall, M., & Haskell, L. (1995). Sexual violence in women's lives. *Violence Against Women, 1*(1), 6–31.

Resnick, H., Kilpatrick, D., Walsh, C., & Vernonen, L. (1991). Marital rape. In R. Ammerman & M. Herson (Eds.), *Case studies in family violence* (pp. 329–53). New York: Plenum.

Richgels, P. (1992). Hypoactive sexual desire in heterosexual women: a feminist analysis. *Women & Therapy, 12,* 123–135.

Riley, A., & Riley, E. (2000). Controlled studies on women presenting with sexual drive disorder: 1. Endocrine status. *Journal of Sex & Marital Therapy, 26,* 269–283.

Rosen, R., & Beck, J. (1988). *Patterns of sexual arousal.* New York: Guilford.

Rosen, R., Lane, R., & Menza, M. (1999). Effects of SSRIs on sexual function: A critical review. *Journal of Clinical Pharmacology, 19*(1), 67–85.

Rosen, R., Leiblum. S., & Hall, K. (1987). *Etiological and predictive factors in sex therapy.* Paper presented at the annual meeting of the Society for Sex Therapy and Research, New Orleans.

Rosenzweig, J., & Dailey, D. (1989). Dyadic adjustment/sexual satisfaction in women and men as function of sex role self-perception. *Journal of Sex & Marital Therapy, 15,* 42–56.

Russell, D. E. H. (1990). *Rape in marriage.* New York: Macmillan.

Sager, C., & Hunt, B. (1979). *Intimate partners: Hidden patterns in love relationships.* New York: Brunner/Mazel.

Salerian, A., Deibler, W., Vittone, B., Geyer, S., Drell, L., Mirmirani, N., Mirczak, J., Byrd, W., Tunick, S., Wax, M., & Fleisher, S. (2000). Sidenafil for psychotrophic-induced sexual dysfunction in 31 women and 61 men. *Journal of Sex & Marital Therapy, 26*(2), 133–140.

Sands, R., & Studd, J. (1995). Exogenous androgens in postmenopausal women. *American Journal of Medicine, 98*(1A), 76s–79s.

Sarrel, P. M. (1999). Psychosexual effects of menopause: Role of androgens. *American Journal of Obstetrics and Gynecology, 180,* 319–324.

Sauber, R., L'Abate, L., Weeks, G., & Buchanan, W. (1993). *The dictionary of family psychology and family therapy* (2nd ed.). Newbury Park, CA: Sage.

Schaefer, M., & Olson, D. (1981). Assessment of intimacy: the pair inventory. *Journal of Marital and Family Therapy, 7,* 47–60.

Scharff, D. (1988). An object relations approach to inhibited sexual desire. In S. Leiblum & R. Rosen (Eds.), *Sexual desire disorders* (pp. 45–74). New York: Guilford.

Schiavi, R., Karstaedt, A., Schreiner-Engel, P., & Mandeli, J. (1992). Psychometric characteristics of individuals with sexual dysfunction and their partners. *Journal of Sex & Marital Therapy, 18*, 219–230.

Schnarch, D. (1991). *Constructing the sexual crucible.* New York: W. W. Norton.

Schnarch, D. (1997). *Passionate marriage.* New York: W. W. Norton.

Schneider, J (2000). Effects of cybersex addiction on the family: Results of a survey. *Sexual Addiction and Compulsivity, 7*(1–2), 31–58.

Schover, L., & LoPiccolo, J. (1982). Effectiveness of treatment for dysfunctions of sexual desire. *Journal of Sex & Marital Therapy, 8*, 179–197.

Schreiner-Engel, P., Schiavi, R., Victorisz, D., & Smith, H. (1987). The differential impact of diabetes type on female sexuality. *Journal of Psychosomatic Research, 31*(1), 23–33.

Schwartz, M., & Masters, W. (1988). Inhibited sexual desire: The Masters and Johnson Institute Treatment Model. In S. Leiblum & R. Rosen (Eds.), *Sexual desire disorders* (pp. 229–242). New York: Guilford.

Segraves, K., & Segraves, R. (1991). Hypoactive sexual desire disorder: Prevalence and comorbidity in 906 subjects. *Journal of Sex & Marital Therapy, 17*, 55–58.

Segraves, R. T., & Althof, S. (1998). Psychotherapy and pharmacotherapy of sexual dysfunctions. In P. E. Nathan & J. M. Gorman (Eds.), *A guide to treatments that work* (pp. 447–471). New York: Oxford.

Segraves, R. T., Kavoussi, R., Hughes, A. R., Batey, S. R., Johnston, J. A., Donahue, R., & Ascher, J. A. (2000). *Journal of Clinical Psychopharmacology, 20*(2), 122–128.

Segraves, R., & Segraves, K. (1990). Categorical and multi-axial diagnosis of male erectile disorder. *Journal of Sex & Marital Therapy, 16*, 208–213.

Shaw, J. (1997). Treatment rationale for internet infidelity. *Journal of Sex Education and Therapy, 22*(2), 29–34.

Sherwin, B. B. (1998). Use of combined estrogen-androgen preparations in the postmenopause: Evidence from clinical studies. *International Journal of Fertility and Womens Medicine, 43*, 98–103.

Sherwin, B., & Gelfand, M. (1987). The role of androgen in the maintenance of sexual functioning in oophorectomized women. *Psychosomatic Medicine, 49*(4), 397–409.

Shifren, J., Braunstein, G., Simon, J., Casson, P., Buster, J., Redmonce, G., Burki, R., Ginsburg, E., Rosen, R., Leiblum, S., Caramelli, K., & Mazer, N. (2000). Transdermal testosterone treatment in women with impaired sexual function after oophrectomy. *The New England Journal of Medicine, 343*(10), 682–688.

Shortland, R. L., & Hunter, B. A. (1995). Women's "token resistant" and compliant sexual behaviors are related to uncertain sexual intentions and rape. *Personality and Social Psychology Bulletin, 21*, 226–236.

Smith, T. (1991). Adult sexual behavior in 1989: Number of partners, frequency of intercourse and risk of AIDS. *Family Planning Perspective, 23*, 102–107.

Sommer, B., Avis, N., Meyer, P., Ory, M., Madden, T., Kagawa-Singer, M., Mouton, C., Rasor, N. O., & Adler, S. (1999). Attitudes toward menopause and aging across ethnic/racial groups. *Psychosomatic Medicine, 61*(6), 868–875.

Spector, I., Carey, M., & Steinberg, L. (1996). The sexual desire inventory: Development, factor structure, and evidence of reliability. *Journal of Sex & Marital Therapy, 22*, 175–190.

Sprecher, S., Hatfield, E., Cortese, A., Potapova, E., & Levitkaya, A. (1994). Token resistance to sexual intercourse and consent to unwanted sexual intercourse: College students' dating experiences in three countries. *The Journal of Sex Research, 31,* 125–132.

Sternberg, R. (1986). A triangular theory of love. *Psychological Review, 93,* 119–135.

Strong, S., & Claiborn, C. (1982). *Change through interaction: Social psychological processes of counseling and psychotherapy.* New York: Wiley.

Stuart, F., Hammond, D., & Pett, M. (1986). Psychological characteristics of women with inhibited sexual desire. *Journal of Sex & Marital Therapy, 12,* 108–115.

Sue, D. (1979). Erotic fantasies of college students during coitus. *Journal of Sex Research, 15,* 299–305.

Talmadge, L., & Wallace, S. (1991). Reclaiming sexuality in female incest survivors. *Journal of Sex & Marital Therapy, 17*(3), 163–182.

Tenover, J. L. (1999). Testosterone replacement therapy in older adult men. *International Journal of Andrology, 22*(5), 300–306.

Tiefer, L., & Melman, A. (1987) Adherence to recommendations and improvement over time in men with erectile dysfunction. *Archives of Sex Behavior, 16,* 301–309.

Trudel, G., Ravart, M., & Matte, B. (1993). The use of the multiaxial diagnostic system for sexual dysfunctions in the assessment of hypoactive sexual desire. *Journal of Sex & Marital Therapy, 19,* 123–130.

Tuiten, A., Van Honk, J., Koppeschaar, H., Bernaards, C., Thijssen, J., & Verbaten, R. (2000). Time course of effects of testosterone administration on sexual arousal in women. *Archives of General Psychiatry, 57*(2), 149–153.

Turner, M. (1995). Addictions in marital/relationship therapy. In G. R. Weeks & L. Hof (Eds.), *Integrative solutions: Treating common problems in couples therapy* (pp. 124–147). New York: Brunner/Mazel.

Van de Velde, T. (1930). *Ideal marriage: Its physiology and technique* (Rev. ed., S. Browne, Trans.). New York: Random House.

Verhulst, J., & Heiman, J. (1988). A systems perspective on sexual desire. In S. Leiblum & R. Rosen (Eds.), *Sexual desire disorders* (pp. 243–270). New York: Guilford Press.

Waring, E. (1981). Facilitating marital intimacy through self-disclosure. *American Journal of Family Therapy, 9,* 33–42.

Warnock, J., Bundren, J., & Morris, D. (1997). Female hypoactive sexual desire disorder due to androgen deficiency: clinical and psychometric issues. *Psychopharmacology Bulletin, 33*(4), 761–766.

Warnock, J., Bundren, J., & Morris, D. (2000). Female hypoactive sexual disorder: Case studies of physiologic androgen replacement. *Journal of Sex & Marital Therapy, 25,* 175–182.

Weeks, G. R. (1987) Systemic treatment of inhibited sexual desire. In G. Weeks & L. Hof (Eds.), *Integrating sex and marital therapy: A clinical guide* (pp.183–201). New York: Brunner/Mazel.

Weeks. G. R. (Ed.) (1989). *Treating couples: The intersystem model of the Marriage Council of Philadelphia.* New York: Brunner/Mazel.

Weeks, G. R. (1994). The intersystem model: An integrative approach to treatment. In G. Weeks & L. Hof (Eds.), *The marital-relationship therapy casebook:*

*Theory and application of the intersystem model* (pp. 3–34). New York: Brunner/ Mazel.

Weeks, G. R. (1995). Inhibited sexual desire. In G. Weeks & L. Hof (Eds.), *Integrative solutions: Treating common problems in couples therapy* (pp. 215–252). New York: Brunner/Mazel.

Weeks, G., & Gambescia, N. (2000). *Erectile dysfunction: Integrating couple therapy, sex therapy, and medical treatment.* New York: W. W. Norton.

Weeks, G. R., & Hof, L. (Eds.) (1987). *Integrating sex and marital therapy: A clinical guide.* New York: Brunner/Mazel.

Weeks, G., & Hof, L. (Eds) (1994). *The marital-relationship therapy casebook.* New York: Brunner/Mazel.

Weeks, G., & L'Abate, L. (1982). *Paradoxical psychotherapy: Theory and practice with individuals, couples, and families.* New York: Brunner/Mazel.

Weeks, G., & Treat, S. (2001). *Couples in treatment: Techniques and approaches for effective practice* (Rev. ed). New York: Brunner/Mazel.

Weingarten, K. (1991). The discourses of intimacy: Adding a social constructionist and feminist view. *Family Process, 10,* 185–192.

Weiss, D. L. (1998). Conclusion: The state of sexual theory. *The Journal of Sex Research, 35,* 88–99.

Westaby, D., Ogle, S. J., Paradinas, F. J., Randall, J. B., & Murray-Lyon, I. M. (1977). Liver damage from long-term methyltestosterone. *Lancet, 8032,* 261–263.

Westoff, C., Bumpass, L., & Ryder, N. (1969). Oral contraception, coital frequency, and the time required to conceive: Data from the Princeton Fertility Study and National Fertility Study. *Social Biology, 16,* 1–10.

Widom, C. (1999). Posttraumatic stress disorder in abused and neglected children grown up. *American Journal of Psychiatry, 156,* 1223–1229.

Wiederman, M. (2000) Women's body image self-consciousness during physical intimacy with a partner. *The Journal of Sex Research, 37*(1), 60–68.

Wincze, J. P., & Carey, M. P. (1991). *Sexual dysfunction.* New York: Guilford.

Winters, S. J. (1999). Current status of testosterone replacement therapy in men. *Archives of Family Medicine, 8*(3), 257–263.

Wolpe, J. (1991). *The practice of behavior therapy* (4th ed.). New York: Pergamon.

Woodrum, S. T., & Brown, C. S. (1998). Management of SSRI-induced sexual dysfunction. *Annals of Pharmacotherapy 32*(11), 1209–1215.

Young, K., Griffin-Shelly, E., Cooper, A., O'Mara, J., & Buchanan, J. (2000). Online infidelity: A new dimension in couple relationships with implications for evaluation and treatment. *Sexual Addiction and Compulsivity, 7*(1–2), 59–74.

Zilbergeld, B. (1992). *The new male sexuality.* New York: Bantam.

Zimmer, D. (1987). Does marital therapy enhance the effectiveness of treatment of sexual dysfunction? *Journal of Sex & Marital Therapy, 13,* 193–209.

Zumoff, B., Strain, G., Miller, L., & Rosner, W. (1995). Twenty-four hour mean plasma testosterone concentration declines with age in normal premenopausal women. *Journal of Clinical Endocrinology and Metabolism, 80,* 1429–1430.

# Index

abandonment, fear of, 66–67, 137
Abraham, G., 103
acquired hypoactive sexual desire, 3–4
Adams, K., 72, 77, 81
addiction, treatment of, priority over sex
  therapy, 128
Adler, S., 94
adultery, virtual, on the Internet, 49
affair, current, as a contraindication to sex
  therapy, 127–28
affection
  absence of, in hypoactive sexual desire, 139
  creating, advanced techniques in therapy,
    196–205
  display of, in clients with hypoactive sex-
    ual desire, 42
  expressing to improve intimacy, 162–63
  fusion of, with sex, 41–42
affirmation, to improve intimacy, 163
Alberti, R. E., 173
Alford, P., 79
Allgeier, E., 22
Alpert, J., 99
alprostadil, 102, see also Caverject
alternative treatments, 102–4
Althof, S., 130

American Psychiatric Association, 1, 6, 27
analysis, integrative and comprehensive, 1
Anderson, C., ix, 9, 10–11, 21, 43, 44–45,
  55, 115
Anderson, E. J., 88
androgen deficiency, symptoms of, 82
andropause, 87–89
anger, fear of, 61–63
  and intimacy, 169–71
anger iceberg, 170
antidepressants, effect of, on sexual desire,
  50, 98–99
antidotes, for antidepressant-induced sexual
  dysfunction, 99–100
anxiety
  and depression, 50
  from lack of information, 39
  reducing with information, 75
  sexual, desensitization exercises, 198
  and sexual difficulties, 35–37
anxiety disorder, association with hypoactive sexual desire, 45–46
Apfelbaum, B., 32–33, 35, 36, 133, 210,
  211, 212
apomorphine, 102

227